THE
SCOTTISH
GOLF BOOK

MALCOLM CAMPBELL *with photographs by* **Glyn Satterley**

This book is dedicated to the pioneering Scots
who brought the shining light of golf to a darkened world...
and to Janey who brings brightness to my every day.

A **SPORTS** MASTERS Book

ISBN 1-58382-053-1

Printed in Hong Kong

99 00 01 02 03 5 4 3 2 1

Library of Congress Cataloging-in-Publication Data available

Published in the USA by Sports Publishing Inc
804 North Neil St, Champaign, IL 61820, U.S.A.
www.Sportspublishinginc.com

First published in Great Britain in 1999 by
Lomond Books

Produced by Colin Baxter Photography Ltd
The Old Dairy, Woodlands Industrial Estate,
Grantown-on-Spey, Moray, PH26 3NA, Scotland.

Page 1 photograph: Durness   Page 4 photograph: Cruden Bay

THE SCOTTISH GOLF BOOK

MALCOLM CAMPBELL

with photographs by **Glyn Satterley**

Foreword by **Sir Michael Bonallack,**
Secretary, The Royal & Ancient Golf Club, St Andrews

Sports Publishing Inc.
Champaign, Illinois
www.Sportspublishinginc.com

CONTENTS

FOREWORD

As Secretary of the Royal & Ancient Golf Club, my office in St Andrews, with its attached balcony, overlooks a flat narrow strip of land, in the shape of a shepherd's crook, on which for over half of this millennium players of all ages and nationalities have played and enjoyed the game of 'gowf'. I refer to the 'Old Course', the most famous course in the world, which has played such a large part in creating the history of this royal and ancient game.

Essentially golf was, and still should be, a simple game. It is easy to imagine shepherds passing the time of day betting with each other as to who could hit a stone, or possibly a lump of sheep's dung, into a rabbit-hole, using their crook as a club. In addition, the sheep for whom they were caring would scrape a hollow in the sandy soil to shelter from the wind and so form the first hazards or bunkers to add to the difficulty of their challenge.

I am not sure if my simplistic image of how golf was born has any substance or not, but I would like to think it has, as it provides a far more attractive background to emulate than that typified by modern courses with sleepered bunkers and tarmacadam cart paths.

To take the time to travel around Scotland and experience the delight of playing the country's numerous natural golf courses is something that both my wife Angela and I look forward to. It reminds us, as does Malcolm Campbell's inspiring book, that the game which Scotland and Scots gave to the rest of the world is still there to be enjoyed in its original beauty and splendour.

Players and champions come and go, but the challenge of the game, and its beautiful courses, many of them evocatively illustrated here, will still be there halfway through the next millennium.

Sir Michael Bonallack, OBE
February 1999

Carnegie Club,
Skibo Castle, Dornoch.

7

INTRODUCTION

Golf is part of the very fabric of Scottish life. It is in Scotland after all that the game has its roots and its soul, and where it is better understood and appreciated than anywhere else in the world.

This is hardly surprising, for the Scots have been playing the 'gowf' definitely since the fifteenth century, and almost certainly a century or two before that, although no official record exists before King James II – or 'Jimmy the Roman Numeral' as American golf writer Dan Jenkins was wont to call him – infamously banned the game by Act of Parliament in 1457.

Golf has survived more than one attempt at Royal proscription; it has survived war and pestilence, internecine clan conflict, invasion and feud. It is in the Scottish blood and, pointedly, remains one of the few unbroken threads running through the historical tapestry of a land of so much bloody history and so little romantic interlude.

But Scotland is more than just the historical and cultural home of the game; it is its epicentre. It is to Scotland that thousands make pilgrimage every year to sample the truest form of this preadamic game. They come for the great diversity of the courses and for the Scottish golf culture; they come to feel and try to understand what it is that makes golf in its native heath so different to any other place on earth, save Ireland perhaps where there is in any event some common bond.

Where else in the world could the visitor play on one day the most famous course in the world, the Old Course at St Andrews, and on the next a delightful and deserted course in the heart of the Scottish Highlands, where sheep still keep the fairway grass short, and visitors are trusted to put their green fees in the 'honesty box', for there is no one there to collect them?

Where else can the golfer find such treasures as the Shiskine course on the Isle of Arran, where the game remains as it did when Willie Fernie and Old Tom Morris were kings, where irrigation still comes from the sky alone, where the 12 holes confirm that the accepted circuit of 18 is only arbitrary and where the test of patience to get there involves an hour-long ferry trip and a ten-mile journey across the mountain, for there is neither airport, railway system nor helicopter service to ease the journey.

Where else can the golfer stand on the last stop between Scotland and the New World and wonder and marvel at the view from the first tee at Machrihanish, and the shot that goes with it across as much of the Atlantic Ocean as he dares?

Where else can the golfer strike out into the Highlands and be confronted with such spectacular golfing surroundings as to take the very breath away; where the deer run free, the eagle still soars in the sky and the air is as clear as the mountain burn beneath?

Golf in Scotland is not simply a game; it is a way of life.

This is a book devoted entirely to golf in Scotland. It is, therefore, an unashamedly Scottish book looking at golf from the Scottish perspective, and yet not denying it in other places.

It is about the history of golf, the great Scottish players and the Scottish golfing missionaries who took the light of their great game into a darkened world for the betterment of all.

It is about wonderful Scottish courses, and the great events and dramas and famous matches that have been played out upon them in the land that gave the game its birth. It is about a pastime that crosses the social divide in a way that it singularly still fails to do in many corners of the globe, where they play the game but often miss the point of it.

With but few exceptions, golf in Scotland has remained true to the traditional principles of the game handed down over the generations. There are, thankfully, few examples of the tricked-up wares of self-styled golf course architects – mostly it has to be said, American – who arrogantly proclaim their creations as 'Scottish-style' championship links, when in fact they are as often as not nothing more than vaguely planned dumpings of dirt that turn honest countryside into fields of upturned egg-boxes to boost the sales of real estate.

Scotland has escaped, by and large, the multi-million dollar disasters of commercial golf course farming that have done nothing to enhance the game in many parts of the world, not least south of its borders. And even the golf buggy, that infernal machine which has bred all over Europe and North America with the intensity of rabbits on Viagra, has found the terrain of Scotland not at all to its liking. Sightings of the beast are thankfully as rare as a smile on the face of an impecunious Aberdonian who has lost a 'bob' and found a 'tanner'.

Golf remains in Scotland what it is supposed to be: a healthy outdoor exercise that in the words of the great club maker of the nineteenth century, Robert Forgan, 'affords the opportunity to play the man and act the gentleman'. It opens up the joys of the great outdoors, the chance to pit one's skill against nature, an opponent and most importantly, one's self.

In Scotland golf is the game for all classes and for all ages. There is hardly a village in the country without a golf course and it is still a common sight, even in this age of computer games and the television culture, to see youngsters of all ages headed for the golf course, pencil bag over shoulder or wheeling golf clubs on trolleys almost as big as they are.

In its homeland, golf is the game for the hardy soul prepared to take on the elements of a climate which can unveil, and often does, all four seasons on the same day. It is the land where the game is still more about 'feel' and 'eye' than the yardage chart, as anyone who has tackled the mighty links of Carnoustie in anything more than the most modest of breezes will readily testify.

Scotland is regarded the world over as the historic and cultural centre of golf and the very Home of the Game. Dismiss any notion that the claims of the French or the Dutch or even the Chinese that golf originated from some stick and ball derivative from within their borders, have any relevance. Their claims are flawed in the one specific that separates the royal and ancient game from all other distractions. It is the element crucial to the whole exercise; the object of the player's progress from tee to green; the target of his exertions. It is the round excavation in the ground, four and one quarter inches in diameter, known quite simply as the 'hole'.

Without the hole golf would not be golf. It might be jeu de mail, or chole, or crosse, or the Dutch game of kolven played on ice or in a court. It might even be the Roman game of paganica, but it most certainly would not be golf. The hole is central to the game and it was the Scots who put it there centuries ago and in so doing turned a simple pastime into the frustration that absorbs millions around the world to this day.

If what follows succeeds in helping the reader understand what golf means to Scotland, and to the Scots who preserve its heritage, and at the same time encourages some insight into the great treasure box of golf courses that is Scotland's gift to the world, then I will rest content.

Malcolm Campbell
Lower Largo
Scotland

THE HISTORY OF GOLF IN SCOTLAND

If history is merely a collection of fables that have been agreed upon, as Voltaire astutely observed a couple of centuries ago, then in the annals of golf he could hardly have found a surer example to emphasise the point. The embryonic phase of this human frustration we now consider as the royal and ancient game is shrouded in much more fable than fact. Whoever and wherever man (it is unlikely that woman would have been so irrational as to invent such an infuriation) first put club to ball, and advanced it across a stretch of turf towards a hole into which it was dispatched, remains a mystery to this day.

It will remain so forever, one suspects, for the best evidence brings us inevitably to the conclusion that it was not invented at all but simply emerged over the centuries from other club and ball games which could have existed since Roman times, or even long before that. There is a romantic vision sometimes aired of the shepherd boy tending his flock on the windswept shores of the Firth of Forth, easing the boredom of his day by swatting at stones on the ground with his shepherd's crook. He propels a round pebble carefully between the sand scrapes worn away by his sheep searching for shelter from the cold blasts of the east-coast wind. One stone takes a final bound into a rabbit hole and the royal and ancient game of golf is invented at a stroke.

It could have happened that way of course, but there is no evidence to support the abstraction and not many, it is safe to assume, would wager the family silver upon it.

The beginnings of the game of golf in Scotland are part fact and a much greater part fable. The fact is rather easier to recount.

The most enduring image of golf in the latter half of the nineteenth century. Old Tom Morris and his son Young Tommy who won eight Open Championships between them.

In the Beginning

A painting by Adriaen Van de Velde of the Dutch game of kolven being played on ice near Haarlem in 1688.

The game of golf developed on the east coast of Scotland for the very simple reason that the ground was perfectly suited to it. From the far north beyond Wick in Caithness to well south of Edinburgh, the east coast of Scotland has mile upon mile of land known as 'links'. This ground was unsuitable for arable farming because the sand was never very far from the surface, but its gently undulating contours, covered in beautiful springy turf, were just made for the game of golf.

Over the centuries the long tracts of exposed sand, left when the sea receded, were blown by the wind into great dunes that constantly moved until, gradually, wild grasses took a hold and stabilised the constantly moving mass. Natural fertiliser from birds and animals, and water provided by the Scottish climate, then encouraged the establishment of finer grasses, the bents and fescues, which form the natural turf of linksland.

It was turf that was hard wearing, that grew on acid soil, was tolerant of drought and was relatively slow growing. It was the natural food of rabbits and grazing sheep and cattle who kept it cropped short in the centuries before mechanical grass cutters were even thought of.

The land, then valued only for the grazing of animals and for leisure purposes, became known as 'links' most likely because it formed the 'link' between the sea and the more fertile agricultural land behind the dunes.

It was, in fact, land just waiting for golf courses to be built upon it.

Often described as an early 'golfer' this illustration from a Flemish manuscript of 1384 is more likely to be of players also involved in the game of kolven. The implements and the size of the ball are the clues.

When it was first used for this purpose is a matter for pure conjecture, but it is possible that some form of the game of golf was being played on the links of St Andrews from as early as the twelfth or thirteenth centuries. In what form it may have been played then we do not know for sure.

It may have developed from the Roman stick and ball game, paganica, in which the ball was made by stuffing feathers into a leather pouch. It was the game taken by the Romans to northern Europe and from which it seems likely that derivatives were developed to suit the particular whim of the local populace.

There are claims from the Dutch that golf originated in the Low Countries and not in Scotland at all. They cite the ancient game of kolven as the forerunner of golf, claiming that it was taken to Scotland in the course of trade between Holland and the east coast. There are claims by the French that golf's beginnings are to be found across the English Channel; they cite chole and jeu de mail in support of the theory.

The Dutch claims for kolven cannot stand much scrutiny for in truth there is very little similarity between it and the royal and ancient game as we know it today. Little may be known about the very beginnings of golf but much is known about kolven, a game which is still played to this day in Friesland in north Holland.

Although it was occasionally played outdoors

on frozen canals in winter, kolven was essentially an indoor pastime played on a purpose-built court with the players playing to fixed marks or posts. The ball was much bigger than a golf ball, more the size of a cricket ball, 'made perfect round and elastic, covered with soft leather and sewed with fine wire' according to an account of the game by the Rev. Walker in 1795. The clubs were long and had heavy, stiff shafts with heads made of brass, perfectly smooth and with no loft.

There exist many Dutch paintings depicting the game being played on frozen canals and rivers, inviting speculation that kolven owed more to the games of hockey and ice hockey than it ever did to golf.

The French claims for chole and jeu de mail are similarly flawed and remain discredited because of the one simple, but essential aspect of the game of golf that separates it from other pastimes of club and ball, the hole. It is the existence of the hole that establishes golf as a totally different game and it is the hole that is the vital factor in locating golf's origins firmly in Scotland.

The early history of golf as it can be verified is contained within the record of Scottish golf.

It is known that the game was a national pastime of the Scots before King James II's abortive efforts to ban it by Act of Parliament in 1457. It is also clear that His Majesty was virtually ignored and that his command to his subjects to spend more time practising their archery for defence of the realm than in pursuit of the 'gowf', fell upon deaf ears.

Less than 60 years later, Scottish archers were no match for their English counterparts in their ignominious defeat at the Battle of Flodden in 1513. Scotland not only lost its king but the flower of its noble families on Flodden Field in that historic battle, and it is not hard to make a case that the pursuit of golf, instead of the practice of archery, may have been a contributing factor.

It did not, however, halt any advance in the popularity of the game. Even Royal displeasure had to give way to its onward march, and by 1552 – 15 January to be precise – the citizens of the town of St Andrews were given, by charter right, the use of the links for 'golf, futball, shuteing at all times with all other manners of pastime'.

Golf was official but not always approved of. The church did not countenance golf being played on the Sabbath and to this day the Old Course at

Lauthier's 'Nouveaux Règles pour le Jeu de mail' of 1717 shows the flexible wooden mallet used to strike a wooden ball quite long distances. There were similarities to golf in that jeu de mail was an individual game and the player retained his own ball, unlike chole in which all the players played the same ball.

St Andrews remains closed for play on a Sunday.

There are accounts in Kirk Session records of the sixteenth and seventeenth centuries of parishioners being punished for violating the church ban on Sunday golf. There are accounts as far back as 1599 of miscreants being fined small sums of money for the first two offences of playing golf 'at the time of the preaching of the Sermon', and of 'the repentance pillar' being used to bring persistent offenders to justice. For those who still flouted the Sabbath ban, excommunication from the church was the next step!

The first golf courses were rudimentary indeed and very far from being anything like the courses of the present day. There were no greens or tees as such and the hole was a crude affair cut roughly with a knife. It served not only as the ultimate resting place for the ball but as a supply of sand for teeing the ball for the next drive.

Golf is unique in that the object of the game is

fairways and the areas around the holes, worn by continual play, eventually became designated areas, or greens, that were allocated for the more delicate task of putting the ball into the hole.

As the game developed, separate teeing grounds were eventually established and the golf course in the form we know it today gradually began to emerge.

The players relied on the rabbits and the sheep to keep the grass short-cropped, for it was not until the early part of the twentieth century that mechanised grass cutting began to take over from the animals in golf course management. Indeed many of Britain's seaside links, Saunton Sands in Devon being a classic example, relied exclusively on rabbits to keep their fairways tightly cropped until well into the second half of the twentieth century when the myxomatosis epidemic of the 1950s killed so many of the rabbits off.

There were no club makers of course in the early

This anonymous painting of St Andrews shows players on the Old Course around 1720. The distinctive St Andrews skyline is in the background. This is thought to be the earliest image of golf in Scotland.

to progress a ball across country from a point which is above the ground, to a final resting place below it. In the early days of golf the ball was perched in the air for the drive or tee shot, on a small mound of sand extracted from the hole to which the players had just played.

A pinch of sand from the bottom of the hole was sufficient to make a suitable platform for the tee shot, and therefore the tee was immediately beside the previous hole. However, the removal of many pinches of sand inevitably made the hole deeper until a point was reached when a new hole had to be cut.

There were no fairways as such, just relatively smooth stretches of turf, probably created in the first place by the continual tracking of rabbits and foxes and by the locals who hunted them. Golfers extended the tracks further into

John Charles Dollman's 'The Sabbath Breakers' depicts events of 1593 at a time when the church ban on Sunday play often resulted in fines for the miscreants or excommunication for repeated offences.

days of the game but golfers found that the skills of the weapons makers could be pressed into service, particularly those of the bow makers who made the bows which King James II was so keen for his populace to use in preference to golf clubs.

The bow makers became the first club makers, manufacturing crude but effective implements first for the wooden balls used until the early seventeenth century, and then more sophisticated clubs to deal with the feather ball, the first major development in golf equipment.

The bow makers who first began the development of the slender, fragile, long-nosed wooden clubs that held sway until the arrival of the gutta percha ball in the middle of the nineteenth century, were club makers in their own right, and examples of the fine work of the best of them, such as McEwan and Philip and Tom Morris himself, command considerable sums in the present day.

A top hat was the recognised measure of feathers, which were then boiled and stuffed into a leather pouch to make a 'featherie' golf ball. The feather ball was an expensive commodity but was the only golf ball available for two centuries until the gutta percha ball superseded it in 1848.

THE BALL MAKERS

In the beginning the golf ball was made of wood, probably of beech, but the feather ball, or 'featherie', came into existence around 1618, marking the first ball improvement in golf.

The feather ball was made in Scotland for more than 200 years until it was superseded by the gutta percha ball in 1848.

It was expensive and easily damaged and the single element that dictated that the game was played in its earliest stages by the wealthier sections of the community who could afford the price of the golf balls.

The task of crafting a featherie was not only arduous for the ball makers of the time, but very detrimental to their health. The ball maker's lungs were filled with feather dust and the constant pressure on the chest of forcing the boiled feathers into the small leather pouch with a special crutch-handled filling rod, took its toll.

Even the most experienced ball maker could only manufacture four feather balls in a day, which accounted for their price of three to four shillings, a huge sum at the time and more even than the cost of a golf club.

Golf Gets Organised

The game of golf as we know it today did not really emerge from its crude beginnings on the east coast of Scotland until it began to become organised around the middle of the eighteenth century. Clubs began to be formed devoted exclusively to golf, and with them the development of a generally accepted set of rules.

The first golf club for which there is definite proof of origin is the Gentlemen Golfers of Leith, now the Honourable Company of Edinburgh Golfers at Muirfield, instituted in 1744.

In that year 'several Gentlemen of Honour skilful in the ancient and healthful exercise of Golf' petitioned the Edinburgh City Council to donate a silver club for their annual competition on Leith Links. The winner of the competition was declared Captain of the Golf for the year, and a silver ball with the date and the Captain's name inscribed upon it, was attached to the silver club. The date of the first ball attached to the silver club has now become recognised as the most reliable evidence of the inaugural date of the very earliest clubs devoted to golf.

There have been claims from other clubs that they are older than the Honourable Company, for example the Royal Burgess Golf Club in Edinburgh and the Royal Blackheath Golf Club in England, but no evidence to substantiate their claims has ever been found. The Royal Blackheath Club claims to date back to 1608 but the date of the purchase of their silver club was 1766 when the first ball was attached.

The Royal Burgess Club claims 1735 as its inaugural date, but when the Society of St Andrews Golfers, now the Royal & Ancient Golf Club, first put their silver club up for competition in 1754 it was, according to the R & A's minute book, open for competition to all clubs in Great Britain and Ireland. There was a response from the Gentlemen Golfers of Edinburgh but none from the Royal Burgess Club not far along the road, which must be considered strange if the club had been in existence for almost twenty years before that.

There is no record of any rules attaching to the earliest form of the game of golf, although it is safe to assume that there had to be some from the very beginning. It was not until a formal competition among players arrived with the presentation to the Gentlemen Golfers of Leith of a silver club from the City Council of Edinburgh for annual competition, that there was a need to agree a set of rules under which the competition would be played.

Compared with the Rules of Golf as they stand today, the 'Articles & Laws in Playing Golf' drawn up by the Leith golfers in 1744 were brief indeed. There were 13 in all, compared to the 34 Rules with scores of subsections, 48 Definitions, four Appendices plus the Rules of Amateur Status, that now govern the game of golf.

Among those instrumental in drawing up the first set of rules was John Rattray, an Edinburgh surgeon who won the first Silver Club in 1744 and therefore became the Gentlemen Golfers' first

The Silver Club presented to the Honourable Company of Edinburgh Golfers by the City of Edinburgh, and first played for in 1744, was paraded through the streets of Edinburgh before the annual meeting to the beat of the drum. (D. Allan, 1787).

Captain. Clearly he was a player of considerable skill for he won again the following year, but his golf was interrupted when he was called from his bed to act as Surgeon to Bonnie Prince Charlie's troops at the Battle of Prestonpans.

He followed the Prince, some say reluctantly, on his march to Derby and thereafter to the famous defeat at Culloden where he was taken prisoner. It was only the intervention of his fellow Leith member, Duncan Forbes, that saved him from the gallows and allowed him to resume his duties as Captain of the Club in 1747.

The competition for the Gentlemen Golfers' Silver Club in 1744 is arguably the first championship in golfing history, although it was a relatively modest affair contested by a dozen souls over two rounds of the five-hole course at Leith. It would be more than a century later before the beginnings of professional golf made their appearance.

By the middle of the nineteenth century professional golf was still very much in its infancy. At that time two of the great centres for golf were St Andrews and Musselburgh, and there was great rivalry between the players native to both places. Money matches became the forerunners of the tournaments of the present day and it was as a result of these matches that professional players came into being.

At Musselburgh the Dunn brothers Willie and Jamie, the Park brothers Willie and Mungo, Bob Ferguson and Dave Brown were the main golfers who played for money, while St Andrews had Allan Robertson, Tom Morris Snr, David Strath, Bob Martin, Jamie Anderson and Tom Kidd.

All were either club makers, ball makers or caddies and Allan Robertson was regarded as the doyen of them all – the champion golfer of his time and the first golf professional.

Tragically, Allan Robertson did not live to play in that first Open Championship at Prestwick in 1860. He had been the undisputed king of the links through the middle of the nineteenth century and it was widely held that he had never been beaten in a serious singles match on the links. That remains debatable

A group of the early professional players at St Andrews in 1856. From the left: James Wilson, Willie Dunn, Bob Andrew, Willie Park, Tom Morris Snr, Allan Robertson, Daw Anderson and Bob Kirk. (Photo: Thomas Rodger)

Old Tom Morris looks on in the background, interested in this player's attempt to escape from the sand dunes. The date is c.1890.

and has to be considered in the light of what constituted a serious match, but the fact is that for many a long year Allan Robertson was virtually invincible.

It is known that when paired with Tom Morris Senior the pair were never beaten in foursomes play, and they were involved in some very serious matches for sums of money that were, for the time, a king's ransom. The most famous of them, perhaps, was the 1849 match between Allan and Old Tom on the one side and the Dunn brothers Willie and Jamie of Musselburgh, on the other. The purse was a staggering £400 and was played for over three courses, St Andrews, Musselburgh and North Berwick Links. It was by all accounts a Titanic battle with Allan and Tom Morris taking the final two holes for victory after having been four down with eight holes to play.

The oldest championship in the world is the Open, first played at Prestwick in 1860, but first suggested at the October meeting of the Prestwick Golf Club in 1856. It took four years for the Championship to get off the ground at all and it has to be conceded that it attracted little more than local attention at the time.

Alas, the first Open Championship came too late for Allan Robertson. He died in September 1859 at the age of 44 from an attack of jaundice.

There were only eight entrants, all of them pro-

fessionals of sorts, in that they were caddies or club or ball makers, for that first Open Championship. The Prestwick Club, which had recognised the gathering importance of professional golf, had proposed that the tournament should be 36 holes of medal play and be open to professional golfers from all clubs. It had further suggested the tournament be played at either St Andrews or Prestwick and that the prize might be a piece of plate or silver.

In the event the idea was greeted with little enthusiasm by all the clubs circulated, and Prestwick in the end decided to go it alone. The Club commissioned a fine red leather belt with silver decoration, including the Burgh of Prestwick's Coat of Arms, from James and Walter Marshall, Goldsmiths, Jewellers and Watchmakers of Edinburgh, at a cost of £25.

Play was over three rounds of the Prestwick links, a total of 36 holes in all, and to ensure that the Rules of Golf were strictly obeyed, the Prestwick Club appointed markers to accompany each pairing. A committee of four very experienced gentleman golfers was selected to settle difficult problems 'in the spirit of the game'.

In the end there were as many officials as there were entrants, for only eight professionals contested the first Open Championship at Prestwick.

It was a mark of the low esteem in which professional players were held at the time that the markers were appointed to oversee play. In the second year of the Championship amateur gentlemen players were allowed to compete, but while the professionals were still required to have markers accompany them, the amateurs were not; a clear indication of the demarcation between gentlemen and players that existed at that time.

The pairings for the first Open Championship in 1860 were: Thomas Morris (Prestwick) and Robert Andrews (Perth); William Park (Musselburgh) and Alexander Smith (Bruntsfield); William Steel (Bruntsfield) and Charles Hunter (Prestwick St Nicholas); George D. Brown (Blackheath) and Andrew Strath (St Andrews).

The first players teed off at 12 noon and the entire field completed the 36 holes before dark in the month of October, in marked contrast to the four days it now takes to complete the Championship.

Willie Park won the first Open with a score of 174, beating Tom Morris, who had moved to Prestwick from St Andrews to be Keeper of the Green in 1851, into second place by two strokes. Andrew Strath finished in third place, six strokes behind the winner.

Prestwick also has the distinction of having been involved in the first Amateur Championship. The idea of the Amateur was first suggested by the Honorary Secretary of the Royal Liverpool Club at Hoylake, Thomas Potter, in 1884 but because only a limited number of clubs were invited to take part it was not officially recognised

as the Amateur Championship until 1886.

Prestwick was one of three clubs chosen to host the event and did so for the first time in 1888.

A portrait of Willie Park Snr, the first champion golfer after the inaugural Open at Prestwick in 1860. (Artist unknown.)

THE R&A BECOME THE RULING BODY

From the middle of the nineteenth century the Society of St Andrews Golfers, which became the Royal & Ancient Golf Club of St Andrews after the award of the title by King William IV in 1834, emerged as the most influential club in Scotland.

There was then an obvious need for a standardisation of the rules of the game, and in 1897 the R & A was invited by the leading clubs of the day to compile a uniform code. It created a Rules of Golf Committee of 15 of its members, with powers to deal with proposals

on and the interpretation of the rules, and that in all such matters the R & A was to be the final authority. The Committee's terms of reference have remained the same ever since.

In the United States, three years before the Rules of Golf Committee was actually formed, the United States Golf Association had been founded to, among other things, 'establish and enforce uniformity in the rules of the game...'

During the first half of this century the R & A and the US GA both

applied the same basic rules – with one or two exceptions – but made separate interpretations of decisions on them. At a special conference in 1951 these differences were largely resolved, with the only stumbling point ball size and some minor points on play.

A Joint Decisions Committee was set up to establish uniformity, and a book of Decisions on the Rules is now jointly published by the two organisations, ensuring that golfers all over the world play to the same set of rules.

Scottish Supremacy

Today golf is an international game played in every corner of the world. It owes that popularity to the pioneering efforts of Scottish golfers in the nineteenth century who built upon the early framework of organisation and spread the gospel of golf with the enthusiasm and dedication of missionaries.

As we have already seen the game had witnessed some early movement out of Scotland to other golfing outposts, taken by royalty to England as far back as the early seventeenth century, by Scottish merchants to far away places like India, where the Royal Calcutta Golf Club dates back to 1829, and by the armed forces to South Carolina in the United States, where golf was played long before the famous Apple Tree Gang founded the first American golf club at Yonkers in New York in 1888. These, however, were isolated pockets; golf was very much vested in the hands of the Scots, and virtually confined within Scotland's borders, until well into the nineteenth century.

The reasons were simple: only the Scots knew how to play, they had the skills to manufacture the clubs and balls required to play; they were the only nation then with any experience of laying out a course upon which to play and relatively poor communications and transport had, broadly speaking, left the game as yet unexposed to the wider world.

Two things changed all that. Firstly the discovery that the rubber from a gutta percha tree could be easily and cheaply moulded into a much more serviceable golf ball than the expensive 'featherie', the only option until 1848, thus opening the game up to a much wider audience. Secondly there was the rapid expansion of the Victorian era which brought new prosperity to an English middle-class and with it an improved transport system. Many of this now mobile middle class imitated the royal family by holidaying in Scotland, where they discovered the delights of golf and then took the game back with them south of the border.

In terms of playing the game, Scotland's professional players, nearly all of whom were also caddies for the gentlemen players of the time, dominated.

A typical late-nineteenth- century scene at North Berwick shows the intense interest among the general public in the matches of the time. Ben Sayers, Hugh Kirkaldy and Sandy Herd were involved in this match on the 4th hole on 9 September 1891. Old Tom Morris was one of the referees.

For the first 30 years of the Open Championship, after its inauguration in 1860, none but a Scot took the title. It was not until the great English amateur, John Ball from Hoylake, won the Open at Prestwick in 1890 that the Scottish stranglehold, first on the Championship Belt and then on the famous claret jug, was loosened.

In the first decade of the Open the Morris family from St Andrews, father and son, won the Championship Belt seven of the 11 times for which it was played. Tom Morris Snr, who became the most recognisable figure in the history of Scottish golf, fastened on the old leather Belt four times; his son Tommy captured it three times in a row, and in so doing won the Belt outright.

That was in 1870, and there being no trophy to play for the following year there was no Open Championship until 1872, when the Royal & Ancient Golf Club of St Andrews, Prestwick Golf Club and the Honourable Company of Edinburgh Golfers, subscribed for the challenge cup we now know as the famous claret jug.

The second half of the nineteenth century was the heyday of Scottish golf. For a decade Old Tom and Young Tom Morris dominated the game, with young Tommy undeniably the finest player of his age, the finest in the history of the game to that point, and some would argue even longer afterwards. What he might ultimately have achieved will never be known, for the great and terrible tragedy of that era was the untimely death of Young Tom at the age of 24, only a few months after his wife had died in childbirth. The young Tom Morris was inconsolable and it was widely held that he died of a broken heart.

There were other great players, too, of course, like the Parks of Musselburgh, who did battle with Old Tom and Allan Robertson, the game's first recognised professional, in many famous matches. Willie Park Snr won the first Open in 1860 and was

champion again in 1863, 1866 and 1875. His brother Mungo won in 1874 and Willie's son, Willie Jnr won in 1887 and again two years later. There were legendary figures like Jamie Anderson from St Andrews and Bob Ferguson from Musselburgh, and Willie Fernie from Dumfries, all of whom have

The famous claret jug, the Open Championship trophy, subscribed for by the Royal & Ancient Golf Club, the Prestwick Club and the Honourable Company of Edinburgh Golfers after Young Tom Morris had won the Championship Belt three times in succession from 1868 and it became his property. The challenge cup was first played for in 1872 when Young Tom was again the winner.

PLAY-OFF

The most unusual outcome to the Open Championship in those early days of the great Scottish professionals, was the victory of Bob Martin from St Andrews in 1876.

David Strath, another St Andrean, and younger brother of the 1865 champion, tied Martin over the Old Course at St Andrews.

It was alleged, however, that Strath had played to the 17th green before the players in front had left it, and as a result Strath took umbrage and refused to compete in the play-off. Bob Martin became Open Champion by default.

their names etched on the old claret jug.

There was Jack Simpson, one of six brothers, and champion golfer in 1884. Brother Archie was a great player too, although never the Open Champion. They were born in the village of Elie in Fife, but their names will always be more closely connected with Carnoustie, that famous links on the Angus coast.

There was Andrew Strath, another native of St Andrews, who won the Open in the sixth year it was played, 1865, and a decade or so later Bob Martin, another St Andrean, who was twice a winner and twice runner-up.

Prestwick, where Old Tom Morris had moved to from his native Fife to become Keeper of the Green in 1851, was a major golfing centre in the second half of the nineteenth century, Musselburgh, near Edinburgh, had been such for much longer still, but there was no argument that St Andrews was then, as it remains today, the undisputed capital of the golfing world.

It was from St Andrews and Fife, and from Carnoustie across the Tay Estuary, and from North Berwick and Musselburgh across the Forth Estuary, from as far north as Dornoch in Sutherland and from villages all along the east coast of Scotland, that golf moved outwards to the rest of the world. The latter half of the nineteenth century was the era of golf's evangelists; the players and the course designers who took the game in its earliest, barely organised form, to other parts of the British Isles and outward to the rest of the world.

Their mission continued well into the twentieth century, and the Scottish influence on the development of golf around the world, its culture and traditions, the ethics and values that set golf apart as the game of dignity and integrity, has been immense and profound. It is a measure of the evangelical strength of these pioneers that these same values still largely prevail, even in the face of the commercial forces that have so drastically changed – few for the better – most other major sports.

It was not only professional golfers who led this spread of golfing knowledge to the wider world. In fact the professional golfer of the nineteenth century and the early part of the twentieth was considered little more than a labourer. Most were caddies who carried the clubs of the gentlemen players of the day with the better among them playing in the few tournaments that existed at the time,

A very early photograph of a golf tournament at St Andrews in 1858 when the Royal & Ancient clubhouse was still a single storey building.

but mostly in matches for often considerable purses and upon which their patrons wagered considerable sums on the outcome. Professional players did take their knowledge further afield, more so as transport and communications improved, but many unsung amateur players, too, made considerable contributions of their own.

Wherever they travelled Scots took their favourite pastime with them. They set up courses and founded golf clubs. None made a more significant contribution to the mass explosion of golf in the late nineteenth and early twentieth centuries, than two expatriate Scottish school friends from Dunfermline in Fife, John Reid and Robert Lockhart, although neither is likely to have realised it at the time. Reid is regarded as the 'father of American golf', as we will see later, but Lockhart had a significant part to play as well.

While Reid was introducing golf to the United States, essentially for the first time, the game was spreading like wildfire in the British Isles. Scottish professionals were imported south of the border into England and to Ireland and Wales to lay out courses to meet the new demand for the game.

A measure of the demand for their services is the huge increase evident in the number of golf clubs founded in the last two decades of the nineteenth century. Prior to that period the majority of clubs were in Scotland. In 1864 there were about 30 golf clubs in Scotland while in England there were only three – Royal Blackheath, Old Manchester and Westward Ho! By 1880 it is estimated that there were 60 clubs in Britain as a whole; by 1890 there were 387 and by 1900 Britain had 2330 golf clubs.

The Scots pioneers had done their work well.

CRUDEN BAY

The arrival of the railway helped spread the popularity of golf and seaside towns built courses as an attraction to visitors. This is a G.N.E.R. railway poster from the 1920s encouraging visitors to the town and the great links at Cruden Bay.

GOLF GOES BY RAIL

Although there is no written evidence so far traced of golf before James II's Act of Parliament of 1457, there is no doubt that a form of the game was being played in St Andrews as far back as the thirteenth century and perhaps even further back than that.

However, it was not until the latter half of the nineteenth century that the game really began to spread outwards from Scotland with the main reason the improvement in the transport system provided by the expanding railway network in Britain.

The railway gave enthusiasts access to the existing courses in Scotland, and to the newly developed Victorian seaside resorts in England, as well as north of the border. The first trains ran into St Andrews as early as 1850 but towards the latter part of the century, seaside towns built golf courses as an attraction to visitors and the railway gave easy access to them. It is no accident that virtually all of the great links golf courses of Britain have had, or still have, a railway line running along one of their boundaries.

Golf then moved inland where courses were built within train distance of the cities to meet the demand for this newly popular game.

Influential Scots

Over the centuries many Scots have left indelible marks on the game of golf world-wide. It was inevitable that this would be so since Scotland is both the geographical and cultural home of the game. Up until the middle of the nineteenth century there were only a few isolated pockets of golfers playing the game anywhere other than within the boundaries of Scotland itself, and most of these were either Scots by birth anyway, or were considerably influenced expatriates.

King James II

The first Scot who tried to influence the game to any real extent did not attempt to do so for the betterment of the game at all; in fact he went to some lengths to try to stop it altogether. Perhaps it was an early example of the Scots perversity in 'forbidding themselves to do what they want to do', as George Pottinger commented in his excellent account of the history of the Honourable Company, that King James II issued an infamous decree banning the game altogether in 1457.

It had no effect of course, for the Scots had more interest in pitting their wits against the links than in entertaining any fear of His Majesty's wrath because of their refusal to practise archery for defence of the nation at a time when the King was warring on several fronts. Even the threat of being taken by the 'King's officiars' was not sufficient to curtail the golfing desires of the populace.

Fourteen years later another Royal decree, this time by King James II's successor, James III, commanding that 'fute-ball and Golfe be abused in time coming', had as little effect on the population as the first one, and when James IV tried to ban the game again twenty years later he got just as short shrift.

There was at least some salvation for James IV, for he took to the game himself after signing a Treaty of Perpetual Peace with England, presumably making the requirement for archery practice less pressing in the process. His Treaty may have been a victory for hope over experience before or since, but at least it gave him some breathing space after having had the sense to take to the links himself.

If you can't beat them join them was clearly the monarch's view, which clearly he did as records of his having to pay a forfeit for losing at golf to the Earl of Bothwell, as well as accounts paid from the public purse for clubs and golf balls, clearly show.

King James I & VI

It was not until 1834 that golf officially became 'royal and ancient', when that title was awarded to the Society of St Andrews Golfers by King William IV, but it had strong royal connections long before that. Despite the efforts of James VI's ancestors to rid Scotland of the game, it flourished, and when James VI acceded to the English throne in 1603

King James II who infamously tried to ban golf by Act of Parliament in 1457, only for his subjects to virtually ignore his decree.

after the Union of the Crowns, he was already a keen hand at the game.

It was James I and VI who was responsible for the first migration of the game out of Scotland. When he moved south with his court he took his golf clubs with him and introduced the game to the neighbourhood of Greenwich.

It would be a long time before a golf club as such was formed, although golf is known to have been played at Westminster and Molesey Hurst. It was clearly because of the influence of the king and his courtiers, or their successors, that the game was played in both places, St James's Palace being within the confines of Westminster and Molesey Hurst being adjacent to Hampton Court, give the obvious clues.

King James played golf at Greenwich or Blackheath and very probably both. There are accounts of him playing in the fields at Greenwich and on the heath at Blackheath and it seems unlikely that His Majesty, who had played the game in Scotland, would not have had a course or courses of some sort laid out for his pleasure.

The existence of some kind of course at this time could certainly account for claims by Royal Blackheath that their club dates back to 1608, five years after the arrival of King James, but there is no evidence of the club in existence then.

A.J. Balfour

There have been many politicians who have played golf but none perhaps who have had more direct impact on it than a Scot who was British Prime Minister. Again it was a case of a Scot leading the way south of the border, for Mr Arthur J. Balfour undoubtedly did as much as anyone at the end of the nineteenth century to encourage the popularity of golf in England.

He was appointed Chief Secretary for Ireland in 1886, just at a time when an influential weekly journal had published a scathing and outrageous attack on the game of golf claiming that only stupid people played it, and that even among those who played the game well an essential condition was that they should be devoid of imagination and intellect. It was strong stuff.

Arthur Balfour, who was Captain of the R & A in 1894, was neither stupid nor devoid of intellect, and as Secretary for Ireland at a particularly tragic time in that long-suffering country's history, he was very much in the public eye. He was known as an enthusiastic, if not particularly accomplished, golfer but he made a point at every opportunity of striding out round the links, accompanied by his

King James IV was another Scottish monarch who tried to proscribe golf but also got short shrift from his subjects. Realising he could not beat them His Majesty decided to join them and took up the game after signing a Treaty of Perpetual Peace with England.

British Prime Minister Arthur J. Balfour, did much to popularise golf in England and was Captain of the R & A in 1894. He once famously said: 'Give me my books, my golf clubs, and leisure, and I would ask for nothing more'.

Duncan Forbes of
Edinburgh was a major figure
in the early organisation
of golf. His passion for the
game extended to playing
on the beach when frost
and snow made the course
unplayable.

Duncan Forbes

Duncan Forbes was President of the Court of Session in Edinburgh at the time of the Jacobite uprising and was strenuous in his efforts to prevent the 1745 Rebellion which ended in such bloody slaughter at Culloden. He was also a keen golfer and there seems a strong possibility, although there is no real evidence to support the claim, that he was the guiding force behind the formation of the Gentlemen Golfers of Leith, which eventually became the Honourable Company of Edinburgh Golfers.

He had a passion for golf that extended to not allowing even the frosts and snows of winter to deter his play. When such conditions prevailed, and the course was unplayable, he was known to take to the seashore and play along the sands.

In November 1728 he described a match against his son over the links of Musselburgh:

'This day, after a very hard pull, I got the better of my son at the gouf. If he was as good at any other thing as he is at that, there might be some hopes of him.'

Duncan Forbes did not actually play in the first competition for the silver club of the Gentlemen Golfers – he played in the second year – but was a major figure in the early organisation of the game.

two detectives, to contradict the claims of the journal. Because of the regard in which he was held his example discredited the claims of the paper and encouraged many in England to take up the game.

An interesting study of
St Andrews players on the
1st fairway of the Old Course
c.1850. Sir Hugh Lyon Playfair,
saviour of St Andrews, wears
his customary 'lum' hat. On
his right is Robert Cathcart.
Major Moncrieff addresses
the ball and George Whyte-
Melville looks on (far right).

Sir Hugh Lyon Playfair

In the early years of the nineteenth century the city of St Andrews – for city it is despite its modest size – was rapidly in decline, as was the famous University. By the middle of the century it was in danger of extinction altogether and was only saved by two things – the game of golf and the intervention of Sir Hugh Lyon Playfair, Provost of the Royal Burgh, and a former Captain of the R & A.

Sir Hugh instituted sweeping changes in the city in the early 1850s, by clearing out many of the unsanitary buildings and modernising the town to the standards of a health resort acceptable to the growing numbers of middle-class visitors coming to play golf.

He was an eccentric character who always wore a 'lum' hat of the type used to measure the quantity of feathers required for a feather ball, and was renowned for his other foible of having written on his umbrellas, 'Stolen from Major Playfair'.

However, Sir Hugh Lyon Playfair's legacy is that it was he who set about the reclamation of the ground in the area of the present 1st fairway on the Old Course, making it possible for the 1st green as it now stands to be built.

Before this work, which he started and which was continued by another St Andrews benefactor, George Bruce, sand from the sea and at times gravel brought in with the high tides, was blown or washed up as far as the steps leading up to the R&A clubhouse.

It was the reclamation of the land together with the construction of the new first green that made the right hand circuit of the Old Course, as it is played now, possible.

Dr Alister MacKenzie

Alister MacKenzie was a Scotsman in everything but birth. His father was a Scottish doctor of medicine who had moved to Yorkshire where Alister was born. In the great golf boom around the turn of the century, with its huge demand for new golf courses, the profession of golf course architect was born and Alister MacKenzie became one of the giants of the craft.

He trained as a doctor and served as surgeon with the Somerset Regiment in the Boer War in South

Africa where he became fascinated by the art of camouflage, at which the Boers were so highly skilled.

When he returned to Britain he put his acquired knowledge of the subject to good use by becoming more involved in golf-course design. Together with another great golf course designer, Harry S. Colt, they designed Alwoodley, near Leeds, where MacKenzie was secretary.

With the outbreak of the First World War, Alister MacKenzie returned to Army service, but not this time as a medical man, but as an expert in camouflage. After the war he rapidly became known for his golf course design work and his fame spread around the world.

He built the famous Cypress Point golf course in California, opened in 1928, but remains best

Dr Alister MacKenzie trained as a doctor but became a master of camouflage and one of the most eminent golf course architects.

29

Depicted in a painting
by Leland Gustavson, the
pioneers of American golf
rest under the tree which
gave them their 'Apple Tree
Gang' nickname.

remembered for the Augusta National course which he designed with Bobby Jones.

Unfortunately MacKenzie did not live to see his masterpiece completed. He saw the finished construction work but died in rather impecunious circumstances before he saw any grass on the course.

The Apple Tree Gang

It was two Dunfermline school friends who pioneered golf in the United States. John Reid and Robert Lockhart were from Dunfermline in Fife, not far from St Andrews. Reid, a resident of Yonkers in New York, is now generally regarded as the 'father of American golf', although Lockhart, a New York linen merchant, also had a significant role to play.

In the summer of 1887 Lockhart ordered six golf clubs and two dozen gutta percha golf balls from Old Tom Morris's shop in St Andrews to take to his friend John Reid in New York. The order was not completed before Lockhart sailed back to America, and the clubs and balls did not reach him until some time later.

Then, on 22 February, 1888, Washington's birthday, Reid and five of his friends – Lockhart was not among them – took themselves into a cow pasture opposite Reid's house in Lake Avenue, Yonkers and, taking advantage of a sudden thaw, laid out their first course. Their pioneering efforts on this three-hole course lasted only three weeks before a blizzard brought a temporary halt to the golf invasion of America.

Reid and his friends formed the St Andrew's Golf Club, named after its famous Scottish counterpart but distinguished from it by the use of the apostrophe. The Club moved to a new site in 1892

in an apple orchard on the Weston estate, where Reid and his friends became known as the 'Apple Tree Gang' after the apple tree under which they sat for shade and took refreshments.

A branch from the original tree is silver mounted and on display in the R & A clubhouse at St Andrews.

Donald J. Ross

Donald Ross was a founder and the only honorary president of the American Society of Golf Course Architects, and a designer of many of America's most revered courses. However, he was a Scot by birth and by nature, and a prominent example of the influence that Scotland has had on the development of golf around the world.

He was born in Dornoch in Sutherland in 1873 and moved to the United States in 1899 after a brief apprenticeship with Old Tom Morris at St Andrews.

He was both a playing and a teaching professional, but by 1910 had made golf course architecture his primary occupation. Within ten

Donald Ross was both
a playing and a teaching
professional until he found
golf course architecture was
much more rewarding.

years his was the designer label on countless courses across the United States. He was earning $30,000 a year from his design work at a time when Walter Hagen and Gene Sarazen were playing for $1000 purses and he was, as Ron Whitten of *Golf Digest* described him, 'the first superstar of American golf'.

Estimates of how many courses he worked on vary between 400 and 500. He designed many famous courses including Oakland Hills, Seminole, Scioto and Interlachen, but he is best remembered for the wonderful layout of Pinehurst No 2 in North Carolina where he died in April 1948.

Donald Ross was also credited with the creation of the first indoor golf school in Boston soon after his arrival in the United States. He was also responsible for the first practice grounds in the States and built the famous 'Maniac Hill' at Pinehurst, which survives to this day.

P. Mackenzie Ross

Sometimes confused with Donald Ross, Mackenzie

Ross was another Scottish golf course architect who contributed much to the development of course design, but in his own country and in Britain and the continent of Europe rather than the United States.

To some extent he carried on where the legendary James Braid had left off and is remembered particularly for the renewal of the Turnberry courses after the Second World War.

Mackenzie Ross built many other fine courses, including the links at Southerness-on-Solway, before his death in 1974.

The splendid figure of Robert Forgan, founder of the club-making firm bearing his name, seated in his St Andrews workshop. He was a nephew of the famous club maker Hugh Philp, and his assistant from 1852 until his uncle's death in 1856. Forgan was one of the first club makers to use the American wood, hickory, for club shafts.

SCOTTISH STANDARDS

British Prime Minister Arthur Balfour often played at North Berwick where he had a famous caddie by the name of Big Crawford, who also carried for the tiny figure of Ben Sayers in his important matches.

Big Crawford – he was well named for he was a giant of a man weighing well over 17 stone – had a booth at the far end of North Berwick links where he would dispense ginger-beer, and often it was suspected something a little stronger, to passing players.

When he knew that A. J. Balfour would be playing on the course, Big Crawford would hoist a small Scottish standard over his stall near the 8th green in honour of his hero.

One day it happened that the Grand Duke Michael of Russia arrived at the ginger-beer stand, and seeing the Scottish standard flying, approached Big Crawford with a query. Whether he was put up to asking the question in his best Scottish accent history does not reveal, but he is said to have asked of the big caddie, 'Whom is yon flag flying for?'

'A better mon than you!' was the uncompromising reply.

CHAPTER TWO

THE PLAYERS

Golf in the early days as it became organised was very much the preserve of the wealthier classes, professional and military men and the landed gentry who not only had the time to play but the wherewithal to afford the cost of early equipment, particularly feather golf balls which were incredibly expensive.

The first golf club members were therefore gentlemen of substance and it was not until the arrival of the much less expensive gutta percha ball in 1848 that the game had a chance to expand into the wider community. As it did so the demand for more courses and for teachers became imperative, and golf began to see the emergence of the professional. These men who made golf their business arrived from the ranks of the caddies, who had previously carried the clubs of their gentlemen employers, and from the ball makers like the first professional, Allan Roberston, who kept the gentlemen players supplied with their expensive feather balls.

Golf was able to cross the barriers of class as in no other walk of life. Great matches were played between sides composed of gentlemen players and professionals. Allan Robertson and Old Tom Morris and Willie and Jamie Dunn of Musselburgh often did battle with huge sums of money resting on the outcome. Large crowds used to follow the matches and betting was often heavy on the result.

As the game expanded quickly in the second half of the nineteenth century, money matches, and eventually tournaments, were held for professional players only. The first of consequence was the Open Championship of 1860, restricted to professional players and caddies who had to be supervised by gentlemen 'markers' to ensure that the rules of golf were strictly adhered to. When the gentlemen players were allowed to play in the event the following year, the professionals were still required to have markers, but the gentlemen players were trusted entirely to conduct themselves appropriately on the links.

Two-thirds of the Great Triumvirate. Harry Vardon (left) and James Braid, who between them won 11 Open Championships. With the third member of the Triumvirate, J.H. Taylor, they dominated the Open for two decades from 1894 until 1914. Vardon's list of six victories has never been equalled. Braid went on to design or remodel nearly 200 golf courses.

Early Days

Gentlemen Players

The great gentlemen players, perfectly capable of beating the professional players of the day, emerged in force in the last decade of the nineteenth century. In Scotland the dominant figures were Leslie Balfour-Melville and John E. Laidley. Both were prominent members of the Honourable Company of Edinburgh Golfers and Leslie Balfour-Melville won no fewer than six gold and three silver medals of the club. He won the Amateur Championship in 1895 and the jury is still out on whether he was a better player than Laidley.

Leslie Balfour-Melville was Captain of the Honourable Company in 1902 and Captain of the Royal & Ancient Golf Club three years after that. He had the remarkable claim to fame of having played for Scotland at golf, rugby and cricket as well as being Scottish lawn tennis champion.

Johnny Laidley, on the other hand, was less of an all-rounder but a remarkable golfer in his time. He won the Amateur Championship twice, in 1889 and 1891, beating Leslie Balfour-Melville in the first final and the great English amateur, Harold Hilton, in the second.

In the 1893 Open Championship he finished runner-up to Willie Auchterlonie, only two strokes behind.

Laidley won ten golf medals of the Honourable Company at Musselburgh and another ten after the

Huge crowds, including many ladies, turned out to watch the great amateur players of the late nineteenth century, confirmed by this photograph c.1889. Horace Hutchinson (left), Leslie Balfour-Melville and Johnny Laidley are the players on the tee.

club moved to Muirfield. In his long and distinguished career he played for Scotland against England in ten consecutive years.

Freddie Tait

When the great amateur player, Freddie Tait, was killed at Koodoosberg Drift in the Boer War in 1900, a great shadow was cast across golf in Scotland. Lieutenant Tait of the Black Watch was one of the golfing heroes of the day and one of the most popular players in the country.

In 1890 he joined the Royal & Ancient Golf Club and that same year lowered the record on the Old Course at St Andrews to 77. Four years later he reduced it to 72.

Freddie Tait was three times the leading amateur in the Open Championship and won the Amateur Championship in 1896 and again in 1898.

His father was Professor of Natural Philosophy at Edinburgh University and conducted many experiments into the aerodynamics of the golf ball. He enlisted his son's help in these experiments, taking advantage of Freddie Tait's reputation as a long and consistent hitter of the golf ball.

Freddie Tait had once driven a gutty ball 280 yards, all carry, at St Andrews and in 1893, on frozen ground, he hit a drive at the long 14th a distance of 341 yards. The carry was measured at 245 yards.

Allan Robertson

When Allan Robertson died at the early age of 44 in 1859, the year before the first Open Championship, he was the finest player in St Andrews, consequently in Scotland and therefore in the world. When news of his death after an attack of jaundice travelled round the 'auld grey toon' one member of the Royal & Ancient Golf Club was moved to say: 'They may shut up their shops and toll their bells, for the greatest among them is gone'.

Such was the regard in which Allan Robertson was held in his home town of St Andrews.

He is generally regarded as being the first golf professional, for not only was he a remarkable player but also a skilled feather ball maker and a caddie to important members of the Royal and Ancient Club and visitors to the town. Tom Morris Snr was apprenticed to Allan Robertson as a ball maker and eventually they became a formidable partnership playing together in matches for some-

35

Joyce Wethered

(Lady Heathcoat-Amery) putting out in her match against Phyllis Lobbett in the 1929 Womens' Open at St Andrews. Bobby Jones once described Miss Wethered as having 'the best swing of either man or woman' he had ever seen.

times very large stakes. They were never beaten.

It is often said that Allan Robertson was never beaten in singles play either, but this is not strictly true. He is known to have lost twice to 'Old Tom' but neither match was for anything substantial in the way of winnings.

In 1858, the year before his death, Allan played a match against Mr Bethune of Blebo and holed the Old Course in a score of 79, the first time 80 was ever beaten. Allan Robertson had been born in the

month of September, his record score had been achieved in September and he was lost to the game on a sad September day.

Old Tom and Young Tom Morris

The Morrises, Old Tom and Young Tom, are the two most easily identifiable figures from Scottish golf in the second part of the nineteenth century. Old Tom was a four-times winner of the Open Championship and an institution in his home town of St Andrews.

In 1851, at the age of 30, he left St Andrews to become Keeper of the Green at Prestwick on the west coast. It was widely held at the time that he had left after a disagreement with his employer and great playing partner, Allan Robertson, the feather ball maker, over the new gutta percha ball.

Old Tom was instrumental in setting up the first Open Championship at Prestwick in 1860 and although he was favourite to win, he finished runner up to Willie Park. However, he won for the following two years and again in 1864 and 1867 after which his son, Tommy, took over and dominated the event.

Old Tom was brought back to St Andrews in 1865 by the Royal & Ancient Golf Club as Keeper of the Green and subsequently became honorary

FIRST WOMAN GOLFER

Scottish women have made a significant contribution to the development of golf since the middle of the nineteenth century. The Ladies' Golf Club of St Andrews was formed in 1867 and by 1886 there were 500 members.

By 1872, the St Andrews Ladies' Spring and Autumn Meetings had become important events with a gold medal and the Douglas Prize open for competition. Miss Mary Lamb and her sister Miss May Lamb, Miss A. Boothby and Miss F. Hume McLeod were the leading players in the early days of the club and regular winners of the medals.

However, we have to go back much further than that to find the first woman player in Scotland.

That honour belongs to Mary Queen of Scots, mother of James VI of Scotland and I of England, and a notable player around the middle of the sixteenth century. Evidence of her keenness on the game is revealed in the account of one of her matches with one of her attendants, Mary Seaton, which the Queen lost; she presented her conqueror with a famous necklace.

The Queen most famously encountered the wrath of the Church for playing golf on the fields at Seton in 1567 only a few days after the death of her husband, Lord Darnley, father of James VI.

professional to the Club until his death at the age of 87 after a fall down stairs in the New Golf Club in St Andrews.

His son Tommy, 'Young Tom', was the greatest player of his age. At the age of 16 he tied Willie Park Snr, already a winner of three Open Championship titles, and Bob Andrew, another well established player, in a match at Carnoustie. Young Tom won the play-off and was on the way to immortality.

He won his first Open Championship at the age of 17 in 1868, recording the first hole-in-one in the championship on the way. He won again the following year and when the Championship Belt was his for the third year in succession in 1870, it was his to keep under the rules of the event. There being no trophy to play for the following year there was no championship, but after the famous claret jug, still played for today, was subscribed for by the R & A, the Prestwick Club and the Honourable Company of Edinburgh Golfers, Young Tom won that too. His winning run of four consecutive Open titles has never been equalled since.

While playing in a match, partnered by his father, at North Berwick in September 1875, a telegram arrived to say that his young wife of barely a year, who was pregnant, was seriously ill. Father and son made as best speed they could back to St Andrews across the Firth of Forth in a yacht made available to them by a resident. The boat had barely cleared the harbour when word arrived that Young Tom's wife and child had died in childbirth.

Young Tom never recovered from the shock and Old Tom found his son dead in his bed on Christmas Day 1875. He had been suffering from pneumonia, but the world of golf believed that the greatest player of the age had died of a broken heart.

The Parks of Musselburgh

The Park brothers, Willie and Mungo, were the standard bearers for the town of Musselburgh at the same time and in the same way that Old Tom Morris and Allan Robertson carried the flag for St Andrews. There were many great matches between them in the days before the Open Championship was instituted in 1860.

Willie Park won that famous inaugural Open at Prestwick and was champion again in 1863,

'A Grand Tournament by Professional Players' at Leith Links on 17 May, 1867. From the left: George Morris, Alex Greig, Andrew Strath, David Park, Willie Dunn, Old Tom Morris, Young Tom Morris (leaning on rail), Bob Kirk, Willie Dow and Jamie Anderson.

Willie Park Jnr at the top of his back swing c.1896. His famous caddie 'Fiery' looks on.

1866 and 1875. His brother, Mungo, was champion in 1874. For 20 years Willie Park had an open challenge to any other golfer for a stake of £100 and he had many famous battles with his old rival Tom Morris.

Willie Park's son, Willie Park Jnr learned quickly from his father and was not only a gifted player but a highly successful businessman. He expanded the family club and ball-making business in Musselburgh and became a golf course designer of much distinction, an inventor of new golf clubs and an author of books on golf instruction.

Willie Park Jnr won the Open Championship twice, in 1887 at Prestwick and again on his home course at Musselburgh in 1889. He was a renowned match player with his most famous encounter a match against Harry Vardon at North Berwick and Ganton in 1899. Special trains were run to take the spectators to watch. A crowd of 10,000 turned up at North Berwick to cheer on their hero but Vardon ran out a comfortable winner.

In 1896 Willie Park Jnr published a book, *The Game of Golf*, the first complete book on the game by a professional player.

Willie Dunn Jnr

Born in 1865 and a member of the famous Dunn family of Musselburgh, Willie Dunn Jnr was a player ahead of his time. As early as the turn of the century he was experimenting with steel-shafted clubs and wooden tee pegs instead of the pinch of sand taken from the hole that was then the standard practice.

He became an innovative golf course designer, moving first to France, where he helped his brother lay out a new course at Biarritz, and then to the United States. He crossed the Atlantic in March 1891 and within three months of his arrival built a 12-hole course at Shinnecock Hills on New York's Long Island with very little equipment and using Indian labour from a nearby reservation.

Huge crowds watched the famous home and home match between Willie Park Jnr and Harry Vardon played at Ganton and North Berwick in 1899. The Scottish leg should have been played at Musselburgh but Vardon refused to play there because he feared problems with the partisan Musselburgh crowd. The stake was £100 a side and Vardon won by 11 and 10.

His layout was later extended to 18 holes and was the first seaside course to be developed in America. Shinnecock also set a trend as the first incorporated club in the United States and it had the first American clubhouse.

Willie Dunn Jnr is considered to have been the first golf course designer of the new school and as such had a significant effect on the development of golf in America.

Andrew Kirkaldy

'Andra' Kirkaldy was one of the great characters of Scottish golf in the latter part of the nineteenth century. He enlisted in the Black Watch at the age of 18 and fought in the Battle of Ytel-el-Kebir in Egypt in 1882. When he returned from war he was professional at the Winchester Club for a short time but his professional career was centred on St Andrews for most of his life.

Famous names gathered for a match at Leith Links in 1867. From the left: Andrew Strath, David Park, Bob Kirk, Jamie Anderson, James Dunn, Willie Dow, Willie Dunn, Alex Greig, Old Tom Morris, Young Tom Morris and George Morris.

ORIGINS OF THE VARDON GRIP

Six-times Open Champion, Harry Vardon, was responsible for the popularisation of the overlapping grip but, although his name is always associated with it, it was not in fact he who invented it.

It is known to have been in use by several leading players before Vardon's time. The great Scottish amateur, Johnny Laidley, who was at the height of his powers a decade or so ahead of Vardon,

used the overlapping grip.

Another great Scottish amateur, Leslie Balfour-Melville, who was six years older than Laidley, and Amateur Champion in 1895, also used an overlapping grip.

Vardon's contemporary and a member with Vardon and James Braid of the Great Triumvirate which dominated the Open Championship from the beginning of the twentieth century to the First

World War, J. H. Taylor was also an exponent of the grip.

Quite how the grip came to be known as the Vardon grip, is not quite certain. One clue may be found in Harry Vardon's book *The Complete Golfer* in which he said: 'My grip is one of my own inventions'.

Clearly, however, it was not, and the origins of the overlapping grip, in universal use today, are most likely to be found in Scotland.

Sandy Herd lived rather in the shadow of the Great Triumvirate of Vardon, Braid and Taylor but was a fine St Andrews player. Bernard Darwin said that the number of his waggles was only exceeded by that of his friends.

Bob Ferguson

Bob Ferguson was another of the great Musselburgh players who made a major mark on the early Open Championships. Ferguson is one of only four players to have won the Championship three times in a row, which he did between 1880 and 1882. In 1883 he tied with Willie Fernie at Musselburgh, by taking only nine strokes to play the last three holes, but lost the play-off by one stroke after taking four at the last when Fernie took only two.

His speciality shot was the long approach using a putter – the 'Musselburgh Iron' as it became known – which he mastered a century before the Americans invented the Texas Wedge.

Sandy Herd

Sandy Herd was a fine St Andrews player who would have been much better known today had he not been a contemporary of the Great Triumvirate of Braid, Vardon and Taylor. He had several victories over Harry Vardon in match play but could rarely beat him in stroke play. He did succeed, however, in 1902 when he won the Open Championship at Hoylake beating Vardon and Braid by one stroke.

In his youth he was known as a 'bonny fechter' (good fighter), a player of dash, courage and stamina, but his habit of waggling the club many times before playing a stroke prompted golf writer Bernard Darwin to once comment: 'The number of his waggles is only exceeded by that of his friends'.

Sandy Herd played tournament golf until he was almost 70.

He was a fine player and tied for the Open Championship in 1889, only to lose in the play-off to Willie Park Jnr. He played in many famous matches, often with his brother Hugh, and was never slow to voice an opinion. His view that Muirfield was nothing more than 'an old water meadow' did not endear him to the members of the Honourable Company.

He was also very sensitive about the spelling of his name and when the letter 'c' was incorporated into it he used to say 'I'm a man, no' the linoleum toon', referring to the town by the same name further down the east coast of Fife. When Andrew Kirkaldy returned from England he was a playing professional until he was appointed Professional to the Royal & Ancient Golf Club.

James Braid

In the space of a single decade the remarkable James Braid became the first player in history to win five Open Championships. This tall, elegant man from the village of Earlsferry in Fife, not far from St Andrews, was one of the greatest players in the history of the game. In 1908 he set the record for the Open with 291, a score that stood until Bobby Jones beat it in 1927.

Braid moved to the famous Walton Heath Club in England as professional when it opened in 1903 and remained there for the rest of his professional career. He was an honorary member of the club for 25 years but it was typical of his unassuming nature that he always insisted on entering the clubhouse by the back door.

He was a true ambassador for professional golf, a founding member of the Professional Golfers' Association and later its president, a position to which he took great wisdom and the voice of moderation.

Braid's legacy to golf was much more than as a player. He remains one of the best and most prolific of all golf course designers and was instrumental in much of the early development of the profession. His best known creations are the King's and Queen's Courses at Gleneagles, the Rosemount course at Blairgowrie, the medal course at Carnoustie and the wonderful links at Nairn in Morayshire, but he was involved in close to 200 projects, either as the original designer or in remodelling work.

George Duncan

George Duncan, the Open Champion of 1920, was the son of the village policeman in Methlick, Aberdeenshire. He was renowned as a very fast player and may well have won more than one Open had the First World War not interrupted his career.

His victory at Deal was remarkable in that he opened with two disastrous rounds of 80 and was well down the field. However, on the second day – the Open was then played over 36 holes on each of two days – he returned wonderful scores of 71 in the morning and 72 in the afternoon, for victory.

George Duncan played against the United States in 1921 and 1926 and in the first three official Ryder Cup matches. He was captain of the side in 1929.

In all these international matches George Duncan won every singles match, beating the great Walter Hagen twice, the second time in 1929 at Moortown, by the remarkable score of 10 and 8.

A bemused Ben Sayers ponders how to extricate himself from a bunker c.1895. In those days bunkers were not raked as they are now and were even more of a hazard.

The Modern Era

Tommy Armour was blind in one eye, an Open Champion and the fastest machine gunner in the British Army.

Jock Hutchison was a diminutive and nervous man who, according to Bobby Jones, might well have won more than one Open Championship had he displayed a 'little more Scottish dourness'.

Tommy Armour

Tommy Armour is one of the most remarkable characters from the early days of the modern era. He was probably the first university educated professional in the history of golf and attended Edinburgh University before leaving to join the Tank Corps in the First World War where he served with great distinction and was highly decorated. He was the fastest machine gunner in the British Army and was congratulated personally by King George V for his efforts at the front line.

Bobby Cruikshank, a fellow professional who grew up with Armour and served with him in France, often recounted how Armour once captured a German tank single-handed, and when the German officer in charge refused to surrender, Armour strangled him with his bare hands.

Armour was blinded in one eye in a gas attack during the Great War but it did not affect his golf game. He emigrated to the United States in 1923 and quickly made a name as a great teacher after winning a dozen tournaments between 1927 and 1935 against big name professionals of the time.

It did not hurt that three of these victories were in major events, the US Open in 1927, the US PGA in 1930 and the Open Championship at Carnoustie in 1931.

Armour had wavy black hair and was given the name of the 'Black Scot'. In time, after he went prematurely grey, it was modified to the 'Silver Scot', the name he is remembered by today.

Tommy Armour was the last Scottish-born professional to win the Open Championship.

Jock Hutchison

Jock Hutchison from St Andrews was one of the best of the stream of Scottish professionals who went to the United States at the beginning of the twentieth century. He was a nervous man of slight stature. Bobby Jones once expressed the opinion that if Hutchison had had more Scottish dourness instead of a ready wit, he would have won many more championships than he did.

In 1916 Hutchison was runner-up in the first US PGA Championship and also runner-up in the US Open with Harry Vardon, Leo Diegel and Jack Burke. In 1920 he won the US PGA, beating J. Douglas Edgar, one up. The following year he returned to his native St Andrews and won the Open Championship in a famous play-off with the amateur, Roger Wethered.

In the first round Hutchison played the 8th and 9th in a remarkable total of three strokes. He holed his tee shot at the short 8th and then unleashed a huge drive at the 270-yard, par-4 9th which lipped the hole, almost went in, and lay stone dead for a two. His playing partner was Bobby Jones, playing in his first Open Championship.

Wethered took three from the Valley of Sin in the final round or would have won. Hutchison almost made the birdie three he needed to win outright but failed and a four meant a 36-hole play-off. There was a suggestion that Wethered would not contest the play-off because he was due to play in a cricket match elsewhere and had been granted an early start time for the final rounds to allow him to catch a train.

Play he did, however, but the amateur was no match for the seasoned professional over 36 holes, and Hutchison won by nine strokes.

Macdonald Smith

Macdonald Smith was the youngest of three brothers from Carnoustie who emigrated to the United States before the First World War. Brothers Alex and Willie were first to leave Scotland and Macdonald, then in his late teens, joined them after they had become settled.

Mac Smith, as he was known in America, was always reckoned to be the best player of the three, despite the fact that Alex and Willie were both US Open Champions.

In the 1910 US Open at Philadelphia Macdonald, still only 20 years old, came through the field with a fine 71 in the final round to fight his way into a play-off with his brother Alex and Johnny McDermott. Macdonald lost the play-off to his brother but it looked certain there was another US Open Champion just waiting in the wings. It did not happen that way, however, and Macdonald Smith became the eternal bridesmaid but never the bride.

John Panton, the quiet man of Scottish golf, and now the honorary professional to the Royal & Ancient Golf Club.

He was runner-up to Bobby Jones in the US Open and the Open Championship in Jones' Grand Slam year of 1930. Two years later he finished second to Gene Sarazen in the Open Championship at Prince's, Sandwich.

However, Macdonald Smith will always be associated with the famous Open Championship at Prestwick in 1925 when he led going into the last round by five strokes and looked a certain winner. Unfortunately the over-enthusiasm of the Scottish crowds to see a Scot beat another expatriate, Jim Barnes from Cornwall, also resident in America, denied him.

Smith was almost trampled underfoot by the huge crowds and it was reported that he never once saw one of his long shots land. He needed only a 78 to win or a 79 to tie but finished with 82 after being engulfed by the crowd.

It was the last time the Open was ever played at Prestwick.

John Panton, MBE

John Panton has always been the quiet man of Scottish golf. Born in Pitlochry in 1916 he turned professional in 1935 and dominated Scottish professional golf for close to two decades.

Macdonald Smith was reckoned the best of the three Smith brothers who emigrated to the United States before the First World War. His brothers both won US Open titles but he did not, and over-enthusiastic crowds trampled him out of victory when he should have won the Open Championship at Prestwick in 1925.

Eric Brown was known as the 'Brown Bomber' and famous for his fiery temper.

Ken Brown played for Scotland on many occasions although, like Sandy Lyle and Brian Barnes, he was born south of the Border. He, like his namesake Eric, had his brushes with authority, most famously during one of his five Ryder Cup appearances. Tall and very slim, Ken Brown was often known as the 'walking one iron', because of his mastery of that particular club. He also used an old wooden-shafted putter to great effect.

He was the leading British player in the 1956 Open at Hoylake and won the PGA Matchplay Championship the same year.

Panton is renowned as one of the finest iron players of the modern game and although his many victories were won mainly on home soil, he did win the Woodlawn Invitation Open in Germany three years in succession from 1958 to 1960.

John Panton was Scottish Professional Champion no fewer than eight times between 1948 until the middle 1960s; he also had seven victories in the Northern Open and won the West of Scotland PGA Matchplay four times.

He joined the Senior ranks in the 1960s and won the Pringle Seniors in 1967 and again two years later. He also won the World Seniors title in 1967.

John Panton was three times a Ryder Cup player, in 1951, 1953 and again in 1961. It was his number of appearances in the World Cup, however, that was remarkable.

He played in a total of 12 matches for Scotland in the event between 1955 and 1968. In addition, he won the Harry Vardon Trophy in 1951, the Association of Golf Writers' Trophy in 1967 and has been awarded the MBE in recognition of his services to golf.

Since 1988 John Panton has been the Honorary Professional at the Royal & Ancient Golf Club in St Andrews.

Eric Brown

Eric Brown turned professional after winning the Scottish Amateur Championship in 1946 and was the leading Scottish player in Europe in the 1950s. He won the Irish, Italian, Portuguese and Swiss Opens between 1951 and 1953 and together with John Panton had a stranglehold on the Scottish Professional Championship for many years.

Between them they won the Championship 13 times in an 18-year period with Brown winning five times. Brown had one of his best ever victories in the 1957 Dunlop Masters.

Always a mercurial character, Eric Brown had a reputation as a fiery competitor, which manifested itself particularly in Ryder Cup matches against the United States.

He played on four Ryder Cup teams between 1953 and 1959, winning all his singles matches, and was non-playing captain of the side in 1961 and 1971.

He had a famous battle with Tommy Bolt in the 1957 Ryder Cup, the last time Great Britain and Ireland beat the Americans before European players were brought in to bolster the side and save the event.

Brown beat Bolt 4 and 3 in a sometimes ill-

tempered exchange. Just before they were due on the tee neither Brown nor Bolt could be seen, prompting a famous comment from fellow professional Jimmy Demaret: 'Oh, they're out there on the practice ground throwing clubs at each other from fifty paces.'

Bernard Gallacher, OBE

Bernard Gallacher turned professional at the age of 23 in 1967 and made an immediate hit on the European Tour. He won two tournaments in 1969 and the Martini International in 1971. He has also won the Dunlop Masters twice, the Carrolls' International and Tournament Players' Championship among a host of other titles. He was Scottish Professional Champion four times, represented Scotland six times in the World Cup and seven times in the Double Diamond Tournament.

It is his contribution to the Ryder Cup for which he is still best remembered. He was involved as a player, assistant and Captain in every Ryder Cup team between 1969 and 1995. He played in every match between 1969 and 1983, eight in all, and was Tony Jacklin's chief lieutenant from 1985 to 1989 when the European team had its first victory over the Americans at The Belfry in 1985 and on American

soil for the first time the following year.

Gallacher replaced Tony Jacklin as Captain in 1991 and lost a narrow match against the Americans at Kiawah Island in South Carolina. However, he led his team to victory at Oak Hill, Rochester, New York in 1995 before handing the Captaincy over to Seve Ballesteros.

Bernard Gallacher has been one of the most highly respected of all Scottish professionals in an outstanding career which also included many years as professional at the Wentworth Club in Surrey.

Brian Barnes

Brian Barnes was actually born in Addington in Surrey, but like Sandy Lyle has always considered himself a Scot and has always been a popular figure north of the border. Barnes was a Millfield scholar and took to golf on the encouragement of his father who was secretary at Burnham and Berrow Golf Club.

As an amateur Barnes won the English and British Youths titles in 1964 before he turned professional that year. He became one of the 'Butten Boys', a group of young professionals brought together for special coaching, and was a pupil of former Open Champion, Max Faulkner, who is now his father-in-law.

Barnes has always been a controversial character and once famously ran into trouble with the PGA for marking his ball with a beer can in the Scottish Professional Championship at Dalmahoy. It was good publicity for the sponsors but bad news for Barnes, whose fondness for alcohol became a problem for him on more than one occasion during his career.

A winner of eight tournaments in a decade on the European Tour, Brian Barnes is best remembered

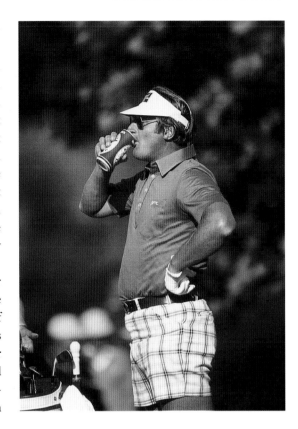

Brian Barnes was a Millfield scholar, a victor twice in one day over Jack Nicklaus in the Ryder Cup and is now enjoying a new lease of life on the Seniors' Tour.

Bernard Gallacher led his Ryder Cup team to victory at Oak Hill in America in 1995 before handing the captaincy to Seve Ballesteros.

for the Ryder Cup match at Laurel Valley in 1975. The Britain and Ireland side took a terrible drubbing at the hands of the Americans but Barnes, smoking his ever-present pipe, beat the mighty Jack Nicklaus twice on the same day in the singles, 4 and 2 in the morning and 2 and 1 in the afternoon.

Barnes has always been a popular player with galleries and the news that he was setting out on a new career on the Senior Tour, where he continues to play with distinction, was widely welcomed.

Sandy Lyle, MBE

Although from a distinctly Scottish family, Sandy Lyle was actually born in England, however he adopted his father's Scottish nationality after he turned professional in 1977. When he won the Open Championship at Royal St George's in 1985 he was the first Scot to win in more than 60 years and the first Briton since Tony Jacklin in 1969.

His crowning glory was to be the first Briton ever to win the Masters Tournament at Augusta in 1988, which he did with the help of a remarkable 7-iron shot from a bunker on the final hole. It was one of the greatest bunker shots ever seen at Augusta. It landed behind the pin and rolled back to within ten feet of the hole. Lyle needed a birdie to beat Mark Calcavecchia and he calmly rolled in the putt for victory.

Lyle has always had an individual style and Seve Ballesteros has said of him: 'When he is good he is the best and there is no one to touch him, but when he is bad he is almost the worst.'

He has a fine record in European golf, having won the European Open and the World Matchplay Championship as well as being the individual winner in the World Cup in 1987. He has twice played in the Ryder Cup and is a three-times winner of the Harry Vardon Trophy. In his career he has experienced many ups and downs and always bounced back, but into the 1990s Sandy Lyle's game began to go into a more serious decline, one from which it seemed he would never fully recover.

Sam Torrance

Apart from Colin Montgomerie, Sam Torrance has been the most successful Scottish-born professional since Eric Brown in the 1950s. He was Rookie of the Year in 1972 and has won a string of major events in Europe, including the Martini International, the Benson & Hedges International and the German Masters, since he turned professional in 1970.

In 1995 he won the Italian and Irish Opens and the British Masters and was within reach of achieving his ambition of finishing European number one. Going into the last nine holes of the Volvo Masters in the last week of the season, Sam was ahead of Colin Montgomerie after a fascinating struggle but was pipped at the post by a single stroke at Valderrama.

Like Bernard Gallacher, Sam Torrance has made a major contribution to the Ryder Cup in a long

Sam Torrance holed the winning putt in the historic Ryder Cup matches at The Belfry in 1985 and was a stalwart of the European team in every Ryder Cup from 1981 to 1995.

Sandy Lyle's crowning glory was victory in the Masters in 1988 at Augusta, the first Briton ever to win the famous green jacket. He also won the Open in 1985 but in the 1990s he suffered a serious decline in form.

forthright comments, often darkened countenance and open body language reveal not only a burning desire to succeed but perhaps a hint of his west of Scotland background.

Montgomerie is often misunderstood and has been the victim of some scandalous outbursts, particularly in the United States. On the golf course no one shows more dedication of purpose but off the course Colin Montgomerie is one of the nicest people it would be possible to meet in a day's march.

Gordon Brand Jnr was born in Burntisland, Fife, and enjoyed a remarkable amateur career until he joined the professional ranks in 1981. He won the English, Scottish and Swedish Amateur Strokeplay Championships as well as the Portuguese Amateur title and played in both the Walker Cup and the Eisenhower Trophy. As a professional he has twice won the European Open and many other prestigious titles. Brand Jnr – he uses the Jnr to avoid confusion with Gordon J. Brand – has twice played in the Ryder Cup and has made a host of appearances for Scotland in the World Cup and the Alfred Dunhill Cup.

Colin Montgomerie is another Scot who had an illustrious amateur career. Monty has dominated European golf in the 1990s just as Nick Faldo did in the decade before.

and distinguished career. He played in every Ryder Cup match from 1981 to 1995, eight in all, and the photograph of Sam Torrance in his red sweater holding his arms aloft after holing the winning putt, is the most enduring image of the historic European victory at The Belfry in 1985.

He scored three points in the 1995 Ryder Cup at Oak Hill which Europe won by a single point in dramatic fashion, and then he led Scotland to its first Alfred Dunhill Cup victory at St Andrews.

He has also a remarkable record of 11 appearances for Scotland in the World Cup.

The son of renowned Largs professional Bob Torrance, who has been a teacher to several top European players, Sam pioneered the broom-handle putter when it made its appearance in Europe and it has become his trademark.

Colin Montgomerie

Until Tom Kite made a late charge in the 1992 US Open at Pebble Beach to win his first major championship, he had for many years been known as the best player never to win a major. Today that mantle is worn by Scotland's Colin Montgomerie.

'Monty', as he is better known to golf galleries around the world, is a controversial figure whose

That he is one of the great players of the modern era there is no question. He has dominated golf in Europe for most of the 1990s, taking over where Nick Faldo left off at the end of the 1980s. In the world context he has ranked as high as No 2 in the official World Golf Ranking, a position he earned after winning the Dubai Desert Classic in 1996.

Colin Montgomerie grew up with golf, his father having been a long-serving secretary at Royal Troon, before retiring just after the Open Championship there in 1997.

Colin had an illustrious amateur career in which he won the 1985 Scottish Strokeplay Championship and the 1987 Scottish Amateur title. He played in the 1985 and 1987 Walker Cup teams before turning to the professional ranks in 1987.

Since then he has been a dominant winner of European Tour events and become a major player on the world stage. No one will forget his valiant effort at the 1997 US Open when he came up only one stroke short of Ernie Els in an amazing finish.

In the early part of 1998 Colin Montgomerie took some time off to be with his family and be present at the birth of his son Cameron in May, a few weeks after a disappointing tilt at the first major of the year, the Masters Tournament at Augusta. However, he returned to competitive golf with his

career remains over-shadowed by the lack of a major championship victory. He has come close, very close, but by the end of 1998 his name was still missing from that exclusive club of players with a major title to their name.

Colin Montgomerie knows that he is good enough to be a major winner, his one hope is that it does not take him as long as it did Tom Kite to get that particular monkey off his back.

Andrew Coltart has been widely tipped as a natural successor to Colin Montgomerie.

Belle Robertson, MBE, has been one of the truly outstanding figures in Scottish women's golf since the late 1950s. She has been Ladies' Champion of Britain and Scotland, Match Play Champion in New Zealand, British Women's Stroke Play Champion among a host of championship titles and has played no fewer than seven times in the Curtis Cup matches against the United States, and twice been non-playing captain. Belle Robertson has represented Scotland no fewer than 16 times in the Home internationals between 1958 and 1982, was honoured as Scottish Sportswoman of the Year four times between 1968 and 1981 and was voted Avia Woman Golfer of the Year in 1985.

biggest win on the European Tour, victory at the Volvo PGA Championship at Wentworth. He then went on to finish the season as the leading money winner on the European Tour for an unprecedented sixth successive time.

Despite his domination of European golf, and his standing world-wide, Colin Montgomerie's

Andrew Coltart

Andrew Coltart is one of the new breed of Scottish professionals making a big mark on the European Tour and tipped to be the natural successor to Colin Montgomerie. He established himself as one of the rising stars in professional golf when,

partnered by Gordon Brand Jnr, he won all three of his matches in his first appearance for Scotland in the Alfred Dunhill Cup at St Andrews in 1994. He also won the Australian PGA Championship that year, which established his reputation internationally.

Although originally from the Scottish Borders, Coltart now lives in Richmond, Surrey, but retains his Scottish connections with an attachment to the St Andrews' Old Course Hotel & Spa in St Andrews. He comes from a golfing family. His father is still a one-handicap player and his great-uncle was a founder member of the Thornhill Golf Club.

As an amateur he played in the Walker Cup and the Eisenhower Trophy before turning to the professional ranks in 1991.

In 1995 he won four of his five matches and partnered Sam Torrance and Colin Montgomerie to Scotland's first victory in the Alfred Dunhill Cup. He also tied third in the World Cup in China, again partnered by Sam Torrance.

Raymond Russell

It is on the shoulders of young players such as Raymond Russell that rests the future of Scottish professional golf, but it was a long struggle before the young man from Prestonpans could establish himself on the European Tour.

When he left school he worked on fruit and vegetable stalls to raise money to fund his golf and made many five-hour round trips by bus and train from his home near Edinburgh for golf lessons from Bob Torrance at his Largs headquarters.

Russell turned professional after playing the Walker Cup side that lost to the Americans at Interlachen in 1993. The year before he had won the Scottish Youths' Championship and he served a two-year apprenticeship on the Challenge Tour before finishing 16th at the Tour Qualifying School in 1995.

His determination and hard work paid off when he won his first European Tour event, the Air France Cannes Open at Royal Mougins, in 1996.

Raymond Russell turned professional after playing in the Walker Cup in 1993 and is one of Scotland's brightest prospects for the future.

51

CHAPTER THREE

SCOTLAND'S HISTORIC COURSES

Scotland is so steeped in the history of golf it is difficult to avoid stumbling over golf courses that have historic importance.

St Andrews is the most famous golf course in the world and generally regarded as the most historic, having changed little in five or six centuries; however there are many others which have historic claims to fame.

No attempt has been made here to try to identify the most important clubs in Scottish golf history, or, worse still, to place them in any order. Rather, the objective has been to select courses or clubs that have made their own particular and important contribution to the game.

Often the club attached to the course is the more historic element. For instance, Prestwick is of relatively modest antiquity as a club compared with the Royal & Ancient or the Honourable Company, but its historical importance is immense. Apart from the Open Championship, first played there in 1860, the club has pioneered many other great events including the first amateur foursomes event, but more particularly its members were revolutionary thinkers during the early days of organisation of the game. Similarly, the Honourable Company of Edinburgh Golfers is recognised as the oldest club in the world of golf, yet its course at Muirfield only dates back to just before the end of the nineteenth century, and was not then as widely acclaimed as it is now.

The eight courses and clubs featured in this section represent, therefore, a wide spectrum of the clubs and courses that are perhaps in George Orwell's terms, 'a little more historic than others'.

The most famous view in golf: the historic Swilcan Bridge at St Andrews with the Royal & Ancient Golf Club in the background.

Carnoustie

CARNOUSTIE CHAMPIONSHIP

Established
c.1839-1842
Course details:
18 holes
6941 yards
SSS 75
Address:
Links Parade
Carnoustie DD7 7JE

Tel: 01241 853249
Fax: 01241 853789

Right: A beautiful prospect at Carnoustie's 13th but intimidating bunkers surround the green.

Below: Deep bunkers threaten at the 2nd.

Since Scotland is the Home of Golf it follows naturally that the vast majority of the historic golf courses of the world carry the imprint of a Scottish hand. As golf developed and spread from Scotland the first golf course developers sought out the talents of Scottish golf course builders to help them with the task.

The most prominent players of the day were called on for advice on how to lay out golf courses, which is why Allan Robertson, Old Tom Morris, Willie Park and James Braid have left such an indelible mark on the history not only of championship golf, but of golf course design as well.

When St Andrews became not only the spiritual but the legislative Home of Golf it was the obvious place to seek advice on most matters concerning the royal and ancient game. So it was to St Andrews that the golfers of Carnoustie turned in the middle of the nineteenth century when they wanted a course laid out at the time of the formation of Carnoustie Golf Club. The actual date is not precisely known but is variously accepted as between 1839 and 1842.

Carnoustie called in Allan Robertson, the first of the great early professional players, to lay out ten holes.

Certainly Allan Robertson did not have to travel very far as the crow flies to undertake his commissioned work at Carnoustie. It is only a few miles from the Old Course at St Andrews across the Tay Estuary to the links of Carnoustie, although in Allan Robertson's day there was not the advantage of the modern road bridge. Today the journey time by road between these two great championship courses is less than one hour.

The course Allan Robertson laid out at Carnoustie formed the basis for what is today one of the truly great championship courses in world golf, while the town itself is hugely significant to the development of the game on an international scale.

If it was St Andrews that gave golf a home, then it was Carnoustie that gave the game many of its ambassadors. As golf became ever more popular, and spread out from Scotland like ripples on a pool, a small army of golfers left the old town of Carnoustie to seek golfing fame and fortune in far-flung lands.

Many of them went to the United States, taking not only their talent as players but their experience of club making and golf course design. These sons of Carnoustie were golfing missionaries spreading the gospel in a land desperate to embrace the faith. Several of them became prophets.

Although Allan Robertson is credited with having laid out the first formal holes at Carnoustie around 150 years ago, golf had been played there for centuries before that. As with most of the courses which developed on the east coast of Scotland there is little in the way of recorded history, but it is known that golf was played on the Barry Links next to Carnoustie as early as the sixteenth century. Sir Robert Maule, whom history records as being one of the first players, is known to have enjoyed the 'gouff' on the Barry Links, and parish records confirm the existence of the game there in 1560.

The ten-hole course that Allan Robertson originally laid out was subsequently extended to 18 holes by Old Tom Morris in 1867. Old Tom had the

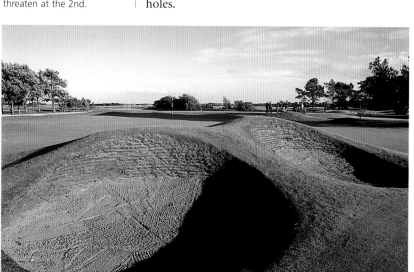

satisfaction of seeing his son Tommy Morris win a tournament open to all comers there the same year when the lad was only 16 years of age. It was a remarkable victory and one of the most famous in the long history of Carnoustie.

Young Tommy tied with Willie Park Snr, already a three-times Open Championship winner, and Bob Andrew, another formidable professional of the day. Tommy beat them both in the play-off and was on his way to immortality.

James Braid, winner of the Open five times, a member of the Great Triumvirate of Vardon, Braid and Taylor and just as famous a golf course builder as a player, was called in to revamp the Carnoustie course in 1926.

Five years later Tommy Armour, a Scot from Edinburgh who had emigrated to the United States to earn himself a famous reputation as a player and a drinker, and just as famous a reputation – although less well deserved perhaps – as a teacher, won the first Open Championship played at Carnoustie.

In 1937 Henry Cotton, the greatest British player after the Triumvirate, took on a field which included the entire United

CARNOUSTIE COURSE RECORD

64 Colin Montgomerie, A Tait

PAST OPEN CHAMPIONS

1931	Tommy Armour
1937	Henry Cotton
1953	Ben Hogan
1968	Gary Player
1975	Tom Watson

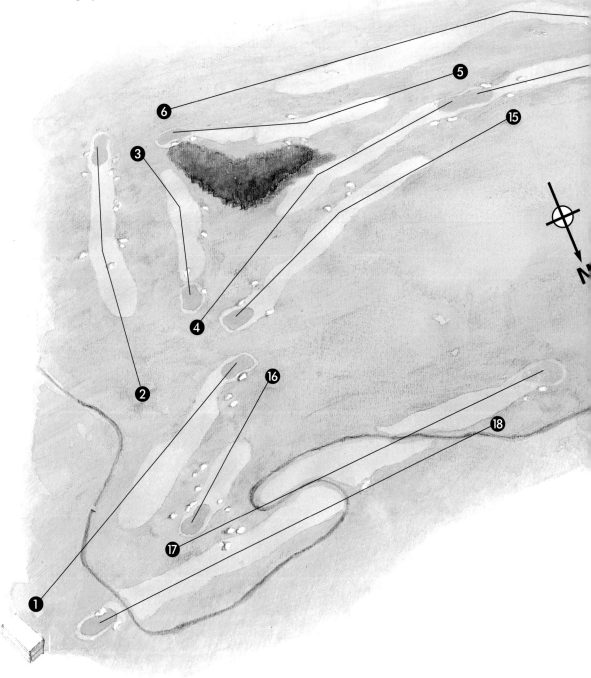

States Ryder Cup team and beat them all in appalling weather conditions. His 71 in the final round, when play was in danger of being abandoned because of the deluge, ranks as one of the great rounds in Open Championship history.

In a golfing world where the word 'championship' has become devalued by golf course builders and architects who produce 'championship' courses as if from a sausage machine, Carnoustie remains the true test for those who would be real champions, and one of the greatest challenges in world golf.

To the names of Tommy Armour and Henry Cotton as Carnoustie champions have been added those of Ben Hogan, Gary Player and Tom Watson, to reinforce the point. It is a roll call which stands as a fitting testimony to the quality of the challenge.

Between them their winning scores average out at as close to the nominal par of the course as does not matter. Holes have been

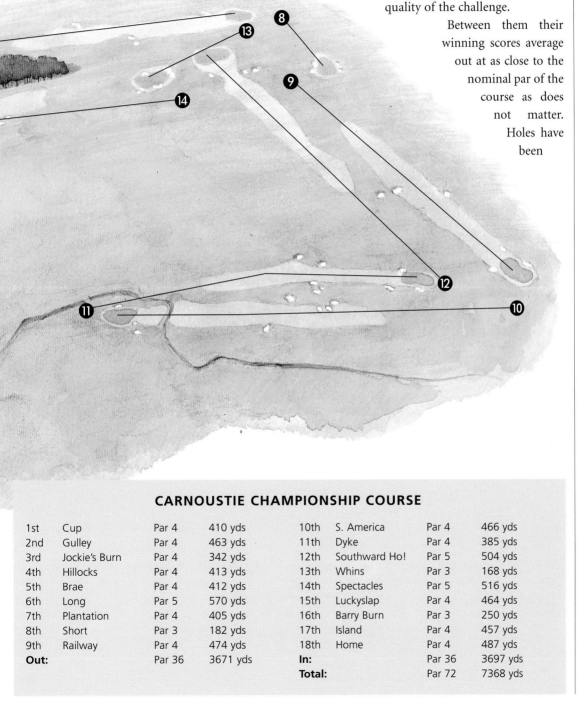

CARNOUSTIE CHAMPIONSHIP COURSE

1st	Cup	Par 4	410 yds	10th	S. America	Par 4	466 yds
2nd	Gulley	Par 4	463 yds	11th	Dyke	Par 4	385 yds
3rd	Jockie's Burn	Par 4	342 yds	12th	Southward Ho!	Par 5	504 yds
4th	Hillocks	Par 4	413 yds	13th	Whins	Par 3	168 yds
5th	Brae	Par 4	412 yds	14th	Spectacles	Par 5	516 yds
6th	Long	Par 5	570 yds	15th	Luckyslap	Par 4	464 yds
7th	Plantation	Par 4	405 yds	16th	Barry Burn	Par 3	250 yds
8th	Short	Par 3	182 yds	17th	Island	Par 4	457 yds
9th	Railway	Par 4	474 yds	18th	Home	Par 4	487 yds
Out:		Par 36	3671 yds	**In:**		Par 36	3697 yds
				Total:		Par 72	7368 yds

The Barry Burn snakes its way across the 17th fairway, creating an island target from the tee. In 1968 Jack Nicklaus carried his drive over the island in a famous Open Championship finish but still lost to Gary Player.

changed and some pars altered over the years but the undeniable fact is that four rounds of 72 on the Championship course at Carnoustie is a standard which only the greatest players have managed to achieve in top-class tournament play. Carnoustie is where the cream always comes to the top.

Like all the great and historic links courses of Britain the challenge of Carnoustie is governed by the weather. Wind is what makes the difference, and when it blows on this famous Angus links not only is the course unrelenting, unforgiving and often underrated, it can be virtually unplayable. There is no place here for the faint of heart.

It is a course without weaknesses. It is laid out in such a way that never does it have more than two holes consecutively running in the same direction. The battle is as much with the elements as with the course itself.

The great Walter Hagen, winner of 11 of golf's major championships, once described Carnoustie as the 'greatest course in the British Isles'. The British magazine *Golf Monthly* voted it second

behind only the Old Course at St Andrews itself, in its 1998 list of Britain's Best 100 Courses.

Over the years there has never been any doubt about Carnoustie's credentials as a great examination of golf but after it hosted the Open Championship in 1975 it went into something of a decline, resulting in the course being bypassed as an Open venue. However, considerable improvement work was carried out over many years to return the course to its former splendour and that has been rewarded with a return to the Open Championship rota in 1999.

The great challenge is the ever-changing nature of the course. There is no such thing as a simple hole at Carnoustie, and the very difficult ones are among the fiercest to be found anywhere.

With the wind against you, the 1st hole, played to a blind green over a high mound, often requires a stinging blow with a long iron to reach the green, while in calmer conditions a modest stroke with a short iron will more than suffice. From this point Carnoustie only gets tougher with a demanding drive at the 2nd, now made even tougher by a new bunker on the right side of the fairway to take account of the increased distances the modern professionals drive the ball.

The 3rd demands a delicate pitch over a stream to a smallish and severely sloping green. From there the course strikes out into the prevailing wind again and the battle is well and truly joined.

The stream known as Jockie's Burn comes into play on four of the first six holes and the infamous Barry Burn, where many have come to grief either playing into it or trying and failing to physically jump over it, gives this majestic course its famous finish.

At the 9th changes have been made to tighten up the green. Bunkers have been added to make the drive, already demanding because of the out-of-bounds down the left side, even more testing. This is the one hole at Carnoustie played downhill, for this great course is one of the flattest stretches of linksland anywhere in the British Isles.

Many wonder when they reach the tee at the 10th why it is called 'South America'. Legend has it that a young caddie, intent on seeking his fortune in that far-off country, departed on the first stage of his journey suitably fortified with Scotch whisky for his long travel, but progressed no further than the copse of trees by the 10th hole where he slept until he awakened to find himself still in his native Scotland.

Before tackling the 11th there is time for a cup of hot tea from the old refreshment hut that has saved many a life in the battle round Carnoustie. The hut occupies a new location since its former site was utilised to build a new tee to lengthen what was perhaps the least demanding of the holes. The 11th is now a bit longer with the introduction of that new tee and the removal of the green to a new site well beyond the old one.

To hit the green at the 161-yard 13th requires a steady nerve to avoid the dangerous ring of bunkers which surround it, while the second shot at the long, curving 14th must carry the famous 'Spectacle' bunkers cut from the face of a sand dune. When the wind is blowing hard from the west the carry is not difficult but stopping the ball on the large double green anywhere near the flag is a test for anyone.

Then there is the famous Carnoustie finish, three holes that strike fear into the stoutest hearts. The par-3 16th is simply one of the toughest single shot holes in world golf, while the Barry Burn snakes its way all over the 17th, calling for a carefully placed tee shot to the 'the island' before any sanctuary can be found.

The 18th is now a demanding par 4 when once it was a relatively easy par 5. Water runs in front of the green and bunkers down the right make the tee shot very demanding.

It was in one of these bunkers that Johnny Miller ended his hopes of victory in the 1975 Open when he tried and failed to reach the green from the sand, leaving the way open for Tom Watson to win his first Open after a play-off with Jack Newton.

A re-sited green and new bunkering at the 11th are relatively recent alterations to the Carnoustie Medal course.

Muirfield

THE HONOURABLE COMPANY OF EDINBURGH GOLFERS

Established
1744
Course details:
18 holes
6601 yards
SSS 73
Address:
Muirfield
Gullane EH31 2EG

Tel: 01620 842123
Fax: 01620 842977

It is not difficult to understand why so many of the world's great players believe that Muirfield, near Edinburgh, is the fairest examination of golf among all of Britain's great and historic championship courses.

If the definition of fairest is that there are no hidden bunkers, or subtle humps and hollows as at St Andrews, or the blind shots which make up the character, for instance, of Old Prestwick, then there can be little argument.

Muirfield, home of the Honourable Company of Edinburgh Golfers, is an honest but hugely demanding test where the dangers are in open view for all to see. Good shots are usually handsomely rewarded, while the penalties for imperfection can be severe indeed.

Classic seaside golf.
The view across the links at Muirfield emphasises the rolling landscape and the fearsome rough.

The great Jack Nicklaus paid Muirfield the ultimate compliment by naming his own course in Dublin, Ohio, Muirfield Village out of respect for the course where he won his first Open Championship in 1966, and about which he has been warm and generous in his praise ever since.

He is not alone among the great players who have rated Muirfield so highly. The late Sir Henry Cotton, who won his last Open at Muirfield in 1948 and was not given to over-effusive comment on courses in general, privately admitted that Muirfield had been his favourite course in more than sixty years as a professional. Most of his modern counterparts share that view.

However, Muirfield has not always enjoyed such

A typically dangerous Muirfield bunker. This one is at the 17th.

a fine reputation among the leading players of the day. Andrew Kirkaldy from St Andrews, the outspoken Scottish professional of the latter part of the nineteenth century, may well have been one of the finest players of his day, although he never won the Open Championship, but he was certainly no lover of the Muirfield links.

He once incurred the wrath of the gentlemen of the Honourable Company by describing their beloved course as 'nothing but an old water meadow'. Andrew Kirkaldy was the last survivor of that rugged old school of Scottish professionals who pioneered the game at the end of the nineteenth century and were never slow to express candid opinions. There may have been little in the way of diplomacy in Andrew Kirkaldy but nonetheless he eventually became the honorary professional to the Royal and Ancient Golf Club at St Andrews.

The Honourable Company of Edinburgh Golfers is generally recognised as the oldest golf club in the world. It has continuous records of its existence since 1744 when 'several Gentlemen of Honour skilful in the ancient and healthful exercise of Golf' petitioned the Edinburgh City Council to donate a silver club for their annual competition on Leith Links outside the Scottish capital. There were then only five holes and the members had to share the ground with the local citizens, and occasionally the military.

The Honourable Company had set out the first official rules of the game of golf in the year of their formation – ten years before the Royal and Ancient

The well-guarded plateau green at the 13th where the approach shot must be played with the utmost precision.

third year in succession, as laid down in the rules of the competition.

There then being no trophy to play for in 1871 there was no Open Championship held, but thereafter the Honourable Company, the Royal & Ancient Golf Club of St Andrews and Prestwick Golf Club subscribed together for the present trophy and jointly managed the event.

For the next 20 years the Championship rotated around Prestwick, St Andrews and Musselburgh. In

Golf Club of St Andrews was founded – and the first winner of the handsome silver club was John Rattray, a surgeon who, with his victory, was appointed 'Captain of the Golf'.

The links eventually became too populated for the Club to continue to play happily there. In 1836, they moved to the town of Musselburgh six miles along the coast to the east to share the course there with the members of the Musselburgh Golf Club.

The golfers used the grandstand of the Musselburgh racecourse as their meeting place until they acquired their own clubhouse in 1868. Through time, however, even the Musselburgh links became too crowded and the Honourable Company moved east again, down the Firth of Forth, to the present course at Muirfield.

At first there was little general enthusiasm for the new course. Apparently it was neither long nor testing in its original guise. A grey, stone wall surrounded the course and there was much in the way of water about. It was this combination that had prompted Andrew Kirkaldy to dismiss Muirfield in the expressive terms that he did, but there may have been another reason for the anti-Muirfield feelings.

When the Honourable Company moved to Muirfield they took with them the Open Championship, which had first been played for at Prestwick in 1860. Willie Park of Musselburgh won the handsome morocco leather challenge belt that year. Ten years later Young Tom Morris made it his own property by winning the Belt for the

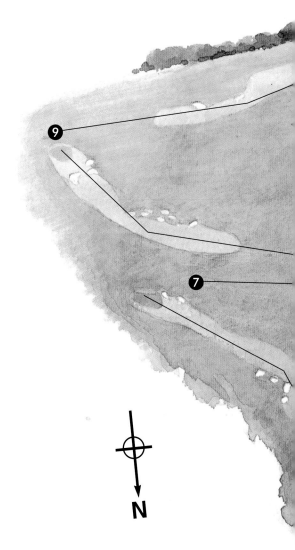

MUIRFIELD CHAMPIONSHIP COURSE

1st	Par 4	447 yds	10th	Par 4	475 yds
2nd	Par 4	351 yds	11th	Par 4	385 yds
3rd	Par 4	379 yds	12th	Par 4	381 yds
4th	Par 3	180 yds	13th	Par 3	159 yds
5th	Par 5	559 yds	14th	Par 4	449 yds
6th	Par 4	469 yds	15th	Par 4	417 yds
7th	Par 3	185 yds	16th	Par 3	188 yds
8th	Par 4	444 yds	17th	Par 5	550 yds
9th	Par 5	504 yds	18th	Par 4	448 yds
Out:	**Par 36**	**3518 yds**	**In:**	**Par 35**	**3452 yds**
			Total	**Par 71**	**6970 yds**

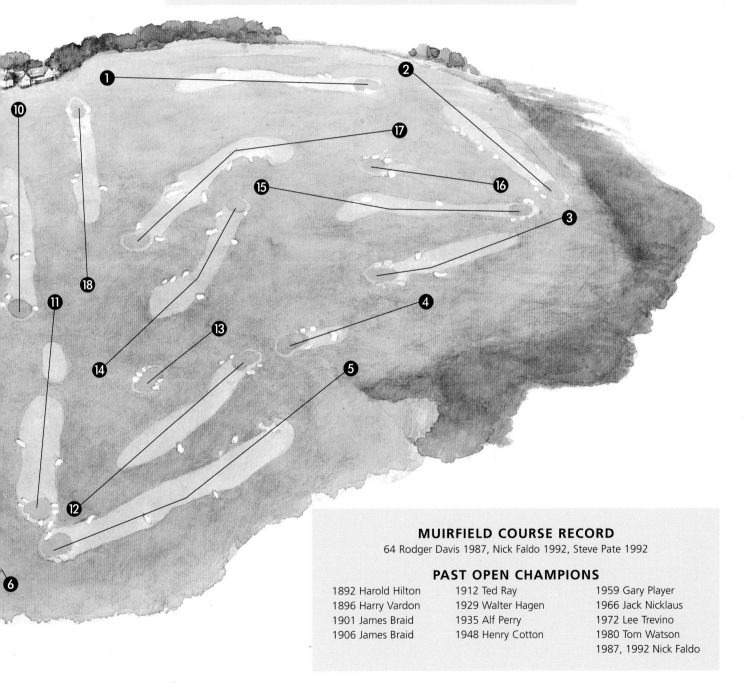

MUIRFIELD COURSE RECORD
64 Rodger Davis 1987, Nick Faldo 1992, Steve Pate 1992

PAST OPEN CHAMPIONS

1892 Harold Hilton	1912 Ted Ray	1959 Gary Player
1896 Harry Vardon	1929 Walter Hagen	1966 Jack Nicklaus
1901 James Braid	1935 Alf Perry	1972 Lee Trevino
1906 James Braid	1948 Henry Cotton	1980 Tom Watson
		1987, 1992 Nick Faldo

The short 13th at Muirfield is a demanding challenge with thick rough to contend with as well as a coterie of bunkers.

1892 the Open was taken to the new home of the Honourable Company at Muirfield much to the displeasure of the golfers of Musselburgh.

However, it immediately found a place in golfing history when, for the first time, the Open was played over 72 holes instead of the previous 36. The winner was the fine amateur player from Hoylake, Harold Hilton, whose score of 305, playing the gutta percha ball, was considered to be remarkably low. Five years later Hilton won the Championship again but since then, with the exception of the remarkable Bobby Jones, no other amateur has won golf's greatest prize.

Muirfield soon threw off its early criticisms and evolved into one of the world's outstanding courses. At regular intervals down the years, it has been the setting for one or other of the great events in British golf.

Harry Vardon won the first of his six Open Championships at Muirfield in 1896 after a play-off with J.H. Taylor, while the other member of that Great Triumvirate, James Braid, also won the first of his Championship titles at Muirfield in 1901.

Ted Ray won his single Open Championship at Muirfield in 1912, the last before the First World War, and the last played on the links before major changes had to be made to take account of modern advances in the game. The present layout owes much to the changes made by Harry S. Colt and Tom Simpson in the mid 1920s. Unlike the great links of St Andrews or Carnoustie, however, Muirfield is in no way a public course. The home of the Honourable Company of Edinburgh Golfers is a very private place where the members play on uncrowded fairways and where the great traditions of the royal and ancient game are jealously preserved.

Muirfield has more than 160 bunkers, many of them built with great walls of turf in the face, which not only make for a pleasing effect but make escape a perilous task if the ball lies too close to them. Jack Nicklaus once commented that they were the most fastidiously built bunkers he had ever seen.

'The high front walls are faced with bricks of turf fitted together so precisely you would have thought a master mason had been called in'. he once said.

It is not just the number of these hazards that presents the problem. The Muirfield bunkers are so designed as to gather the wayward shot. Seldom does a ball heading for one of them jump over or escape, for the surrounds are meticulously prepared to make sure that it does not.

To land in a fairway bunker from the tee is almost certainly to surrender a stroke, for there are none from which it is possible to reach the green. The greenside bunkers parade in packs to consume anything a little off line and they instil fear in even those who are masters of the sand iron.

Occasionally they relent a little, as in the case of Lee Trevino in the memorable Open Championship of 1972 when he holed from off the green no fewer than three times and none more remarkably than his shot from the greenside bunker straight into the hole at the short 16th. That Open at Muirfield in 1972 produced one of the most dramatic finishes of the modern era and arguably brought about the subsequent decline in the fortunes of Tony Jacklin after his earlier successes in winning the Open titles on both sides of the Atlantic inside the one year.

Much of the quality of Muirfield is in its test of driving. The fairways are not menacingly narrow but the rough, unlike on most other links courses, is consistently lush and totally unforgiving. To land in it is almost certainly to lose a stroke, even for the strongest players.

When the late Sir Henry Cotton won his third Open title at Muirfield in 1948 he missed only four fairways in 72 holes, a feat of wonderful precision greatly admired during the second round by His Majesty King George VI.

Muirfield does not conform to the usual rules for classic seaside links courses. There is no wide and desolate sprawl of linksland, with holes that are sometimes hard to define. Instead the course is confined by a wall on three sides and is almost claustrophobic by comparison with St Andrews, Carnoustie or Turnberry.

There are, however, some wonderful views across the great sand dunes to the north of the course, out across the Firth of Forth towards the Kingdom of Fife where can be seen on a clear day the ever-changing patterns of patchwork fields.

It is a course enveloped by stories of its legendary one-time secretary, Paddy Hanmer, who would often gaze across the empty expanses of the Muirfield links through his binoculars before telling visitors hopeful of a game that they could not play because the course was 'too busy'.

It is the home of a club of great history and importance to the development of the game, and a course which every golfer worth his clubs wants to play. Only the fortunate few, however, are ever afforded the opportunity.

The famous Muirfield clubhouse, home of the Honourable Company of Edinburgh Golfers and the lair for many years of its legendary secretary, Capt. Paddy Hanmer, R.N.

Musselburgh

OLD COURSE

Established
c. 17th century
Course details:
9 holes
5380 yards
SSS 37
Address:
Silver Ring Clubhouse
Millhill
Musselburgh EH21 7RG

Tel: 0131 665 6981

A lone figure approaches the 2nd green on the historic links of Musselburgh. Today it is a curio from an almost forgotten past; now the race horse is king and the course is hemmed in by the track.

Like St Andrews, the old Musselburgh links east of Edinburgh are a relic from the very cradle of golf and hold their own special, even if sometimes chequered place in the history of the game in Scotland. There has been golf played on this strip of golfing ground for centuries, although today, sadly, there is little to remind the world of the part it played in the early days of the game.

Where once were seen the great deeds of Old Tom Morris and Allan Robertson, the Parks and the Dunn brothers, the race horse is now king. The old course is hemmed in by the Musselburgh race track and although valiant work has been done to try to restore some of the old course's former lustre it remains a largely abandoned monument to golf's antiquity.

It was the scene of six Open Championships after the event moved away from the Prestwick monopoly from 1860 to 1870.

The first Open played at Musselburgh was in 1874 for the now familiar claret jug, when Mungo Park won with a score of 159 in the biggest field thus far entered for the Championship, 32 in all.

Of the other five Musselburgh Open Champions, three were Musselburgh men, Bob Ferguson, David Brown and Willie Park Jnr Interestingly, Brown, who won in 1886 was not really a professional at all but worked in Musselburgh as a slater.

Originally the Musselburgh course was seven holes, but an eighth was added in 1832 and another shortly afterwards. The Royal Musselburgh Golf Club was established at Musselburgh in 1774, although there is fairly good evidence that the club dates back further than that, probably as early as 1760. In 1774 a Silver Cup was subscribed for by gentlemen golfers of the Musselburgh Club, 20 years after the R & A first played for its silver putter and 30 years after the formation of the Gentlemen Golfers of Edinburgh.

The Edinburgh Burgess Society also shared the Musselburgh links and various dates, and indeed a variety of names, are attached to that particular club. It has been variously known as the Society of Golfers in and about Edinburgh and at one time the Edinburgh Golfing Society. Today it is the Royal Burgess Golfing Society of Edinburgh, with its Royal prefix having been granted in 1929.

The Royal Musselburgh Golf Club, however, had royal connections much further back than that; as far back as 1876, in fact, when Prince Arthur, Duke of Connaught and godson of the Duke of Wellington, granted the Royal title and remained Patron of the Club until his death in 1942. The Connaught Cup was presented to the President of the Club, Sir William Hope, in 1887 at a ceremony attended by His Imperial Highness The Grand Duke Michael of Russia, a keen golfer himself, who had previously been made an honorary member of the Club.

Around that time there were half-a-dozen golf clubs using the Musselburgh links and the management of the links became a pressing problem. The four senior clubs, The Honourable Company, Burgess, Bruntsfield and Royal Musselburgh agreed that there should be a Green Committee to take over full control of the golf course. Each club was given two representatives on the committee and had to contribute funds according to the size of the membership. It was the end of 100 years of control of the links by the Musselburgh Golf Club.

Musselburgh had been the scene of many great matches before that time. There had been the first leg of the famous foursomes match in 1849 between Allan Robertson and Old Tom Morris from St Andrews against the Dunn brothers, Willie Snr and Jamie, pride of Musselburgh, for the huge sum in these days of £400. Much to the satisfaction of the locals the Dunns held up the honour of Musselburgh by trouncing the St Andrews pair by 13 and 12 over the 36 holes.

For 20 years Willie Park, winner of the first Open Championship at Prestwick in 1860, had a standing challenge in the magazine *Bell's Life*, to play any golfer in the world for £100 a side. He had many famous battles with Old Tom Morris between 1856 and 1882, none more so than the last one.

The Musselburgh supporters had by then gained something of a reputation for rather overzealous support of their favourites. They were known to interfere with the balls in play and the outspoken professional from St Andrews, Andrew Kirkaldy, scathingly dismissed them as 'they damned miners'.

In any event this last great tussle between Park and Morris came to a dramatic end when old Willie Park stood two up with six holes to play. Robert Chambers, head of the Edinburgh publishing house, and himself a player of note, having been a previous Amateur Champion, was refereeing the contest and stopped play because spectators were taking judicious kicks at the golf balls in their efforts to help the Willie Park cause.

Chambers and Morris retired to Mrs Forman's public house, leaving Willie Park on the course. Some time elapsed before Park sent in the message that if Tom Morris did not come out and finish the match, he would play the remaining holes and claim the stakes. That is exactly what happened for Old Tom and the referee stayed put.

Sadly, it was not the only time that the Musselburgh spectators blemished the honour and integrity of the game over many years.

J.H. Taylor suffered similarly badly at the hands, or more correctly the feet, of the Musselburgh faithful in their efforts to influence the outcome of his match against young Willie Park in 1895. His experience prompted Harry Vardon to refuse to play young Willie at Musselburgh in their great challenge match of 1899, when one leg was played

A quiet view of the 5th hole at Musselburgh where once the members of half-a-dozen golf clubs created such a jam that one by one the clubs abandoned the old links for pastures new.

in England and the other in Scotland. The Scottish leg was eventually played at the 'neutral' venue of North Berwick.

One of the greatest finishes in the Open Championship was played out at Musselburgh in 1883 when Musselburgh hero, Bob Ferguson, was attempting to win the Championship for the fourth year in succession. Had he been able to do so he would have equalled Young Tom Morris's record of four in a row which still stands to this day.

Willie Fernie from Dumfries scored 159 for the 36 holes despite a ten at one hole. Ferguson looked out of it but finished with three threes to force a play-off, and was then a stroke ahead playing the last. The Musselburgh man made his regulation four at the finishing hole but Fernie drove the green and then holed out for a two to snatch an unlikely victory by one stroke.

As the pressures on the little course began to build up with the increasing numbers of players, the clubs sought out alternative venues and a move to territorial independence. The Royal Burgess Club

moved to Barnton in 1894 and the Bruntsfield Club moved to their own course in 1898.

The Honourable Company decamped to Muirfield in 1891, and took the Open Championship with them, but the Royal Musselburgh Golf Club continued to play over the old Musselburgh links until they too abandoned the old course in favour of a new layout designed by James Braid at Prestongrange House, Prestonpans, further down the coast, where the club remains to this day.

The emigration of the last of the great clubs from Musselburgh signalled the rapid decline of the Musselburgh links and there was a time when the course decayed into a very poor state indeed. Improvements have been made but further intrusion by the race course and a lack of any serious effort to preserve this historic site has left Musselburgh links now little more than a curio from an almost forgotten past.

When the last of the great clubs left Musselburgh for good the course went into decline. But there have been efforts to restore this historic golfing site and improvements have been made. The race course is a constant hazard at Musselburgh as can be seen here at the 3rd.

North Berwick

NORTH BERWICK

Established
1832
Course details:
18 holes
6420 yards
SSS 71
Address:
West Links
Beach Road
North Berwick EH39 4BB

Tel: 01620 892135
Fax: 01620 893274

The links of the West Course at North Berwick belong to what Sir Guy Campbell (1885-1960), golf administrator, journalist and prominent golf course designer, once described as the 'Primitive Age' of golf, that period from the very beginnings of the game until the arrival of the gutta percha ball in 1848. Far from being depreciative of the merits of this venerable links, his 'primitive' classification was a reflection of the course's antiquity and its place among that very special group of golf courses which evolved naturally and owe very little to the hand of man.

North Berwick stands among very elevated company, for among the others in Sir Guy's list are the Old Course at St Andrews and the links of Dornoch, Montrose, Barry (Carnoustie), Scotscraig, Elie, Leven, Musselburgh and Dunbar.

These were the sites of the earliest courses down the eastern seaboard of Scotland where the sea had receded and left in its wake sandy wastes broken and divided by channels into which the tides ebbed and flowed and where, over the centuries, a new ecology developed. Burns and rivers found their way to the sea down these channels, depositing on their journey silt and sediment, creating an environment in which grass could grow.

The sand as it dried out was blown by the wind into the sand hills or dunes which characterise these courses and which, despite the efforts of mechanical man in the form of the golf course architect, has never been successfully replicated no matter the amount of effort or money expended.

It was on these sand hills and exposed dunes that vegetation in the form of course grass eventually took a hold. It became more fertile as flocks of birds utilised the area for resting, nesting and breeding, and the combination of the bird droppings and the seed they deposited encouraged the growth of other

The beach is a companion for much of the round at North Berwick. Here, at the 2nd hole, it could not get much closer.

grasses from the seed blown there by the wind.

Where the soil became suitable, whins, broom and heather and even trees grew on this land reclaimed from the sea.

North Berwick is typical of that evolutionary pattern, indeed it is a classic example of it for it has changed very little over the centuries. The North Berwick Golf Club was founded there in 1832 and is one of Scotland's oldest clubs. It is a private club, but visitors are permitted by charter to play at a reasonable fee, and well worth paying it is.

Golf is played here on one of the game's most remarkable courses. It is classic and ancient links as we have seen, but it has the additional elements of blind shots, great ridges across fairways and even walls that have to be negotiated on more than one occasion in the course of the round.

A full appreciation of the merits of North Berwick is not usually gained on first acquaintance, and perhaps not on the second either. Rather like the Old Course at St Andrews, or new neighbours, this is a links that needs a little time to get to know. Once the learning curve shallows out, however, it is a course that tempts the visitor back, if not for the ultimate challenge of it, then the eccentricity and the wonderful views that are attached to it.

In its earlier days it was not a very long golf course and it prompted the eminent golf writer, Horace Hutchinson (1859-1932), to describe it once as 'the sporting little links of North Berwick', adding, 'You might as well leave your driver at home. If you are even a medium driver, it is scarcely in your hand.'

The great amateur, Johnny Laidley, once required only 33 strokes for the first ten holes and the course was renowned for producing players who were master pitchers and short game players. Eventually, however, the course was lengthened and while today it is not overly long by some standards it is quite long enough to produce as good a test as anyone would want, particularly when the wind blasts across the exposed ground.

The West Course at North Berwick has been regularly used as a qualifying course for the Open Championship when it reaches Muirfield on its rota.

Some of the holes at North Berwick have wonderful names. 'Point Garry Out', 'Mizzentop' 'Bos'n's Locker', 'Carl Kemp' and the 'Pit' are among them. 'Point Garry Out' is the first hole on the course and at one time shared a green with the 17th, 'Point Garry In'. This was the double green that Bernard Darwin (1876-1961), doyen of golf writers, described as 'a terrible place' sloping down to the rocks and to the beach.

One of the great golf hotels, the Marine Hotel at North Berwick, enjoys commanding views over the ancient links and across the Firth of Forth to the hills of Fife.

Far right: Lengthening shadows emphasise the rolling linksland of North Berwick which has not changed in centuries.

'And we come to it, besides,' said Darwin, 'at two of the most agitating moments of the round; at the first hole, when we have not had quite enough golf, and at the 17th, when, if the match has been a fierce one, we have perhaps had too much.'

The problems set today by the Point Garry green at the first may not be as severe as they were in Mr Darwin's time but they remain fierce enough.

The wall comes into play for the first time at the long third, when the second shot has to be played over it. In many ways it is the only point of interest in the hole but at close to 460 yards it is a tough par 4 and aptly named the 'Trap'. It follows the 'Sea' hole, another 450-yards-plus hole with the constant danger of the sea on the right-hand side.

The third of the long par 4s on the way out is the 'Linkhouse' hole where in days long gone by the renowned North Berwick caddie, Harry Crawford, had his ginger beer stall. 'Big Crawford' as he was known, caddied for Ben Sayers in all his important matches and also for Conservative Prime Minister,

Arthur Balfour, who was his hero and a regular player at North Berwick. When Lord Balfour was playing on the links, Big Crawford raised a small Scottish standard on his stall in his hero's honour.

The front nine is more than two hundred yards longer than the back nine and mostly played into the prevailing wind, making it a demanding par of 35. The back nine is shorter with the real interest coming in the final six holes.

The 13th is known as the 'Pit', a modest-of-length par 4 of less than 350 yards, where we have stonework to contend with again, this time in the shape of a low wall which separates the green and the fairway. The fairway runs down the right side of the wall but the long narrow green is sited on the other side of it. Anything driven down the right from the tee leaves a very difficult pitch across the wall and across the width of the green rather than up its length. The sea awaits those who miscalculate the process.

The most famous hole at North Berwick is the 15th, the 'Redan' hole. This long par 3, played to a

plateau green set at an angle to the line of the play and guarded by a deep bunker in the front left, is a classic one-shotter that has been copied, or used as inspiration, many times; copied most eminently by Charles Blair Macdonald when he built the National Golf Links on Long Island and by A.W. Tillinghast on the 2nd hole at Somerset Hills in New Jersey. Both the 7th and the 17th at Shinnecock Hills are said to have been inspired by the Redan and certainly there are similarities. The 17th at Pebble Beach is also associated with the Redan, though the green runs upward, not from front to back.

There have been many great matches played at North Berwick and few better attended than the Scottish leg of the famous match between Harry Vardon and Willie Park in 1899. It was a home and home match for £100 a side with 36 holes to be played at Ganton in England and 36 holes originally scheduled to be played at Park's home course at Musselburgh. Vardon refused to play at Musselburgh because of the well known partisanship of the locals who had a reputation for interfering with golf balls during play, usually in favour of their home players on whom large sums were usually wagered, and the Scottish leg was moved to North Berwick.

Firm and fast greens and classic seaside links are the hallmarks of North Berwick. The huge outcrop known as the Bass Rock, top right, is never far from view.

Old Course, St Andrews

OLD COURSE

Established
15th century
Course details:
18 holes
6566 yards
SSS 72
Address:
St Andrews Links Trust
St Andrews KY16 9SF

Tel: 01334 466666
Fax: 01334 477036

No matter where in the world the golfer may travel he will find no other more thrilling sight than the historic city of St Andrews with its backdrop of ancient buildings and dramatic spires. Approaching the town from the west, past the little towns of Guardbridge and Leuchars, the old town springs suddenly into view to send a shiver of excitement down the spine of even those of the most frugal spirit.

Here in the ancient Kingdom of Fife lies the cradle of the game of golf, its cultural home, the Mecca to which every golfer aspires to make pilgrimage at least once in his or her golfing life. It is here that the ghosts of Old Tom Morris and Allan Robertson roam the ancient links, and where the rules and standards that have set golf apart as

The widest fairway in world golf. The 1st and 18th fairways on the Old Course at St Andrews are more than 100 yards wide but even the greatest players, the most notable example in recent times being Ian Baker-Finch from Australia, have somehow managed to find the road on the right from the 1st tee under the windows of the R & A clubhouse.

the game of highest principle and personal integrity, have long since been laid down.

Golf has been played on the Old Course at St Andrews for more than 400 years, and on the ancient links of the town for centuries longer still than that. The charter giving the citizens of the town the right to use the links for 'golf, futball, shuteing at all times with all other manner of pastimes' is dated 25 January 1552.

According to Dr J.B. Salmond's *The Story of the R & A,* published in 1956, the charter was bought for one shilling by an Edinburgh bookseller, who later sold it to the University library for 45 shillings, surely one of the shrewdest pieces of literary business ever conducted. In 1922 it was presented

to the Town Council of St Andrews and it is an interesting coincidence that the date of this charter of freedom for the citizens of St Andrews matches that of the birthday of Robert Burns, Scotland's national poet, 200 years later.

The Old Course is unique in that it owes little to the hand of man in its design and layout. It has evolved over the centuries at the whim of time and tide to become the masterpiece that Mother Nature herself created.

With the exception of Ben Hogan – and he was never to know what he missed – all the great names in the history of golf have walked at one time or another across the famous little stone bridge over the Swilcan Burn onto the final fairway to stand on the most famous stage in world golf.

Crossing that historic little bridge and looking towards the Royal and Ancient clubhouse standing guard over the vast expanse of the fairway shared between the first and last holes, there lies to the left the wide stretch of the West Sands utilised in more recent times for the opening titles of the film *Chariots of Fire.* To the right is the ancient town itself, home not only of the game of golf but of Scotland's most ancient seat of learning, the University of St Andrews, and in more turbulent times a main centre of the Scottish Reformation.

The Old Course is the classic seaside links. The sea, however, is seldom in view apart from at the first and last holes where the view of St Andrews Bay is dramatic. There are no great dunes as there are at Royal Birkdale or Royal Aberdeen, or Ballybunion in Ireland. The fairways are wide with

One of the Old Course's main defences is gorse. It threatens everywhere, and nowhere more dangerously than here at the 13th where banks of the impenetrable bush flank the right side of the fairway along the entire length of the hole.

The approach shot to the short par-4 10th is one of the trickiest on the Old Course. The green slopes sharply from front to back but the problem is always to get the ball up to the hole on the huge and deceptive green.

little elevation and interrupted at intervals by huge double greens.

There are only four single greens on the Old Course, the 1st, the 9th, the famous 17th Road hole, and the Home hole, the 18th.

To stand on the 1st tee immediately in front of the big window of the Royal & Ancient clubhouse is to stand on the most inviting fairway in the game of golf. It is shared with the 18th and is 100 yards wide, and yet despite this tempting expanse the stroke from the 1st tee on the Old Course at St Andrews remains the most nerve-wracking opening shot in golf. The famous Bateman cartoon, depicting 'the man who missed the ball on the 1st tee at St Andrews', still hangs today in the R & A clubhouse as a constant reminder.

If the first shot to the 1st is the most frightening shot in golf then the second to the 1st comes a very close second. To have any chance of success at what looks the most innocuous of short iron shots on a calm day, the player must carefully judge which club to play, add one more and then one more still to be sure of getting over the wicked little stream known as the Swilcan Burn, running immediately in front of the putting surface.

Once across the Swilcan Burn the course turns right and follows the sweep of St Andrews Bay, sharing fairways and greens along the way, until it turns right again at the start of what is known as the Loop. It is here, starting at the 7th and finishing at the 11th, where the fairways of these two holes cross, that scores on the Old Course have to be made.

It is within this run of five holes that the Old Course's only two short holes are found, the 8th and the wickedly difficult 11th, known as the 'High Hole In'. From here the course starts for home back along the path already trodden, often sharing the fairways of the outward journey and playing to the 'other side' of the huge double greens. White flags mark the pins on the outward journey while red distinguishes the homeward stretch. The exception is the last hole where tradition demands that white is the order of the day.

The course has changed little over the years and apart from a new tee here and there it was much the same for John Daly when he won the 1995 Open Championship as it was for Tom Kidd when he won the first Open over the Old Course in 1872. A few additional tees have been added in preparation for the Open in the year 2000.

Avoiding the bunkers is the key to survival round the Old Course. There are dozens of them, described so graphically by Bernard Darwin as 'these greedy, lurking enemies'. Most of them are hidden from view, a result of the fact that in days past the course was played in a clockwise direction, known as the left hand circuit, and not as it is now, anticlockwise, on the right hand circuit.

Many of these treacherous obstacles have fascinating names, with the most famous, Hell bunker, a huge pit of sand which guards the 14th, the Long hole. However, there are others often less obvious but just as dangerous. In front of the 7th green, the High hole out, is the huge Cockle bunker while a few yards to its left Strath bunker eats into the front of the 11th.

At the 16th, the Corner of the Dyke, a group of three bunkers are known as the Principal's Nose. Only one of them is visible from the tee and it lies in the very centre of the fairway. Many are those who have felt confident they have driven sufficiently well to pass the Principal's Nose only to find their ball nestling deeply in the bunker known as Deacon Sime, a nasty little pot some 30 yards further on.

The notorious Road bunker, which eats into the front of the 17th, the famous Road hole, has claimed many a victim, not least of whom was poor Tommy Nakajima, who was well placed in the 1978 Open until he found that bunker. Now his name is etched forever in St Andrews Open

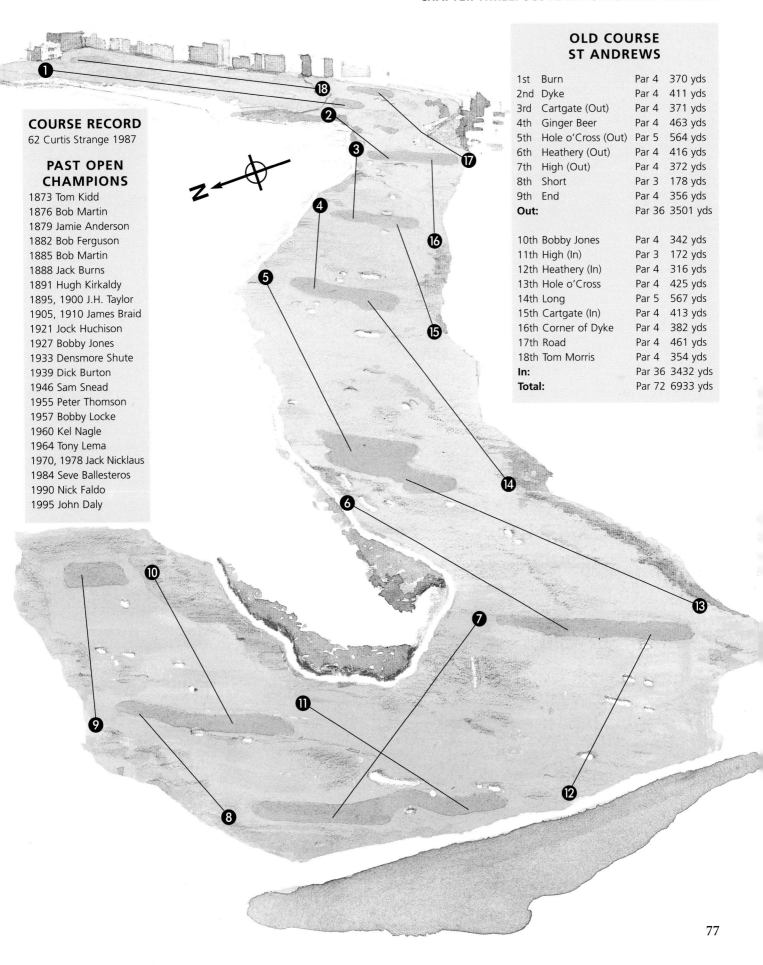

OLD COURSE ST ANDREWS

1st	Burn	Par 4	370 yds
2nd	Dyke	Par 4	411 yds
3rd	Cartgate (Out)	Par 4	371 yds
4th	Ginger Beer	Par 4	463 yds
5th	Hole o'Cross (Out)	Par 5	564 yds
6th	Heathery (Out)	Par 4	416 yds
7th	High (Out)	Par 4	372 yds
8th	Short	Par 3	178 yds
9th	End	Par 4	356 yds
Out:		**Par 36**	**3501 yds**
10th	Bobby Jones	Par 4	342 yds
11th	High (In)	Par 3	172 yds
12th	Heathery (In)	Par 4	316 yds
13th	Hole o'Cross	Par 4	425 yds
14th	Long	Par 5	567 yds
15th	Cartgate (In)	Par 4	413 yds
16th	Corner of Dyke	Par 4	382 yds
17th	Road	Par 4	461 yds
18th	Tom Morris	Par 4	354 yds
In:		**Par 36**	**3432 yds**
Total:		**Par 72**	**6933 yds**

COURSE RECORD
62 Curtis Strange 1987

PAST OPEN CHAMPIONS
1873 Tom Kidd
1876 Bob Martin
1879 Jamie Anderson
1882 Bob Ferguson
1885 Bob Martin
1888 Jack Burns
1891 Hugh Kirkaldy
1895, 1900 J.H. Taylor
1905, 1910 James Braid
1921 Jock Huchison
1927 Bobby Jones
1933 Densmore Shute
1939 Dick Burton
1946 Sam Snead
1955 Peter Thomson
1957 Bobby Locke
1960 Kel Nagle
1964 Tony Lema
1970, 1978 Jack Nicklaus
1984 Seve Ballesteros
1990 Nick Faldo
1995 John Daly

history for the four strokes he took to escape. The bunker was rechristened 'The Sands of Nakajima', by one golfing scribe, and the name has stuck ever since.

Once past the notorious Road hole, the Old Course has done its worst in the bunker department for it has none left to offer before the player makes his way back to the haven of the Home green and into the town itself. The drive at the 18th, the Home hole, is straight at the clock on the right hand side of the R & A clubhouse looking from the tee, and the acres of space enjoyed at the first are there again for the finish.

The final green, built by Old Tom Morris himself, with its white fence on two sides, the R & A clubhouse on the north side and the other St Andrews golf clubs, shops, hotels and houses opposite, provides a magnificent finish to the worlds most famous course.

No matter the time of day, the critical eyes of the permanent knot of spectators leaning over the white fences watch the players negotiate the approach over or through the deep depression in the front left of the green known as The Valley of Sin, passing judgement according to the level of failure or success.

The Royal and Ancient Golf Club watches over the Old Course like a jealous old dowager. The Club came into existence in 1754 when the first members gathered for much eating and drinking either at Baillie Glass's or the Black Bull Tavern. It was then known as the Society of St Andrews Golfers and it

was not until King William IV became the Society's patron in 1834 that the title of the Royal and Ancient Golf Club of St Andrews was conferred.

Ten years after the Society was founded it decreed that the number of holes on the Old Course should be reduced from 22 to 18, the standard which has prevailed to this day.

Contrary to popular belief the Royal and Ancient Golf Club does not own the Old Course. The links is the property of the local authority and held in Trust under Act of Parliament, ensuring that the world's most famous course remains, as it always has been, a municipal links open to anyone to play upon payment of a green fee.

St Andrews is the greatest of all the Open Championship venues. When the Open comes to St Andrews the atmosphere in the old town that lives and breathes golf is like that at no other sporting occasion. For weeks before, the talk is of nothing else as the town prepares to welcome the greatest players in the world for the four days that decide who is to be the champion golfer of the year.

Today the great players play for huge prize money and the ancient claret jug, the most famous trophy in golf. In 1860 for the first Open at Prestwick there was, by contrast, no prize money and only a leather belt to play for.

Any professional was allowed to enter, although the rules as laid out by the then Captain of the club, Lord Colville, let it be understood that 'the players shall be known and respectable "caddies"'.

It is still believed in St Andrews that it was the death in 1859 of the recognised professional, Allan Robertson, that was the catalyst for the first Open. Robertson, who was a feather ball maker in St Andrews, was the greatest player of his era and reputed never to have been beaten in any official match, although there is evidence that Old Tom Morris beat him on at least two occasions.

Robertson was the champion player and after his death there were those who sought an official event to find a successor to the unofficial title Robertson had held for years. Prestwick inaugurated the event.

Since the days of the great money matches between the legendary figures of the early days of the game like Old Tom Morris, Allan Robertson, Jamie Anderson and the Park brothers from Musselburgh there have been countless dramas

The medal tee of the 18th hole on the Old Course is only a couple of steps off the green of the famous 17th, the Road hole. It is a relic of the early days when players took a handful of sand from the hole and teed off their ball for the next hole just a couple of steps away.

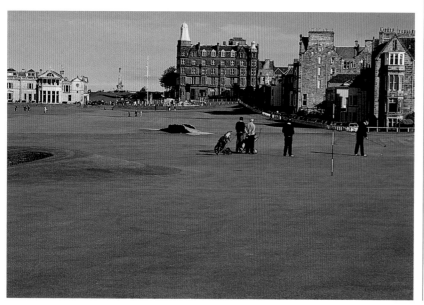

played out over the Old Course.

Bobby Jones, the greatest amateur player of all time, won the Open at St Andrews in 1927 and the Amateur Championship there three years later, the first stage in his remarkable Grand Slam, where he won the Amateur and the Open championships on both sides of the Atlantic in the same year.

It is the 17th or Road hole, the most famous hole in world golf, that everyone who journeys to St Andrews wants to play. It is fraught with danger right from the tee shot over the corner of the grounds of the Old Course Hotel to the green hard against the old road. The approach is a terrifying affair, with the infamous Road hole bunker in the front left of the green as Bernard Darwin once wrote 'eating its way into its very vitals', and the menace of the road itself behind.

The Road bunker has probably ruined more cards than any other in the history of the game and the road has claimed more than its share of victims too, most notably Tom Watson who landed on it with his second shot in the last round of the 1984 Open Championship and lost to Seve Ballesteros as a result.

The notorious 14th hole on the Old Course is another that can strike fear into the heart of the finest players. The drive must avoid the dreaded Beardies bunkers, a swarm of four treacherous chasms, which draw anything struck to the left like a magnet. To reach safety on the vast expanse of fairway to the right of them, known as the Elysian Fields, is difficult because of the close proximity of the old stone wall which marks the boundary of the course.

From there Hell bunker must be avoided, either to the left where there is room or to the right where

there is little. The Grave and Ginger Beer bunkers threaten the approach from the left while broken ground and whin are the menace on the right.

A long list of great champions have come to grief at one time or another on this menacing hole, among them Gene Sarazen. In 1933 when in good position to defend the title he had won at Prince's the previous year, he tried to carry Hell bunker with a brassie (No 2 wood) shot and failed. He buried his shot from the sand into the face of the bunker and needed eight strokes for the hole. Sarazen missed getting into a tie with Densmore Shute and Craig Wood by one stroke.

The great Bobby Locke suffered a similar fate in 1939 when he found the Beardies from his drive, was too greedy with his escape from the sand and failed to come out, and then found Hell with his next. An eight again was the result and he had had to sink a difficult putt for that. Standing on the 14th tee he had been six under fours and he went on to finish in 70.

The following day he tried to find the gap between the Beardies and the wall only to end up with a seven after he drove out of bounds. The news caused consternation at home in South Africa for in four years of championship golf he had never been known to take as much as a six!

A classic view of the Old Course at the start of the Loop where two fairways, the 7th and the 11th, cross. The enormous size of the double greens is obvious with the pin for the 7th to the right and the pin for the 11th close to the infamous Strath bunker almost on the horizon.

Prestwick

The Prestwick Golf Club stands as a monument to the early days of the game. It was the birthplace of the Open Championship, and therefore of professional tournament golf; it pioneered many other great events and remains to this day one of the most revered clubs in the world of golf.

Prestwick has not held an Open Championship for more than 70 years, and yet it has staged more Open Championships than any other course, save for the Old Course at St Andrews, and it was not until 1995 that even St Andrews passed the Prestwick total of 24.

This famous links has been the scene of great golfing deeds and achievements, and it is doubtful if any club ever received a finer compliment than that paid to it by the great golf writer Bernard Darwin. 'A man is less likely to be contradicted in lauding Prestwick than in singing the praises of any other course in Christendom'.

Darwin expressed this opinion when Prestwick was in its heyday and part of the expanding rota of courses for the Open Championship. However, by 1925 the lack of space around the course made it too difficult to control the crowds and Prestwick was removed from the Open rota forever.

Like so many other great clubs of its vintage, the early days of Prestwick Golf Club are sketchy. It is known that the Club was formed by a group of like-minded men who first met in the Red Lion Hotel in Prestwick on 2 July 1851. They were men of substance; wealthy men of property, noblemen with estates, men of the military services and of the professions.

The common factor which bonded them together was not simply their wealth and influence but that they were men of leisure with time to play golf and enjoy other country pursuits such as hunting, shooting and fishing. They were members of the ruling class at a time when Scotland was in the full throes of the Industrial Revolution.

It was also the age of steam and Scotland was expanding its rail network as fast as anywhere in Queen Victoria's Britain. Eleven years before the Prestwick Club was formed, on 11 August 1840, the railway line linking Scotland's industrial capital, Glasgow, with the town of Ayr on the Clyde coast some thirty miles away, was completed. The track ran through Prestwick and it opened up the entire coast along the Firth of Clyde.

Although the club was founded in 1851 it is known golf had been played at Prestwick – or certainly very close by – for many years before. The land on which the club built its first formal course had originally been granted to the men of Prestwick by King Robert the Bruce of Scotland for services rendered during the wars of independence. The ground was 'common land' and records show that the Prestwick Club paid the princely sum of £6 per annum for the use of it.

James Ogilvie Fairlie of Coodham was a leading figure in the formation of the Club and it is likely that it was his idea in the first place. He was a prominent figure in golf at that time, captain of the Royal and Ancient Golf Club of St Andrews in 1850, and a gifted player.

A local man, John Cuthbert, was recruited as the club's first secretary and his letter to 69 gentlemen

PRESTWICK

Established
1851
Course details:
18 holes
6668 yards
SSS 73
Address:
2 Links Road
Prestwick KA9 1QG

Tel: 01292 477404
Fax: 01292 477255

Left: A spectacular setting for the 10th at Prestwick.

Below: The famous old clubhouse at Prestwick where lunch in the Long Room is one of the great delights in world golf.

in all parts of Scotland offering them membership of the new Prestwick Club for an entrance fee of £1 and an annual subscription of £1, brought a response from 50 agreeing to join, including an acceptance from Lord Eglinton.

The Earl's castle was situated not far from Prestwick and His Lordship had privileged rights to stop any train on which he was travelling. He often exercised his privilege to stop the train beside the links to deposit himself and his friends for an informal round some years before the formation of the club.

The rudimentary course then in play was hardly sufficient for the use of the new Prestwick Golf Club and Fairlie was instrumental in persuading Tom Morris Senior to leave St Andrews, design a new 12-hole layout at Prestwick and become the Keeper of the Green, or the golf course superintendent as he would be known today.

Morris brought with him his infant son to settle in Prestwick. Young Tom, as he was later to become known, learned his golf over the course designed by his father before he went on to become one of the greatest champions in the history of the game.

Nine years after the Prestwick Club was founded, and after several important amateur events had been played there at the instigation of Fairlie, it was decided to organise the first professional open event. Again it was Fairlie who had a key role in its organisation.

Prestwick had first suggested the idea of a tournament open to professional players as early as 1856, but had met with very little support from other clubs. On 17 October 1860, the Club decided to go ahead anyway and commissioned a handsome red leather belt as the trophy. The cost was £25.

Only 'known and respectable caddies' were allowed to play in the event and a total of eight players, who passed this test of respectability, were ordered to gather in front of the Red Lion Hotel to

The famous Alps hole, the 17th, where Freddie Tait played a miraculous shot from the bunker in the final of the Amateur Championship against John Ball in 1899. Up to his ankles in water he played his ball, which was floating on top of the water, cleanly on to the green for a remarkable half.

hear the Rules and sign their acceptance of them.

A total of 13 rules were drawn up and the Club appointed markers to accompany each of the four pairs to ensure that the Rules of Golf – and of the tournament – were obeyed. It seems that the committee of Prestwick members assembled to oversee what was in effect the first Open Championship had serious doubts about the ability of the 'professional' players to abide by the accepted rules 'in the spirit of the game'.

A great crowd gathered to watch the three rounds of 12 holes, all to be played on the same day starting at noon.

Many Prestwick members were there for the Club's annual Medal competition to be played the following day. Some had their wives and families with them to watch this new competition for such a valuable prize.

There was also intense betting on the outcome with Tom Morris, the local hero, being heavily backed but there was much support too for Robert Andrew, the man they called 'the Rook'.

However, it was neither Morris nor Andrew who would win the first Open Championship. That honour went to Willie Park from Musselburgh who returned a score of 174 to beat Tom Morris by two strokes, with Andrew Strath from St Andrews third, six strokes behind the winner.

They could not have known then that this event, with its eight honest caddies who then went back to carrying the bags of members in the annual Medal competition the following day, would grow into the multi-million dollar extravaganza it has become today.

Much of the original 12-hole course at Prestwick is still identifiable today almost 120 years after it was extended to 18 holes. When the work was completed in 1882, most other clubs had followed St Andrews' example in establishing a round of golf as 18 holes. However, in Prestwick's case the move to standardisation hardly went smoothly.

There were complaints that the new holes 'were not golf' and never would be, but one of the main advantages was that it provided a start to the new course much nearer to the present clubhouse, which opened in 1866.

Although Prestwick is famous as the birthplace of the Open, and many of the great events that have

happened there have been associated with that particular championship, there have been many other historic events fought out there.

The Amateur Championship has been played at Prestwick on ten occasions, the first as far back as 1888 when John Ball won over Johnny Laidley, and the last, almost a hundred years later in 1987, when Paul Mayo defeated Peter McEvoy over 36 holes.

The first international professional golf match was played at Prestwick in 1903 between Scotland and England. The Scots were the winners by nine matches to eight.

Prestwick had its heyday up until the First World War. Thereafter its lack of space to adequately control the large crowds who wanted to watch championship golf proved to be its downfall as a major tournament venue. The club relinquished any hold on the Open in 1925 after the infamous championship in which thousands of spectators engulfed the play and made it virtually impossible for Macdonald Smith, an expatriate Scot from Carnoustie, to enjoy the victory he surely should have had.

Smith was hustled and jostled all the way round by a crowd estimated at 15,000. He was given very little room to swing, and not once in the round did he see the outcome of one of his longer shots. He left the course 'tired, angry and embittered' – and four strokes behind Jim Barnes.

It was a black day in Prestwick's history. The club that had given golf the Open Championship would never be asked to host it again.

The elevated tee at the 17th, the Alps hole, where the drive must carry a long way to the fairway and where the approach shot is, typical of Prestwick, a blind one.

Royal Aberdeen

ROYAL ABERDEEN

Established
1780
Course details:
18 holes
6372 yards
SSS 71
Address:
Balgownie
Bridge of Don
Aberdeen AB23 8AT

Tel: 01224 702571
Fax: 01224 826591

Dramatic surroundings
at the 6th on the
Balgownie course.

In the league table of golf course antiquity, the name of the Royal Aberdeen Golf Club stands at number six and deserves to be much better known to the wider world than perhaps it is. Here, at the Balgownie links on the other side of the River Don, but hardly a mile from the Granite City, is history indeed, a club which was founded as the Society of Golfers at Aberdeen as far back as 1780 and one of the most testing of all the great Scottish links.

It would be recognised as older still than that if the gentlemen of the Society had felt the need to ballot the membership in regard to new recruits to their number before that date. Almost certainly they could have, because there is little doubt that the gentlemen of Aberdeen were playing golf on the links two centuries earlier than that – including Sundays – although clearly they had felt no need at that time to gather around them the blandishments of officialdom and bureaucracy.

In fact it was not until the eve of the Battle of Waterloo in 1815 that the club as we know it today – but without its Royal prefix – came into being and incorporated the old Society. The Society members brought with them the old ballot box bearing the 1780 date and the president's chair, dated three

years later.

The evidence of golf at Aberdeen from as far back as the late sixteenth century is strong enough, and there is further confirmation of the game in the minutes of the old Town Council written towards the middle of the seventeenth century when John Dickson of Leith was granted a 'licence and tolerance' to make golf balls within the burgh.

Royal Aberdeen's credentials of antiquity are therefore well established and a visit to the course soon confirms its other credentials, those of one of the most testing and spectacular courses in Scotland.

The original course was laid out on a strip of common land between the Don and Dee rivers. In the second half of the nineteenth century the Club acquired the present course on the north side of the river.

There is dramatic scenery here, beautiful expansive scenery all the more easily visible from a variety of tees set high in the sand dunes, most of them offering marvellous views across the wide expanse of Aberdeen Bay.

It would be difficult to find a better outward nine holes in the whole of Scotland, and therefore by extension the whole of the British Isles perhaps, than at Balgownie. Longer than the back nine by close to 400 yards, the opening nine holes are nothing short of superb.

No comfortable opening here to ease you into the round. A 400-yard-plus par 4 is what you have to cope with even before the muscles are fully warmed to the task. It is followed immediately by a classic 530-yard three-shotter to reinforce the point that this is a man-sized golf course not interested in the least in taking prisoners. Those who remain in any doubt require only to step on to the tee at the 3rd and work out how to cover the 223 yards to the hole in the allotted three strokes.

There are occasions on this front nine, standing on several of the tees, when it is difficult to know if there is a fairway to play to at all. All around is

Tees set high in the sand dunes offer spectacular views around the Balgownie course and over the wide expanse of Aberdeen Bay.

topography that would test the resources of astronauts training for a moon walk, and yet when the valleys between and around the sand dunes emerge into view, there is revealed that wonderful crisp turf only found on the true linksland beside the sea.

This majestic front nine winds its way out to the turn with a couple of good two-shot holes, one of them short but tremblingly dangerous, another par 5, shorter of length than the first one but testing enough, a pleasant shortish iron par 3 and a bludgeoning par 4 of 453 yards that completes the first half of the course.

The return journey to the old clubhouse is shorter of length but into the wind most of the time, making it feel much longer than the 3000 yards the score card assures us it is. The short 11th is a test of nerve and club selection and the absence of a par 5 makes the nominal par of 34 a doughty challenge for even the bravest heart and the best of ball strikers.

It did not worry local member John P. Grant many moons ago when he holed the course in 63 strokes in a medal, with the only tragedy for Grant that he had a putt for a 61 and three-putted!

That eminent Scottish golf writer, Sam McKinley, who never tired of quoting Ben Sayers

who said: 'It's no' possible, but it's a fac', was not short to apply that quotation to Mr Grant's remarkable efforts.

It was an amateur record that stood until former US Amateur Champion, John Fought, shot 64 after alterations had been made to the course and he was accredited with the new record. That score has only been bettered by professional Antonio Garrido, who equalled John Grant's 63.

The Club was granted Royal status in 1903, when the then secretary, Colonel M.M. Duncan, read out to the members the letter from Lord Balfour of Burleigh, the Secretary of State for Scotland, informing Colonel James Davidson, Captain of the Club, that King Edward VII had granted the club's petition 'to use the royal title'. His Majesty also became Patron of the Club.

However, it was not the Club's first association with royalty. That began in 1872 when Prince Leopold became the Patron of the Club, which he remained until his death in 1884.

In 1925 James Braid of Great Triumvirate fame but by then firmly established in his role as golf course designer and refurbisher, was due to visit the Forfar Golf Club to redesign the holes Old Tom Morris had first laid out there in 1871. A committee member at Royal Aberdeen learned of his impending visit and suggested to the Club that the five-times Open Champion be approached and asked to give his opinion on the Balgownie links.

Braid visited the Club and then submitted his usual detailed report outlining alterations and additions to the bunkering, together with the levelling of some of the bumps.

It appears that Royal Aberdeen were less impressed with Braid than were the gentlemen of Forfar. The Angus links underwent much in the way of alteration for Braid's nine-guinea fee plus expenses, while Royal Aberdeen adopted only a limited number of the great man's suggestions. The Club remains insistent that Braid did not remodel the course but simply refined it and that such refinements as were undertaken were essentially cosmetic.

Royal Aberdeen has hosted many important tournaments over the decades including both of the Scottish Amateur Championships and the Northern Open.

Sam McKinley, in one of his beautifully crafted accounts of a visit to Balgownie, once recalled an amusing incident in the 1929 Scottish Championship between a presumably Scottish-born competitor and an Anglo-Scot when the tie reached the 14th hole. The ditch running across the fairway was at the distance of a long drive. The Anglo inadvertently teed his ball in front of the tee markers and dispatched his drive down the fairway. His opponent immediately recalled the shot, as he was perfectly entitled to do.

'Surely, I'll play another,' said the rule infringer, 'but I think I ought to tell you I am probably in the ditch.' 'No matter,' replied his opponent and the offender immediately drove again to a safe part of the fairway.

The first ball was of course in the ditch, but the rigorous upholder of the law came out on top in the end, winning on the last green.

They have always been keen on their Rules at Royal Aberdeen and the golfing law now enshrined that players may have only five minutes to look for a lost ball was established at Royal Aberdeen as far back as 1783. It first appeared as Law XII in the *Laws of the Game* drawn up by the Society of Golfers at Aberdeen and was worded thus: 'The Part whose Ball is amissing shall be allowed Five Minutes to search for it, after coming to the Spot where the Ball appeared to drop.'

In the early 1980s, however, the members went for a long time without even getting five minutes to look for their golf balls. A plague of crows descended on the course and whisked the balls away as soon as they landed. Fortunately, the plague left as abruptly as it arrived and the members went back once again to having the luxury of a full five minutes to find lost golf balls.

Deep bunkers and clinging rough guard the 8th green at Royal Aberdeen.

Royal Dornoch

ROYAL DORNOCH

Established
1877
Course details:
18 holes
6514 yards
SSS 73
Address:
Golf Road
Dornoch IV25 3LW

Tel: 01862 810219
Fax: 01862 810792

In a remote corner of Sutherland, on a latitude shared with Hudson Bay and northern Russia, lies a golf course which many know by reputation only, for they have never ventured far enough north to find it. The great links of Royal Dornoch is one of the great outposts of golf and one of the world's finest golf courses.

Remoteness has always been a factor in keeping this magnificent course out of the mainstream of championship golf. If it had been in the central belt of Scotland it would surely have been on the Open Championship rota long ago. This very remoteness, of course, has been at the heart of the romantic aura that has attached to Dornoch since before the First World War, when wealthy amateurs with time to spare took themselves north on the long train journey from more southern parts to the little grey town that clings to the very top corner of Scotland.

Today it retains much of that cult following, although more now among Americans than the well-to-do of southern English society. The transatlantic influence has been fuelled, to some extent at least, by the praises sung of it by luminaries such as Tom Watson, who is an honorary member, and the great American golf writer Herb Warren Wind, neither of whom are bad judges.

The notion that it remains a remote place is also an evaporating fancy. It is true that Dornoch is well over 200 miles from Glasgow or Edinburgh by road but communications with the north have improved out of all recognition over the last couple of decades. New road bridges to the Black Isle at Inverness and over the Dornoch Firth have reduced journey times to very tolerable levels indeed and the expedition is in itself a joyous experience through some of Scotland's most majestic highland landscape.

Among those who seek out this haven of wild beauty and formidable challenge, there are few who fail to rejoice in the sheer glory of the place. Royal

The beautiful links of Dornoch, which would surely have long since hosted an Open Championship were it not for its remoteness from Scotland's central belt.

The 3rd at Dornoch is the classic driving hole: an elevated tee to a sweeping fairway with all the problems in clear view.

Dornoch is very special indeed, and it commands a special place in the history of Scottish golf. Records show that golf has been played on the links here since 1616 and only Leith and the Old Course at St Andrews itself can claim greater antiquity.

Prominent among the discerning few who made the journey to Dornoch by train before the First World War were Roger Wethered, runner-up in the Open Championship at St Andrews in 1921, and his sister, Joyce Wethered, perhaps the greatest woman player of all time, and whom the great Bobby Jones once described as, 'the finest golfer, man or woman, I have ever seen.' Sir Ernest Holderness, Amateur Champion in 1922 and again two years later, was another devotee and regularly took the train north to hone his game on the crisp turf beside the Dornoch Firth.

This is classic links and spectacular terrain with views of the sea from every hole. The holes are strung out along Embo Bay in the mouth of the Firth on a narrow strip of softly contoured duneland where there is just enough room for parallel fairways on two distinct levels. It is completely exposed to the changing moods of weather in this northern latitude, a mere four degrees below the Arctic Circle.

The weather, however, is much less of a factor at Dornoch than might be supposed. The area benefits from a micro climate that resists the extremes of snow and frost in winter and enjoys many more long and warm summer days than might at first be imagined. This is not to say that the full force of the northern climate does not descend from time to

time upon the place, but it happens less frequently than most people believe.

The wind of course is always a factor. There are few days on which it does not sweep over the exposed links to create the classic seaside challenge.

Although golf has been played at Dornoch for centuries, organisation of it did not arrive in the town until the autumn of 1876 when the local Chief Constable, Alex McHardy, originally from Fife, and Dr Hugh Gunn, a graduate of St Andrews University, organised a meeting to form the Dornoch Golf Club. The original nine holes were opened for play the following spring when the club was officially constituted. Ten years later Old Tom Morris was drafted in from St Andrews to extend the course to 18 holes and was immediately taken by the natural plateaux which made perfect green locations.

The major influence on the development of Dornoch came from one remarkable man, John Sutherland, one of the most revered names in the history of Scottish golf. He was an estate agent and factor in the town and was appointed secretary of the club in 1883. It was a position he held for more than fifty years, during which time he made several revisions to the course in collaboration with J.H. Taylor, a regular summer visitor to Dornoch.

It was the coming of the railway in 1903 that really put Dornoch on the golfing map. By that year a sleeping car service could bring those who knew of its mysteries overnight from London and soon the little Sutherland town became a popular resort among the game's rich and famous.

The present course measures a relatively modest 6514 yards with a par of 73. There are four par 3s but only two par 5s on the card. Certainly its remoteness has mitigated against the hosting of major events but the Amateur Championship did go there in 1985 and the Scottish Ladies' Amateur Championship was played there in 1971 and again in 1984.

The relative dearth of major tournament golf does not mean, however, that these famous links have been deprived of a deal of first-class play. Five-times Open Champion, Tom Watson, a self-confessed lover of traditional Scottish links golf, plays at Royal Dornoch whenever he can, and rates it as one of the great courses of the five continents.

'I have played none finer', he is on record as

saying, 'it is a natural masterpiece'. There can be no finer accolade.

The course follows a natural soft 'S' shape along the line of the shore and is of a typical Scottish 'out and back' configuration. As in all classic links the wind is the key factor; when it is in the prevailing west the first eight holes can lull the player into a false sense of well-being, but from the turn at the 9th the battle for home is a hard one indeed with no let up. Only the 17th reverses the direction of the homeward journey, and it contributes little in the way of respite for the drive into a hidden valley is fraught with danger if too much liberty is taken with the bunkers and the gorse on the left side. The pitch to the green will seldom be of much length but requires a deft touch over a gaggle of awkward bunkers to a plateau green very difficult to hold.

The home hole requires two solid blows to reach the open green in normal circumstances; when the weather boils up, as it so quickly can in this isolated corner, it requires three from even the strongest, and all of them precisely struck into the bargain.

Famous golf course architect Donald Ross was a native of Dornoch and took his experience of this classic layout into a great deal of his work. His famed No 2 course at Pinehurst in North Carolina owes a great deal to the Sutherland links. Plateau greens and subtle slopes are its hallmark and, like Dornoch, had it been a little more accessible it might well have entertained more in the way of top tournament golf than it has. Another master American course architect, Pete Dye, has accorded Dornoch the flattery of imitation by designing the short par-4 5th at the Columbus Golf Club in Ohio on Dornoch's 15th, known as Stulaig. Not only have Donald Ross and Pete Dye incorporated the inspiration of Dornoch in their

work, many other architects have used the plateau greens as a theme in their designs. The famous 14th, the Foxy hole, is a recurring influence on courses in the United States. This beautiful 445-yard par 4 does not have a single bunker in its entire length. It relies on simplicity of design in which the natural feature of a substantial sand hill on the right has created a double change of direction. There is no need of artificial hazard and with the green entirely open in front, for the player who cannot reach it in two strokes, for this is a long hole into the prevailing wind, there remains the possibility of a chip and run up on to the plateau green to save par.

The 14th green, like so many others on the course, sits a few feet above the fairway, encouraging the slightly errant shot to roll off, leaving a delicate chipping challenge to get up and down in two. Much of Donald Ross's work in America reflects this principle, so obvious at the Foxy hole, which Harry Vardon once described as, 'the finest natural hole I have ever played.'

There is a rather macabre side to the adjoining Struie course which is very much part of the Dornoch story. The last woman convicted as a witch in Scotland, Janet Horne, was burned close to what is now known as the 'Witch's Pool', over which today's golfers now play at the end of their round.

The 17th at Dornoch is the only hole that reverses the direction of the homeward journey, but it offers little respite from the battle.

CHAPTER FOUR

SCOTLAND'S CLASSIC COURSES

Sculptured fairways and angled greens mark the Monarch's Course at Gleneagles out as a very typical Jack Nicklaus creation. This is the par-5 2nd.

The historic courses of Scottish golf are often more closely identified with the clubs which play over them than the courses themselves, while the classic courses of Scotland remain exemplary in their own right.

Scotland has a seemingly endless supply of these classic venues; wonderful layouts that attract visitors from all over the world to experience the real game in the surroundings where golf was born and has developed over several centuries. They are the crème de la crème of courses to play.

As in the previous section, what follows is not an attempt to create a league table, or to put forward the case for one course over another in terms of quality or standing. It is instead a collection of great courses that have more than earned the description of 'classic'.

The qualities that make them such are many and varied but all have that indefinable quality that sets them apart from others that might be of equal test or spectacular setting but have not yet attained the aura of this particular group.

Most are household names for no such list would be complete without the majestic links courses like Turnberry or Royal Troon, Machrihanish or Gullane, but there are others included which, although a little less widely known perhaps to all but the real cognoscente, are equally deserving of their place.

Scotland is rightly famous for its great links courses but it has many fine examples of the game played away from the seaside. In fact six of the 16 courses in this section are inland courses despite the fact no attempt was made to strike any balance between the traditional game by the sea and the courses inland.

Blairgowrie

ROSEMOUNT

Established
1889
Course details:
18 holes
6588 yards
SSS 72
Address:
Rosemount
Blairgowrie PH10 6LG

Tel: 01250 872594
Fax: 01250 875451

The Rosemount course at the Blairgowrie Golf Club ranks among the very best of all the great inland courses in the British Isles. There is not the grandeur of Gleneagles perhaps, with its wide and glorious vistas, but Rosemount is a spectacularly beautiful place in a totally different way.

It has that wonderful charm, found in so few courses, of having each hole as an individual entity unaffected and untouched by any other. Each hole is played along its own private thoroughfare fringed with heather, pine and silver birch. Wildlife, long since impervious to the intrusion of man in this peaceful setting, roams the fairways and the rough, casting only the occasional glance at the golfing frustrations of the intruders.

With early morning sunlight filtering through the stands of pine, reflecting the morning dew and silhouetting a grazing deer, or red squirrels darting about gathering their winter horde of fir cones, it is easy to see why Rosemount is regarded as one of the game's most beautiful outposts.

Here there is tranquillity where only the players in front, and occasionally the game behind if they are quick enough about it, are ever in view. Even when every tee time is taken this air of peace and isolation remains and is one of the main reasons why so many keep coming back to this very special corner of Perthshire.

It was sad in some ways that part of the original course had to be given up to accommodate the new Lansdowne course opened in 1974, but it was by all accounts an unavoidable price that had to be paid to introduce a badly needed second 18 holes. Dave

The beautiful Rosemount clubhouse, strangely described by the original committee as 'rather rustic' today offers a warm welcome and some of the finest fare in Scottish golf.

Thomas and Peter Alliss were given the task of creating the second course, which they did with the clear intention of offering something of a contrast to the original design.

The Lansdowne course is therefore a much more modern layout, much tighter in the fairways and with more of an American golf course feel to it than the traditional layout of the Rosemount course.

That would have been inevitable anyway considering the pedigree of the original course. Rosemount was the work of Old Tom Morris in its initial form and then of the legendary Alister MacKenzie of Augusta National fame, who lengthened Old Tom's 9-hole layout to 18 in 1923.

Even at that stage in its development the Club was beginning to feel constricted by numbers and an expansion plan was put together for the 42 acres already leased and the further 31 acres purchased from the Lansdowne family.

The Blairgowrie Golf Club shrewdly enlisted the help of James Braid, who at the time was completing work on the new course at Glenbervie, and asked him to remodel Alister MacKenzie's beautiful layout. It needed a delicate touch and an understanding mind, qualities Braid had in abundance.

It is said that Braid required very little time to stride round pegging out new greens and tees before accepting his £10 fee and setting off to catch the overnight train back to Walton Heath. He left behind the skeleton of a masterpiece to be completed by John Stutt, the constructor chosen for the work and it must have been the best £10 the Blairgowrie Golf Club ever spent.

In today's world of multi-million pound design and construction budgets and long timescale projects, it seems incredible how little time Braid actually required to create what is considered to be a golfing work of art. Skilfully bunkered fairways and greens, some of them the originals created by Alister MacKenzie, and one of the hallmarks of Rosemount, the lone pine tree left strategically in the middle of a fairway, reflect the great genius Braid had for golf course design.

Of course he had had plenty of experience by the time he remodelled Rosemount. There were few

trees for him to use to isolate holes when he built the King's and Queen's courses at Gleneagles but he also achieved the same effect of seclusion there through masterful use of the land and his understanding of how to find the most natural way to lay out holes.

Braid's Rosemount course opened in 1934 and he also provided the Club with a short 9-hole course.

A few changes have been made over the intervening years but the major alterations came with the construction of the Lansdowne Course. The 1st and the 18th holes were among those from Braid's

The glorious surroundings of Rosemount are obvious in this shot of the short 17th.

Large greens and bunkering by two of the great masters of the art, James Braid and Dr Alister MacKenzie, are hallmarks of the Rosemount layout.

course taken into the Alliss/Thomas layout and new holes were built at the far end of the course. The land had been farmland and not heathland like the rest of the course. They were at best a compromise. However, there have been moves to restore the course as much as possible to the Braid design with original bunkers being re-opened and greens reshaped to his plans.

In the holes retained from the old course the heathland turf of the fairways is a joy to play from. They are much more generous of width than those of the Lansdowne but the presence and threat of heather is never far away.

The well-kept greens are large and accommodating with subtle borrows never easy to read, and they are of course protected by the bunkering of two of the world's masters of the art, Braid and MacKenzie.

The Blairgowrie Club was founded in 1889 and the members have wanted for little in the way of creature comforts ever since. The clubhouse

is a traditional old building complementing perfectly the beautiful and tranquil setting of the courses.

The powers-that-be of the time described the original building as 'a pretty rustic club-house', which perhaps it is, although there is nothing rustic about the inside workings. There was originally a considerable amount of stabling included in the plans, but this is gone now to make way for the horseless carriage and its much greater demands on space. Blairgowrie has, as a result, a car park of quite extensive proportions.

This is a club that understands the needs of members and visitors alike and makes perfect provision for them. That is why it is so popular with visitors who come back time and time again, and why so many of them vote Rosemount as the finest inland golf course in Scotland.

It also presents one of the finest tables in Scottish golf. Plain golfer's fare it is, and just the way it should be.

Downfield

Like some of the other notable clubs which lie within striking distance of the championship courses of Carnoustie and St Andrews, the wonderful layout at the Downfield Club in Dundee lives a little in the shadow of its more iconic neighbours. The result is that Downfield seldom enjoys the recognition it deserves as one of Scotland's outstanding courses.

Parkland layouts in Scotland in any case tend to be regarded with less approbation than their seaside cousins, no matter how fine they are, but Downfield runs against the tide, boasting an impressive following among those who appreciate the peculiar pleasures of top-quality parkland golf.

No less a personage than five-times Open Champion, Peter Thomson, is among that influential following. The Australian is particularly remembered for the comments he made after the Scottish Open at Downfield as far back as 1972 when he described the Dundee layout as 'One of the finest inland courses I have played anywhere in the world.'

High praise indeed, and Thomson is not a man to make such a statement lightly. His comments are always measured and there are few players in the world whose opinion is more highly respected.

'It's a tough, demanding test of golf amidst some of the most picturesque scenery', said Thomson, 'and you need to drive very long and very straight to have any chance of success here.'

All of which is true, as an ever-increasing number of visitors to the northern outskirts of the City of Discovery are finding out to their great pleasure.

DOWNFIELD

Established
1932
Course details:
18 holes
6822 yards
SSS 73
Address:
Turnberry Avenue
Dundee DD2 3QP

Tel: 01382 825595
Fax: 01382 813111

A peaceful end to the day. Long shadows on the 18th green at Downfield.

Mature stands of trees, lush fairways and a feeling of tranquillity belie Downfield's closeness to the industrial city of Dundee.

It really is one of the treasures of Scottish golf, not only for its wonderful challenge but also for the hospitality and welcome visitors find in the clubhouse. That is after they find it! Downfield is not the easiest golf club in the country to locate and the journey there involves a fairly involved piece of navigation, part of which is through a pretty dense residential area of the city.

However, once the Downfield estate is located the surroundings are nothing short of spectacular, with fairways lined by mature stands of trees, lush rolling fairways and a wonderful sense of peace and tranquillity.

Golf has been played in the village of Downfield since the early twentieth century when the 9-hole Baldovan course was laid out. Records are hard to find today but one story persists from those early days regarding the clubhouse. It is said that the Baldovan players actually used an old horse-drawn tramcar as their clubhouse.

The course reverted to agricultural use during the First World War and it was not until 1932 that any move was made to revive golf in the village.

Three fields were rented from the Camperdown Estate and a 9-hole course laid out for a total cost of £150.

Shortly before the end of the year a general meeting was held and the Downfield Golf Club officially constituted. The course was handed over to the new committee and immediately there was a rush for membership of the new club.

It quickly became clear that 9 holes were not sufficient to keep up with demand and the club took an early decision to extend the course to 18 holes.

However, it was not only the demand for golf that was expanding rapidly in Dundee at that time. The need for new housing was just as strong after the Second World War and housing developments spread at an incredible rate in the outskirts of Dundee. Until then the course had enjoyed open country views, but the march of concrete eventually led to the Downfield Club's course being surrounded by new housing.

Alarmed at the prospect of being engulfed by bricks and mortar the Club entered into negotiations with Dundee Corporation, the local authority at that time, and after three years of discussions an exchange of land was agreed in 1964 when the present course was laid out and opened for play. Five holes from the original course were incorporated into the new design which was the work of the club's green committee with assistance from the respected golf course architect, C.K. Cotton.

It was a spectacular layout making full use of the marvellous surroundings and creating in the process as long and challenging a course as any inland in the British Isles. It was quickly recognised as such and the Club soon attracted many top amateur and professional events.

In addition to the Scottish Open, the Scottish PGA Masters, the Scottish Boys' Stroke Play and the Scottish Amateur Championship have all been played at Downfield and the course was nominated as a qualifying course for the 1999 Open Championship soon after the R & A announced that nearby Carnoustie was back on the Open Rota. It was also the venue for the final of the World Seniors' Professional Championship back in 1968 in which American, Chandler Harper, won the title by two shots from 1951 Open Champion, Max Faulkner.

Following the event the Club played host to a memorable one-day pro-am which featured a host of Open Champions including Bob Charles, Max Faulkner, Tony Jacklin, Peter Thomson and Gary Player.

BBC television chose Downfield as the venue for their successful *Play Golf* series with Peter Alliss which featured club members side by side with top professionals such as Greg Norman, Bernard Gallacher, Tommy Horton and John Panton.

After the Club was reconstituted in 1932 it appointed Fred Walker as the club professional the following year. It was the start of a remarkable 39-year association with Downfield for Walker who served the club with distinction until he retired in 1971. Two years earlier he was voted Club Professional of the Year by the Professional Golfers' Association.

His son Bobby kept the Walker name very much alive at Downfield when he reduced the course record to an incredible 63 at the age of only 14 and then went on later to win the Scottish Professional Championship twice and to represent Scotland in the Canada Cup which is now the World Cup of Golf.

Downfield enjoyed its golden era in the late 1960s and early 1970s but the return of Carnoustie to the Open Championship rota from 1999 has ensured that this much overlooked course will once again draw many admiring glances when it steps into the spotlight of Open Championship qualifying.

Sunlight streams through the trees to illuminate the beautiful Downfield setting.

Duke's Course, St Andrews

DUKE'S COURSE

Established
1995
Course details:
18 holes
7171 yards
SSS 72
Address:
Craigtoun Park
St Andrews

Tel: 01334 479947
Fax: 01334 479456

The Old Course Hotel in St Andrews may have an unrivalled position alongside the famous Road hole on the Old Course but its guests have no more chance of negotiating a tee time on the world's most famous golf course than anyone else. It has been a source of amazement to many foreign guests to the Old Course Hotel over many years to find that their names have to go in the daily ballot with all the other hopefuls.

The hotel's answer to this perennial problem was quite simple; build a course of their own where their hotel guests would have guaranteed times and which would at the same time enhance the standing of St Andrews as the world Mecca for golfers.

In keeping with the hotel's commitment to the best of everything it had to be a golf course of the very highest quality. It was not to be a rival to the Old Course but simply a complement to it to give hotel guests the opportunity to play a top-class inland golf course as an alternative to the traditional links of the Auld Grey Toon.

The hotel was acutely aware that the choice of architect would be critical to any new course in the Home of Golf. They didn't have to look too far, however, to find the right man for the job. Five-times Open Champion Peter Thomson was almost a natural choice. The Australian has had a long love affair with St Andrews – he has a house there – and he won the second of his Open Championships at St Andrews in 1955.

The splendid clubhouse at the Duke's Course stands on the highest point of the course and enjoys spectacular views across the course to St Andrews and far beyond.

He has a much deeper affinity and understanding of British links golf than most of his contemporaries and although the site at the old Craigtoun Hospital was not beside the sea it was an interesting piece of ground, offering wonderful views across the Old Town and over St Andrews Bay.

The result of Peter Thomson's work is the Duke's Course, officially opened by HRH Prince Andrew just before the Open Championship at St Andrews in 1995.

The course lies two miles outside the town and although it would never be the true links course that Peter Thomson would love to have built, it would certainly be true to his long-established philosophy that the game of golf is played on the ground and not in the air.

'The real challenge should be getting to the green, not just landing on it. Once there the putting should be fun,' Peter Thomson has said many times when discussing golf course architecture.

The Duke's Course is a solid testament to his philosophy. The fronts of the greens have been left open to the running approach shot and the greens themselves are contoured, not always very subtly. They can be devilishly quick.

The course, therefore, stands as a tribute to the Peter Thomson philosophy of golf in the traditional vein, although some issue could be taken over the distances between a few of the greens and the following tees. The requirement to make golf buggies available for Old Course Hotel guests, many of whom know of no other way to get round a golf course, was undoubtedly a factor in this element of the design, but it does make it a longer walk round. Add in a couple of tough but unavoidable climbs from the 9th and 18th greens and it's easy to understand why only the stoutest hearts will want to play the course from its full 7171 yards. Played to this length it is the longest inland course in Scotland.

From more manageable tees, however, it is a delightful test, if a little damp underfoot when the weather is not too kind.

Off the fairways the rough is fierce and the visitor will be hard pushed to find anything in there other than, perhaps, the ghost of the infamous Archbishop James Sharp whose phantom carriage is said to thunder past the clubhouse before plunging into the Bay of St Andrews. Occasionally, it is said, his daughter's screams can be heard from the

fairways, although it has to be said they would not be so easily heard from the rough!

The legend is an interesting one. On 3 May 1697, Archbishop James Sharp was travelling the old road to St Andrews with his daughter when his carriage was held up by five assassins who were actually lying in wait for an unfortunate by the name of Officer Carmichael. On the day in question Carmichael escaped the brigands' attention, only to die later for his cruelties.

Sharp was widely known in Scotland at the time as the Judas who betrayed the people of Scotland and the local Laird and, since he was

The hills of Angus make an interesting backdrop to the demanding tee shot at the 14th.

passing, the men felt it incumbent upon them to kill him. They ignored his pleas for mercy, according to the legend, and in front of his daughter, slashed his face, cut off his hands and shot him. For good measure they then rode over his head with his own carriage!

It is a gruesome tale of seventeenth-century St Andrews hospitality but visitors today are assured of a much warmer welcome at the Duke's Course. The new clubhouse is a magnificent building set in a secluded copse not far from the scene of poor Archbishop Sharp's demise.

Like the hotel itself the clubhouse is a five-star facility with a relaxing bar and excellent food in the dining area.

There has long been a need for another top class golf course in the Home of Golf and the Duke's Course fills that requirement perfectly.

Peter Thomson remains a regular visitor to the course to monitor its development, to supervise minor changes and oversee the maintenance

programme. One of the recurring problems he had to deal with was the drainage of the course. Heavy rains have tended to make the golf course very soft at certain times of the year but a major drainage programme representing a considerable investment for the Hotel has now put most of that to rights.

The improvement in drainage has brought the fairways more into line with the quality of the greens which are contoured, sometimes less than subtly, and can be devilishly quick.

Phil Mickleson might stop a lob wedge downwind on one or two of the holes, but he would probably need a 10 compression golf ball, with a paper-thin balata cover and a feather core, to do it.

Mere mortals must rely on a little more cunning and rapid development of their chipping technique to get the same job done.

The Duke's Course stands as a tribute to Thomson's philosophy of golf in the traditional vein.

Dunbar

The site of the present course at Dunbar is said to have been the one chosen by Oliver Cromwell for the camp to rest his troops before the Battle of Dunbar in 1650. Today the battles over the old Dunbar links are more concerned with the golfing challenge and just as fierce they often seem to be too.

This is an area rich in the history of Scotland and in the antiquity of Scottish golf. Dunbar is at the end of the string of ancient links spread out ribbon-like around the southern shore of the Firth of Forth. North Berwick, Musselburgh, Gullane and Luffness are nearer Edinburgh, and face across the Forth to other ancient golfing grounds like Leven and Elie, but Dunbar is slightly more removed. It lies just around the corner of the headland at North Berwick on the coastal route south towards Berwick-on-Tweed.

The first Dunbar golfers played not on the East Links as they do now but on a course to the west of the town at Westbarns. It is known that golf was played in the area more than a hundred years before Bonnie Prince Charlie's defeat at Culloden, for there is record of a local minister being censured for playing 'gouf' in 1640 and a quarter of a century before that of two men finding themselves in hot water for playing 'at ye nyneholis' on the Sabbath.

These early accounts of the game at Dunbar would have been of a basic form of the game for it was not until 1794 that organised golf came to the town. In that year a group of gentlemen with Masonic connections gathered together to form the Dunbar Golfing Society and played on a course at Westbarns. The club fell into decline and was eventually wound up, although the course itself, or certainly parts of it, was still around and being played on until the beginning of the Second World War.

A new club was formed in 1856, the Dunbar

DUNBAR GOLF CLUB

Established
1856
Course details:
18 holes
6426 yards
SSS 71
Address:
East Links
Dunbar EH42 1LT

Tel: 01368 862317
Fax: 01368 865202

Golf Club, and moved to the present site on ground that was formerly part of the Duke of Roxburghe's estate. The members engaged the services of Old Tom Morris, then the Keeper of the Green at Prestwick, to lay out a course of 15 holes. Three additional holes were added in 1880 and in the time since very few changes have been made to the layout.

The Dunbar course occupies a thin strip of land beside the sea and alongside a rocky, exposed beach. Most of the layout is classic links but there is also an inland element to it. The first three holes are played on the south side of the Old Deer Park wall that runs the entire length of the course before the route crosses the wall and heads out on the links proper towards the Barns Ness lighthouse.

The wind is always the main factor. The course itself is not overly long in calm conditions but even a light breeze transforms it into a serious challenge and as stiff a test as any among its East Lothian neighbours. The quality of the challenge is reflected in the fact that Dunbar has been used for many important championships including the final qualifying rounds for the Open when it is played down the road at Muirfield.

All the major Scottish championships have been played here: The Scottish Amateur and Scottish Professional Championships and the Scottish Boys' Championship which almost had its home at Dunbar from 1976 to 1990. The Boys' Amateur Championship was played at Dunbar in 1995 and the Dunbar Golf Club has also hosted the R & A Trophy, played between the juniors of the Home Countries.

The course is unusual in that it starts with two par 5s, although they are not the most testing three-

The spectacular panorama of the 8th at Dunbar hard beside the North Sea with the hills of Fife just visible in the background.

shot holes in this part of the world. A short par 3 completes the trio of holes on the landward side of the wall.

From this point on the going becomes much tougher. The strip of land is narrow and accuracy rather than length pays the best dividend. The 7th is a case in point. It is a par 4 of well under 400 yards in length, but it dog-legs to the right and has the omnipresent wall running the entire length of the fairway. The green is tucked hard against the wall, making it a nightmare in the wind for the right-hander prone to slice.

Just as the Old Course at St Andrews has a loop to change direction for the homeward journey, so too does Dunbar, but in the opposite direction. The holes around the turn, where the layout loops to the left and then back on itself at the 13th before striking for home, are perhaps the most interesting part

of the course.

The long 9th is over 500 yards in length, again with out-of-bounds threatening on the right. It is followed by a formidable par 3 of more than 200 yards often played into the teeth of the breeze. Three very good par 4s complete the left-hand loop before the course strikes out for home alongside the ocean.

At the 14th there is an interesting diversion in the form of a listed building known as The Vaults before the assault on the last four holes.

The 18th brings the course back to the landward side of the old wall and to the front of a very welcoming clubhouse. It is a testing finishing hole of 437 yards, with the wall again a major danger.

A quick calculation reveals that out-of-bounds threatens on no fewer than ten of the holes at Dunbar while the beach can take its toll on nine of them.

It is a strong challenge tempered by splendid views out to sea towards the Bass Rock, and in addition to the excellent golf here there is a fine beach, very good sea fishing and a nature reserve.

An indication of how times have changed since the early days of golf in the late eighteenth century is revealed in the records of the Dunbar Golfing Society's regulations of 1794, which read, 'When the expense of each member for dinner amounts to two shillings and sixpence, the Club shall be dissolved.'

However, whether a sudden rise in the cost of dinner at the Golfing Society was the cause of its demise, history does not, alas, record.

Dunbar is a stiff challenge tempered by splendid views out to sea. This is the 14th green.

Gleneagles

If there is one golf centre almost as well known outside Scotland as St Andrews then it is the majestic Gleneagles Hotel in Perthshire. This celebrated retreat of the rich and the famous is a world-class resort particularly popular with American visitors, many of whom perceive it as the essential Scottish experience.

Certainly there is no shortage of tartan, or plaid as the visitors from the former colony insist on calling it, to massage that feeling of Scottishness, and few hours in the day pass without the skirl of the pipes being heard somewhere around the 850 acres of the estate. It is a place where the transatlantic visitor has no problem in whiling away the odd hour or two in the opulent confines of the hotel bar in contemplation of his Caledonian forebears.

There was a time when golf was the only reason for a pilgrimage to Gleneagles but today, although matters royal and ancient still remain the principal attraction, there are other counter-attractions in which visitors can indulge in that profoundly Scottish way.

Tennis, clay pigeon shooting, off-road driving, fishing and even falconry, not to mention full spa facilities, are all available to guests seeking a little respite from the delights of the King's and Queen's courses or the battle of the Monarch's.

Gleneagles has an interesting history. In 1912 the Caledonian Railway Company began discussing a plan for a hotel in central Perthshire and the Gleneagles site was ultimately chosen for the development. By August 1913 agreement had been reached and it was planned to open the new hotel by Easter 1915.

The plan included the construction of two golf courses with James Braid and Maj. C.K. Hutchison invited to submit plans. Their first visit to the site was made on 29 December 1913 and by the following April they were appointed to design and supervise the construction of the courses at a fee of £120 plus expenses.

The actual construction of the course was handed over to Carters the seed merchants who received £1500 towards the cost of the course and a further £4000 the following year. By 1918 the King's Course was ready for play and so too was the Queen's, then planned as a ladies' course.

The King's Course was officially opened on 1 May 1919 and the first professional tournament, won by Tom Fernie, was played there a year later. The hotel, however, remained uncompleted.

On 6 June 1921 Gleneagles hosted an international match between Great Britain and the United States which was in effect the forerunner of the Ryder Cup. Course designer James Braid played in the match, beating Clarence Hackney by 5 and 4 in the singles, and then in partnership with his fellow member of the Great Triumvirate, J.H. Taylor, halved his foursomes match against Hackney and Fred McLeod. Jock Hutchison, the expatriate Scot from St Andrews who returned to his home town to win the Open Championship that year, also played in the match.

In 1923 the hotel was finally completed, eight years behind schedule, and Gleneagles' reputation began to grow. Many important events have been played at Gleneagles over the years since including,

KING'S

Established
1919
Course details:
18 holes
6471 yards
SSS 71
Address:
The Gleneagles Hotel
Auchterarder PH3 1NF

Tel: 01764 663543
Fax: 01764 694383

Left: A majestic setting for the first hole on the Monarch's course at Gleneagles.

Above: The idyllic surroundings of the King's Course are famous the world over. This is the 8th green.

The glen from which Gleneagles takes its name is clearly seen in this delightful shot looking over the 3rd green on the King's Course.

in more recent times, the Bell's Scottish Open, the McDonald's WPGA Championship of Europe and the PGA Cup matches.

Some changes were made to both the King's and Queen's Courses over the years but many were reversed to return them as nearly as possible to the original Braid/Hutchison layout. The King's Course is a very fine example of moorland golf with generous fairways and greens.

It was never intended to be a particularly testing layout but as a golf experience it ranks very highly among the best of them, particularly when the weather is fair. It can be a miserable place when the weather is not kind but on an autumn day with the sun reflecting the changing colours of the season it is truly a magical place.

The setting of Gleneagles is magnificent in a valley between the Ochil Hills to the south and the Grampians away to the north. Some of the views from the course are quite stunning.

There are good and memorable holes too, like the 3rd where the second shot is played blind over a

huge mound immediately in front of the green, and the short 5th with its upturned saucer green that will hold only the most accurate of tee shots. The most famous of the holes is the 13th, known as 'Braid's Brawest', a long 464-yard par 4 with a ridge running across the fairway in the landing area for the drive and a fairway that narrows appreciably 100 yards or so from the green.

Then there is the King's Course finish with a spectacular 18th hole that is nominally a par 5 but played all the way downhill offering even the most modest of players the opportunity to finish with a birdie.

The Queen's Course is a fine complement to the King's and a much better course than it is often given credit for. There are some fine holes and always the wonderful Gleneagles surroundings.

A third course, the Monarch's, was opened in 1993 at a cost of close to £6 million. Gleneagles brought in Jack Nicklaus to build what is an American-style course which, complete with cart

paths and buggies, is in complete contrast to the traditional layouts of Braid and Hutchison. For hotel guests who prefer to ride than walk, no doubt it has been viewed as a valuable asset to the Hotel but among the traditionalists it raised many an eyebrow when it was completed.

Gleneagles also has a par-3 course known appropriately as the Wee Course. It is the light alternative for beginners and the inexpert and is said to recall the 9-hole course constructed by head greenkeeper George Alexander and staff from the Hotel. There is also a Golf Academy which opened in 1994 and includes a 320-yard double ended driving range with a capacity for 40 players.

For a long time the Gleneagles courses were the restricted preserve of Hotel guests and club members. Outsiders remained behind the imposing wrought iron gates of the entrance. Now, however, the Hotel has reconsidered its policy and opened the gates to visitors with, of course, sufficient wherewithal to meet the not inconsiderable green offering.

For those who want a little escape from the delights of James Braid or the modern test of Jack Nicklaus the hotel has plenty of alternative attractions. Clay pigeon shooting, an equestrian centre, off road driving and a splendid spa are only a few of them.

Above: The tee shot at the 13th on the King's Course is played over a hill and into a hidden valley.

Below: The short par 4 15th on the King's Course is often within range from the tee.

Gullane

GULLANE

Established
1882
Course details:
18 holes
6466 yards
SSS 72
Address:
Gullane EH31 2BB

Tel: 01620 843115
Fax: 01620 842327

It was an accident of geology that created the renowned links of the Gullane Golf Club in East Lothian not far from Edinburgh. Sand from Aberlady Bay blown by the prevailing westerly winds was blocked by the huge mass of basalt rock that lies at the heart of Gullane Hill. Over the centuries the drifting sand stabilised into undulating terrain where marram and bent grasses and later the fine species of fescue ideal for playing golf became established, and the classic linksland of the east of Scotland gradually emerged.

It was a long process, but once established the land around the Gullane Hill was perfect for golf and it has been a principal centre for the game for centuries since. It is known that golf was played at Gullane more than 300 years ago for there are

The ancient links of Gullane are perfect for golf and have been a principal centre for the game for centuries. The hills of Fife are prominent in the background across the Firth of Forth.

records of play between the Weavers of Aberlady and the Weavers of Dirleton in 1650 on the first Monday of the New Year known as Auld Hansel Monday.

Until 1850 there were only seven holes, but with the arrival of the gutta percha ball in 1848 golf became accessible to a much wider audience and the game began to expand in Gullane. Gradually the course was extended to accommodate the growing number of players and in 1882 the Gullane Golf Club was founded. Still there was not sufficient golfing ground to meet the demands of new players and by the end of the nineteenth century a second course had to be built. A third course at Gullane was added in 1910.

The golf here is much hillier than at most Scottish links courses because of the Gullane Hill but the amount of climbing involved is a lot less than the visitor might think at first glance.

Gullane No 1 is the principal of the three courses and has been a venue for many important championships in its long history. As far back as 1897 the Gullane Club organised the British Ladies' Championship and Gullane has been a regular final qualifying course for the Open Championship, as well as a popular venue for both the British Boys' and Youths' Championships, the Scottish Stroke Play and the Scottish Ladies' Championship, not to mention a raft of more minor events.

All three Gullane courses share the same wonderful turf, superb putting surfaces and of course the inevitable climb up the Gullane Hill. The climb, however, is no hardship at all for the view when the summit is reached is quite spectacular. To the right the famous links of the Honourable Company of Edinburgh Golfers at Muirfield stretch out into the distance. Straight ahead to the north is the Firth of Forth with beyond it the hills of the Kingdom of Fife, wherein lurk the ghosts of ancient rivalries.

To the west the sands of Aberlady Bay, which played such a leading role in the formation of the Gullane courses in the first place, stretch away towards Edinburgh and the Forth bridges, rail and road, which are easily seen on a clear day. There are landmarks galore to be spotted. The Bass Rock, the Isle of May closer to the Fife shore, the twin hills across the Forth known as the Paps of Fife, the Ochil Hills and, behind you, the Pentland Hills and

The 18th on Gullane
No 1 Course lies at the foot of the huge mass of basalt rock that lies at the heart of Gullane Hill.

There are spectacular views across the Firth of Forth, with its busy shipping lanes, from the No 2 Course at Gullane.

A modest par 4 gets the round under way, followed by a more demanding two-shot hole as the course begins its move up the Gullane Hill. If the wind is strong, as so often it is, two shots will not be sufficient to reach the green in regulation, despite the fact that it is only 378 yards long.

The 5th and 6th continue the climb until the 7th tee reveals what Bernard Darwin once described as the best view in golf. Atop the Gullane Hill, that

the Lammermuirs. It is a panorama of intoxicating splendour.

The golf to go with it is just as splendid. No question here of turning the ball over in the winter months. The ball is played as it lies at Gullane no matter the time of the year: the greens putt as truly in the dead of winter as they do in the height of summer. This is classic golfing ground and turf of such quality that there are few places left in the game with anything at all to match it.

It seems strange that the courses at Gullane have nothing other than a numerical distinction to separate them. They are crying out for proper names for identification rather than the soulless digits more in keeping with a convict settlement than one of the historic centres of world golf.

It is all the more strange since there are some wonderful and imaginative names to identify the individual holes. Thucket Knowe, Maggie's Loup, Queen's Head and King's Chair come immediately to mind, with Corbie, Traprain and the Roundel all vying for attention too. All, however, have to submit under the collective heading of Gullane No 1 and will continue to do so no doubt for another couple of hundred years.

The first tee of the No 1 course sits on the outskirts of the village beside the professional's shop, a twelfth-century church and a famous golf museum.

wonderful panorama expands and the exertions of the climb are set aside to make way for the delights of a drive downhill to that inviting fairway at the 7th, a feeling to be savoured again at the Hilltop hole, the 17th, where the wide expanse of East Lothian is laid out for all to see.

Among the finishing holes the 15th is one to strike terror into all but the stoutest of hearts. It is a double dogleg par 5 of 540 yards past the Pump House, from which it takes its name, to a fearsome green with slopes enough to test the most diligent putter.

It was to the back of this green that Babe Zaharis famously struck a driver and a 4-iron on her way to victory in the British Ladies' Championship of 1947, an outstanding feat of power and precision.

It was also at Gullane that same year that Zaharis, the most famous woman athlete of her time, and perhaps any other for that matter, ran into trouble with authority.

Officials decided that the red-and-white checked shorts in which she appeared on one of the days were not appropriate for Gullane, or for the championship, and she was politely requested to change her attire. The Babe did so and went on to win comfortably and collect the Ladies' Championship Trophy from the Marchioness of Tweeddale.

Ladybank

The ancient Kingdom of Fife is renowned for its great links golf courses. At its hub is St Andrews, the Mecca that draws golfers from all over the world, while all around the coastline of the county there are dozens of other classic seaside links.

However, Fife has as many courses away from the sea as it has bordering on it, with the best of them unquestionably the wonderful heathland course at Ladybank. Indeed this beautiful layout set among pine, and swathed in deep heather and impenetrable gorse, stands comparison with any of the great inland courses in the British Isles.

Ladybank is that rare combination of immense and superb challenge allied to spectacular surroundings given in such full measure to only a handful of very special places. For many years now it has been a final qualifying course for the Open Championship when the world's greatest golf event returns to St Andrews, and yet it is surprising to find that this fine layout has only been one of a full 18 holes since the early 1960s.

The club itself is much older of course. It was founded in 1879 with only 6 holes to play on, a modest number by today's standards but not at all untoward at that time. Old Tom Morris made the 14-mile trip west from St Andrews to lay out the original course, a task that would have taken him no time at all since he was accustomed to laying out a full 18-hole course in a matter of a couple of days.

Old Tom's fees for his services were £1 a day plus his travelling expenses, which even in those days surely constituted a very modest outlay for the consultant services of a four-times Open Champion. It is not clear whether Old Tom's commitment at Ladybank was charged on a pro rata basis, but if it was then Ladybank's 66p-worth of design fees must surely equate to the best value in the history of golf course construction.

The original 6-hole layout served the Ladybank members well enough until the game became more popular and the course became more congested. Three additional holes were added in 1910 and Ladybank survived quite happily in this form for another half a century.

By the early 1960s the club was in the mood to expand again and a further 9 holes were planned. The club's honorary president, Charlie Samson, was the man mainly responsible for the transformation of Ladybank from a pleasant 9-hole layout into

LADYBANK

Established
1879
Course details:
18 holes
6641 yards
SSS 72
Address:
Annsmuir
Ladybank KY15 7RA

Tel: 01337 830320
Fax: 01337 831505

The green for the long par-5, 7th hole is set among stands of mature trees and typical of several greens at Ladybank, but gorse and heather are the main enemies.

what is today such an excellent course.

It was his vision and his ability to bring together local labour and local ideas for the design that made the expansion possible. His task, and that of those who so ably supported him, was made a lot easier by the simple fact that the ground available to the club was quite perfect for the purpose. Ladybank is pine woodland and virtually unspoiled. The heathland turf drains readily and the course is set in a secluded location hidden from the outside world. The work was completed in May 1961, a date that marked the arrival of Ladybank as a top-class inland golf course.

A couple of changes were made in the mid 1970s when two of the par 4s were converted to a par 3 and a par 5, but otherwise the layout remains as a tribute to Charlie Samson's vision, and proof if it be needed at all that $1 million design tags, famous names and 'signature' holes don't always win the day over honest endeavour and the right piece of golfing ground.

The forward-looking attitude of the Ladybank committee and its members has catapulted the club and the course up the league table of courses that discerning players want to visit. It enjoys an enviable reputation as a welcoming club and there is an honest, down-to-earth approach to be found here. The club has not been slow to move with the commercial times either, and has been very successful in attracting a solid visitor base to fund its operations.

A searching challenge and a wonderful setting are what make Ladybank one of Scotland's finest inland courses. This is the 11th green where the approach is extremely difficult past the tall tree just off the putting surface.

It remains, quite radically, one of the few courses in Fife offering ride-on buggies, although it has to be said, in thankfully modest numbers.

The club gained some notoriety several years ago when it staged an exhibition match between Seve Ballesteros and Jack Nicklaus, sponsored by the Old Course Hotel. The then owner of the hotel, Frank Sheridan, had hoped to play the match on the Old Course at St Andrews outside his hotel but was unable to persuade the then Links Management Committee to allow the match to go ahead, despite the fact that he had acquired a tee time for his famous duo.

It was all a bit embarrassing at the time for St Andrews but Ladybank weren't slow to invite

Mr Sheridan and his displaced superstars to enjoy the delights of classic heathland golf.

Jack and Seve discovered, as everyone who plays there inevitably discovers, that a steady hand with the driver is a must. The fairway is the only place to be, for only a few yards off it no prisoners are taken.

There is a famous story of a very competent golfer who missed one particular fairway at Ladybank and, bag over his shoulder, ploughed into the whins and gorse in search of his ball. When, after several minutes, he had not reappeared his playing partners urged him to give up the search for the missing ball on the grounds that it was futile; the player was heard to respond plaintively that he had long since stopped looking for his ball and was now looking for his golf clubs!

Another interesting aspect of Ladybank is the success it enjoys in staying well secluded. It is not the easiest golf course to find without a little orienteering experience. It sits in a triangle roughly formed by the A914 and A91, a major crossroads in Fife where the road north leads to Carnoustie via the Tay Bridge, while the road to the east leads inevitably to St Andrews. Neither of these great championship links is therefore very far removed from Ladybank.

However, there are two approaches to the club. Find the first and the car park alongside the clubhouse beckons. Find the second and the sanctuary of the clubhouse will only be reached after first crossing the main railway line from Edinburgh to the north.

A deep and unseen bunker lies in wait across the fairway in front of the final green at Ladybank.

Loch Lomond

LOCH LOMOND

Established
1994
Course details:
18 holes
7060 yards
Par 71
Address:
Rossdhu House
Luss
Alexandria G83 8NT

Tel: 01436 860223
Fax: 01436 860265

A difficult drive and a testing short approach are the difficulties to be faced on the 9th at Loch Lomond.

When former Open Champion Tom Weiskopf and his golf-course architect partner Jay Moorish were called in to design what is now the internationally famous Loch Lomond Golf Club, they could scarce believe their eyes. Nature had presented them with a site which Weiskopf described as one of the most beautiful places on Earth.

Weiskopf believes that what he built on the shores of Loch Lomond is his lasting memorial to golf. There has been a long line of voices echoing that sentiment ever since.

Loch Lomond is by any standards stunning. Former Ryder Cup captain Tony Jacklin was so impressed by the course on his first visit he declared it to be '…the most beautiful new golf course I have ever seen', forecasting that one day it would be a venue for the Ryder Cup.

Golf Magazine in the United States immediately ranked the course in 44th place in its top hundred courses in the world after the official opening in 1994.

Few courses have ever made such a major impression so soon after completion, although the initial development was not without its problems. The original development company went into liquidation in 1990 and there was much uncertainty over the long-term future of the course. It was held on a maintenance-only basis for some time until its future was finally settled after its acquisition by the Lyle Anderson Company and DMB, a privately held investment company from the United States.

Weiskopf built his masterpiece in the Rossdhu Estate, home of the chiefs of Clan Colquhoun, on an incredibly picturesque and wooded peninsula guarded on three sides by the loch. It is both a wonderful and historic site.

Rossdhu has been home of the Colquhouns since 1773. The Georgian manor house, which is now the clubhouse, was built by Sir James

Colquhoun to replace the fifteenth-century Rossdhu Castle, the remains of which still stand behind the 18th green of the course.

The Colquhoun Clan traces its ancestors back to 1368 when Sir Robert Colquhoun, chief of a clan that had fought with Robert the Bruce, married the fair Maid of Luss. She brought with her to the union the spectacular mountains and islands of the estate.

Rossdhu House looks out across the enchanted but treacherous waters of Loch Lomond. In the Middle Ages it was on these waters that the then chief, John Colquhoun 10th of Luss, was savagely murdered by a band of Hebridean marauders led by the chief of the Clan McLean. In 1603 the Colquhouns were massacred at the hands of Clan Macgregor at the infamous Battle of Glen Fruin, for which the Clan Gregor were outlawed by a special act of council.

Today there is peace around the loch fabled in song for its bonnie banks and braes. Weiskopf understood the tranquillity and special character of

the place when he set about laying out his course. He treated the site with great sympathy for its surroundings and its inspiring, if often violent, history.

He made full use of the rolling landscape and the mature woodland, the azaleas and the rhododendrons. In April when great splashes of colour

Above: The 18th is one of the most spectacular finishing holes in Scottish golf.

Below: Azaleas on the 9th at Loch Lomond put even Augusta in the shade.

The Bonnie Banks of Loch Lomond create the setting for a golf course that is not only one of the most beautiful in Scotland but anywhere in the world.

light up the surroundings of the old house not even Augusta in all its splendour can rival it.

The great mass of Ben Lomond stands majestic and protective to the north across the Bay of Rossdhu and the views to the islands are breathtaking, making the Loch Lomond course one of the very special places to play in the whole world of golf.

Weiskopf laid out the front nine around the loch, bringing it occasionally into play but always exploiting the beauty of the water. The first four holes offer a reasonably comfortable start although the 2nd, with its approach played over a low wall and up to a double green, can cause no end of trouble unless the drive is struck long and straight.

The full majesty of Loch Lomond comes into view after the testing downhill, dogleg left 4th, where the green is elevated and ringed by trees and dense vegetation lurks just short and to the right. The short walk from this rolling green up a slight incline to the 5th tee gives little hint of the splendour about to unfold.

Standing on this elevated tee there stretches beyond the inviting green below a panorama of the loch and its islands of staggering beauty. It is surely one of the most beautiful settings for a golf hole anywhere the game is played.

The loch then comes into play in its own right as a hazard at the 6th, regarded as the 'Signature hole', a long par 5 which runs along the edge of the loch with more stunning views to the east and north dominated by the imposing mass of Ben Lomond itself. The tee has been built up from the shore of the loch and the drive must avoid not only the water on the right but also the deep undergrowth on the other side of the fairway. A nest of bunkers forces a choice between a lay-up or a carry for the second shot but the green is out of range for all but the longest hitters, or of course the designer himself.

It is aptly named 'Long' Loch Lomond and along with the short 5th these are the two holes that visitors generally remember most after their round.

Wonderful renovation work has been undertaken in the old house to create a masterpiece of a clubhouse. The atmosphere of this historic building is palpable as soon as the main door is entered. The urge to speak in hushed tones is almost compulsive.

Loch Lomond, however, is a very private place. It is not a course that many will ever play and it has incurred some criticism in a land where golf has always been considered the right of all and not the few.

Lyle Anderson's course is the preserve of a mainly international membership who play there only occasionally and where, like Augusta, the fairways lie often silent. They open to the wider throng only once a year when the Standard Life Loch Lomond, an event that draws the world's top players in the week before the Open Championship, arrives in Luss, and the security guards who normally patrol the gates to block inquisitive eyes have an alternative role in checking admission tickets.

Lundin

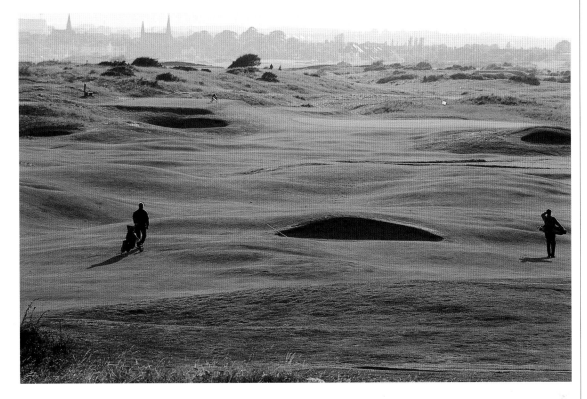

LUNDIN

Established
1868
Course details:
18 holes
6394 yards
SSS 71
Address:
Golf Road
Lundin Links KY8 6BA

Tel: 01333 320202
Fax: 01333 329743

Along the north shore of the Firth of Forth, only a handful of miles from St Andrews, there lies a golf course which, although it is in essence a traditional links, embodies an interesting history out of which has come a blend of styles rather unusual in a seaside setting.

The links of the Lundin Golf Club, and the course of its neighbours across the Mile Dyke at Leven, were in days gone by one and the same and for a time the clubs shared the course, starting at opposite ends.

The Leven players were first to utilise the links for the 'gowff'. The golfers of the old Leven Golf Club were playing as early as 1846 among the sand dunes and the humps and hollows on the west side of the dyke. To begin with only 9 holes were maintained by the members themselves until they were joined in 1867 by the members of the Innerleven Club, a club with a claim to be in the top 16 oldest in the world and now part of the Leven Golfing Society. The Innerleven Club had until that time played on the now defunct Dubbieside links across the River Leven where they had been holding competitions from as far back as 1820.

The course was extended to the Lundin Links side of the Mile Dyke in 1868 when the Lundin Golf Club was founded and the rolling sandhills towards Lundin Mill were brought into the layout, making it 9 holes out and 9 back, very much in keeping with the style of the middle of the nineteenth century.

Three golf clubs were then using the new 18-hole course, the third being the Leven Thistle Golf Club, another of Scotland's historic clubs dating back to 1867 and still one of the strongest playing clubs in the country.

Old Tom Morris is credited with the original layout of the second 9 holes and appears to have had some input into the first 9 holes, although some time after they were first laid out. His son,

The 2nd hole at Lundin
Links with its undulating fairway and menacing burn. The town of Leven lies round the bay.

The upturned saucer green of the 6th hole at Lundin Links is fiendishly difficult to approach. The island bunker in the foreground protects the 10th green.

Young Tommy Morris, won the inaugural competition over the new 18 holes on 2 October 1868, the year of the first of his four consecutive victories in the Open Championship at Prestwick. His score for the 36 holes was 170, one better than Bob Kirk and seven ahead of Davie Strath.

The course continued to be played from both ends as it were until 1909 when congestion forced a revision of the links. The course was divided at the Mile Dyke with the Leven clubs retaining the western side and the Lundin Club taking the eastern side, allowing the development of two separate 18-hole layouts.

Lundin Golf Club brought in James Braid, a native of Elie only four miles along the coast, but by this time resident at Walton Heath in London, to lay out new holes on the north side of the railway line, and remodel several of the holes left from the original course.

Braid was a great admirer of Old Tom Morris's work and retained the best holes from the original layout, including the 1st, 2nd, 17th and 18th. Today the Lundin course has changed little since Braid laid

it out. There have been radical changes to the 3rd hole, some bunkering alterations and the introduction of an irrigation system which has taken much of the keenness from the traditional links greens, but otherwise the course is much as Braid left it.

A legacy of the old railway line, long since a victim of Lord Beeching and his rail cuts, remains in the shape of the railway embankments. These form a natural out-of-bounds barrier through the middle of the course. Over the Mile Dyke at Leven the old railway embankments have been removed, much to that course's detriment.

The 9 holes on the south side of the old railway line are of course the classic links holes of the original course with the 1st, the long 4th, the uncompromising 15th and the wonderful finishing hole, a quartet to stand comparison with almost any other. Rolling fairways that were once keen and fast-running in the summer drought, now enjoy the protection of fairway irrigation and doubtless will never be quite the same again. Such, alas, is the price that comes with popularity, for Lundin Links is now a course of such wide approbation that it draws players from far and wide to sample its undoubted delights.

On the other side of the railway line the fairways take on more of a heathland texture as the course moves away from the shore and eventually on to a plateau to play the interesting par-5, 15th. From here the views across the Firth of Forth to Edinburgh, the Gullane Hill and the Bass Rock further to the east, are quite spectacular.

The drop back down to the old holes by the shore comes at the 14th, a glorious

one-shotter known as 'Perfection' for reasons soon revealed. It is played steeply downhill over gorse to a green surrounded by more bunkers than can be seen from the tee. The green itself slopes to the back and would be hard enough to attack in normal circumstances but with the Mile Dyke threatening out-of-bounds on the right, perfection is very much what is called for.

The finishing four holes at Lundin Links are well renowned for their challenge and ability to easily destroy an otherwise promising score. The wind, as always, is the key factor. Downwind it is often difficult to hold any of these greens with an approach, although less so now than at one time since the intervention of the sprinkler, but into the wind they present nothing less than a fearsome finish.

The boundary of the railway is a constant and distracting companion on the left and the second shot to the final hole is one of the most testing in the whole of golf in the ancient Kingdom of Fife. Against the wind it will be played with a very big club indeed, even if it can be reached at all. The road runs hard against the green on the left as the strip of links narrows almost to a point below the clubhouse, while the beach to the right awaits those who succumb to the blocked or badly cut shot in

the effort to avoid the tarmac. It is by any standards a great finishing hole.

The Lundin Golf Club has been a final qualifying course for the Open Championship when it is played at St Andrews on several occasions, and the club annually hosts the prestigious East of Scotland Stroke Play Championship. In 1974 Lundin was the venue for the World Senior Professional Championship, won that year by Roberto de Vicenzo.

Above: The Mile Dyke separates the Lundin Links course from its next door neighbour, Leven. Until 1909 both sides of the dyke were the same course.

Below: The devilishly tricky 5th hole at Lundin Links demands a precision tee shot to a well-protected green.

Machrihanish

MACHRIHANISH

Established
1876
Course details:
18 holes
6228 yards
SSS 71
Address:
Machrihanish
Campbeltown PA28 6PT

Tel: 01586 810213
Fax: 01586 810221

One of the most
spectacular opening holes
in world golf. The drive from
the 1st at Machrihanish
has to carry as much of the
beach – and the sea when
the tide is in – as the player
has the nerve to take on.

It requires an effort of not inconsiderable will to get to the links of Machrihanish on the southern tip of the Mull of Kintyre but anyone with any feeling for the history of the game, or a desire to seek out one of the best examples of classic links golf still remaining relatively untouched in these days of so-called progress, has to make this journey.

Old Tom Morris believed that the ground on which this famous course is laid out was designed by the Almighty for playing golf, but be that as it may he was still able to leave his own particular mark on this Divine creation. There remains to this day much left of what he laid out back in 1879.

Old Tom did not start with a blank sheet of paper whether provided by Divine providence or not. There had been golf played at Machrihanish as early as 1871, but it was not until five years later that the organised form of the game arrived with the formation of Kintyre Golf Club in 1876.

An account of its formation is eloquently recalled in Sheriff D.J. McDiarmid's centenary history of the Machrihanish club which reports the meeting on Saturday 11 March 1876 in the Argyll Arms Hotel in Campbeltown to form a club for the purpose of playing golf in the vicinity of Campbeltown. The entrance fee was fixed at ten shillings (50p in today's money) and the annual subscription at five shillings. Furthermore the members agreed that the rules of golf in force at Prestwick should be adopted.

Members were keen to get on with the business of playing the game, although they had no course to play on at the time. They were not helped by the fact that the ensuing week was particularly stormy according to the personal diary of Mr David Colville, one of the three members appointed to make up the club's founding committee. There was heavy snow all week and it was not until the snow melted that the members arrived to play for the first time.

On Monday 20 March 1876, Mr Colville and three of his friends assembled at Machrihanish, not only to play their first round as an officially constituted club, but also to build their golf course!

Mr Colville's diary records that the first sod was cut at 10am and that 10 holes made a good course, a course which they created as they went along and there is no evidence they even had official permission to create it in the first place!

'We had 2 rounds – 1 hour to each. Farmer seems agreeable to our playing', commented the diary.

The club prospered quickly and in the first year boasted more than forty members. By November of 1876 the Club had persuaded Charles Hunter, the professional at Prestwick across the Firth of Clyde, to make the journey to Machrihanish to rearrange the 10 holes and add another two. Three years later the club acquired additional ground on the west side of the river and Old Tom Morris made what must have been a daunting journey from St Andrews to advise the

Club on a full 18-hole layout.

In normal circumstances he required no more than a couple of days at a site to lay out the course. In the case of Machrihanish it seems he stayed for four days.

Above: Tackling the 1st.

Below: Classic rolling linksland and firm and fast greens are the order of the day in these remote parts.

Rolling greens, wild and wonderful scenery and no shortage of the product of the local distilleries await the visitor who has made the journey to Machrihanish.

Had it been that Old Tom was no stranger to a glass of whisky it would have been a forgivable assumption that his somewhat protracted stay, at least by his standards, could have been connected to the proliferation of Scotch whisky distilleries that existed around Campbeltown at that time. In truth there was then no shortage of ammunition for lovers of fine single malt.

However, Old Tom was by all accounts a man who eschewed for the most part the delights of the still, although he was keen enough on the company of kindred spirits, particularly in the close proximity of a great seaside links. This could more than account for the extra time he spent there, for Machrihanish is well renowned for its hospitality to visitors.

Today it is not as difficult to reach Machrihanish as it was in Old Tom's time, when the only viable route was by steamer from the mainland to Campbeltown and then by whatever means possible across the peninsula to the golf course. Now there is a splendid road that runs through some of Scotland's grandest scenery allowing a return journey to Machrihanish to be made inside a day quite comfortably.

However, a precautionary overnight bag is always a sound investment when contemplating a trip to the far corners of the Mull of Kintyre. Distilleries may not be as prolific as once they were but there is no shortage of their produce and no shortage of willing and decent company in which to enjoy it.

There have been a few changes made to the course since Old Tom's visit in 1879. In 1914 five-times Open Champion, J. H. Taylor, was brought in to make alterations which the members enjoyed for more than a quarter century until the Second World War. The Royal Navy acquired part of the course for a Fleet Air Arm training centre and later RAF Coastal Command staked their claim. The 9th and 10th holes were lost and the 8th had to be sacrificed. Sir Guy Campbell was given the task of remodelling and it is his design that visitors enjoy to this day.

The very remoteness of Machrihanish is in many ways its most valuable asset. Even with modern transport – it is accessible by regular air service from Glasgow in only a matter of minutes as well as by the much longer road connection – it is by any standards out of the way.

But once there, what joy there is to behold.

The tee shot from the first, which requires to be struck across as much of the Atlantic Ocean as the player has courage to take on, is one of the great experiences in Scottish golf, or indeed any other golf for that matter.

There are blind shots to be played, rolling greens to be carefully read and fairway lies to negotiate that are seldom level. And then there is the turf; pure, crisp seaside links that invite the nipped iron shot and leave behind the slightest sliver of a divot to mark the spot.

If there is a golfing heaven somewhere, then it is a safe bet that Machrihanish will have to be passed on the way to get there.

Montrose

Thanks to the diary of a young man by the name of James Melville, it is known that golf was being played in Montrose long before Mary Queen of Scots, golf's first woman player, was being chastised by the church for playing golf on the fields of Seton shortly after the murder of her husband Lord Darnley. There has therefore been golf played on the links at Montrose for more than four centuries, making the town one of the earliest and historically most important centres of golf in Scotland.

James Melville, born in Montrose, was a gifted scholar who entered St Andrews University when he was only 15 years old. Not only was he blessed with academic gifts but also with a keen interest in golf. His diary records that from an early age he had been interested in many different sports including archery, but the entry describing how he had been taught from the age of six 'to use the glubb for goff' established without question that golf was being played in Montrose in the middle of the sixteenth century. Since James Melville was born in 1556 it can safely be assumed that the game was well established by the time he took to having lessons at the tender age of six.

Golf at that time would have been very much a haphazard game on the links, played in its crudest form and certainly without any formal organisation. It would be another 250 years after James Melville's lessons on the links until any form of formal organisation came into the game with the founding of the Montrose Golf Club in 1810.

According to early records the golfers of Montrose might not have bothered even then to band themselves together into a club. Only word that the Montrose Town Council was planning to build a school on the golf course, and virtually on the first tee at that, galvanised the 'gowfers' into action. The Montrose golfers formed themselves into a club and won their battle against the Town Council. Another location had to be found for the school.

It wasn't the first time the golfers had had to fight to save the golf course. As early as 1785 a tenant of the Town Council had ploughed up part of the common links land and a petition of protest was sent to the Sheriff Depute. After due consideration the Sheriff Depute ruled in favour of the golfers and the links were saved.

Indeed it could be argued that by coming together in common cause against the Town Council tenant in defence of their golf facilities, the golfers of Montrose had actually formed themselves into a club at that stage. However, even if the 1785 date could be verified there was no formal constitution until 1810 and in any case it would not move the club very much further up in the league table of the world's oldest clubs.

Even with the 1810 date the Royal Montrose Golf Club, as it now is, ranks among the dozen or so oldest golf clubs in the world. It had a close association with Royal Blackheath which claims 1608 as its founding date, although there is no documentary evidence before 1787.

However, Montrose does have one unique claim to fame. At one stage in its history it was the links with the greatest number of holes. At a time when

MONTROSE

Established
1562 (Medal Course)
Course details:
18 holes
6470 yards
SSS 72
Address:
Traill Drive
Montrose DD10 8SW

Tel: 01674 672932
Fax: 01674 671800

The 14th green on the ancient links of Montrose.

golfers had to share their course with other sports including football, cricket, archery and horse racing. The right of the citizens to use the links for leisure activities is enshrined in law. For more than three centuries golf was free to them.

Free golf on the links lasted only until the Town Council and the non-golfers insisted on charging the players as the game became

Golf has been played at Montrose since the sixteenth century and parts of the original course are still in play today.

Musselburgh had only five holes, Montrose had five times that number, although they were not all played on every occasion.

In 1866, however, a unique event was organised and advertised in the national press as an 'Open Championship to be held on Montrose Links, over 25 holes, being one round of the Golf Course.'

Two Open Champions entered. Willie Park, winner of the first Open Championship at Prestwick six years earlier, finished second with a score of 115. Andrew Strath from Prestwick, who was then the reigning Open Champion, finished on 119, as did Jamie Anderson who was to win the Open three times in succession from 1875. The winner was T. Doleman from Glasgow who took the first prize of £10 with a score of 112 for the 25-hole course.

Eventually the Montrose golfers did come off worst in a battle with authority and it resulted in the loss of some of the original links. The Industrial Revolution brought demand for industrial and housing development and the Town Council was eventually able, with Parliamentary consent, to confiscate the East and Mid Links for this use. The Council made ground available at the North Links by way of compensation.

Part of the original links was retained and some of the Medal Course as it is still played today has therefore been played on for more than four centuries.

Like St Andrews, the links at Montrose were and still are common ground and for many decades

more organised with the arrival of such refinements as cups for the holes, flagsticks to mark their position and eventually the cutting of the grass around the holes.

There was a proliferation of clubs and club-houses at Montrose by the end of the nineteenth century but after a series of amalgamations only three now remain, the Royal Montrose Golf Club, the Mercantile Golf Club and the Caledonia Golf Club. The Royal Montrose Club emerged from the original Montrose Golf Club which in 1845 was granted the Royal title by Prince Albert and became the Montrose Royal Albert Golf Club. In 1986 the Royal Albert Golf Club merged with the Victoria Club, formed in 1864, and the last Captain of the Royal Albert Club, Mr J.A.C. Clark, wrote petitioning the Duke of Edinburgh to grant the Royal title to the new merged club. Buckingham Palace duly confirmed that His Royal Highness had 'agreed to continue his patronage if the name is changed'.

The present Medal course owes much to the design work of Willie Park Jnr who, in 1903, made alterations to a layout by the Mercantile Club on which Old Tom Morris had given advice.

A second 18-hole course, the Broomfield, was opened in the 1920s and today a Links Trust administers both the courses with representation from the clubs.

Several important events have been played at Montrose including the Scottish Professional Championship in 1967 and 1970 and the Scottish Amateur Championship in 1975.

Nairn

NAIRN

Established
1887
Course details:
18 holes
6722 yards
SSS 74
Address:
Seabank Road
Nairn IV12 4HB

Tel: 01667 452103
Fax: 01667 456328

Among the many great links golf courses for which Scotland is so famously known, there is one that has enjoyed rather less in the way of recognition than it clearly deserves. The great links of the Nairn Golf Club on the Moray Firth are the equal of almost any in the country and yet over the years this wonderful course has been somewhat underrated.

Even today it remains relatively unknown save to the initiated who appreciate traditional golf by the seaside and along with it an uncompromising challenge.

Set among great stands of gorse and heather not too far from Inverness alongside the shores of the Moray Firth, there are spectacular views across the water to the mysterious Black Isle and Easter Ross to the north, and to the mountains to the west.

There is classic links golf to be found here played on crisp seaside turf along fairways that thread their way through the whin and gorse and where the greens are as firm and fast as can be found on any day's march.

Like St Andrews the wind can be fickle, blowing into the player's face on the way out alongside the shore to the west, only to promptly change direction completely just as the long journey home is about to begin. There is no place here for the faint of heart. This is challenging ground; demanding ground, where only those who can find the fairway with rapier precision and carry a putter of unrelenting fortitude can hope to survive.

The Club itself dates back to 1887 when Andrew Simpson laid out the original course for the princely sum of £36. Three years later Old Tom Morris made the journey north from St Andrews to extend the course still further and charged the Nairn members a matter of six pounds and ten shillings for his trouble.

However, the layout as it is played today owes most to the hand of the legendary James Braid, the five-times Open Champion, who expanded and refined the layout in the course

The delightful 14th hole at Nairn is played from a high tee down to this undulating green with stunning views of the Moray Firth in the background.

The modern clubhouse at Nairn is the background of this view across the 14th green.

ground was opened up to create the 9th, 10th and 11th holes, and the 16th and 18th were extended. Work was completed by 1923.

In his report to the Club Braid said, 'The texture of the turf and the character of the greens are unrivalled. With the alterations I have suggested I consider the course will maintain its pre-eminence in the front rank of really first class links and meet all modern requirements both in regard to length and as a thorough test of skill at the game.'

These words apply as much today as they did then.

Braid made another visit in 1926 to build the short Newton course, make a new 2nd tee and move the 5th green to the top of a plateau, but apart from the course being lengthened, little has altered since.

It was the coming of the railway line in the last century that put Nairn on the map and gave the impetus to its development as a holiday resort which became known as the 'Brighton' of the North. It was the combination of wonderful terrain, civic ambition and the determination of the founders of the golf club to create a golf course to stand comparison with any other in the country, that was the foundation for Nairn's ensuing success among more discerning travellers.

Influential patronage was also a help, of course, and it has done Nairn's reputation no harm that over the decades Field Marshall Earl Haig, Ramsay Macdonald, HRH the Duke of Windsor when Prince of Wales, Harold MacMillan and, in more recent times, Lord Whitelaw have all been regular visitors.

Indeed Lord Whitelaw's golfing association with Nairn and the golf club is a particularly long-standing and famous one. He first played at Nairn in the 1920s and was a regular visitor playing in club competitions. In 1933 he won the club's junior championship with a 73, a score which was not bettered for more than 50 years.

The Club celebrated its centenary in 1987 by hosting the men's and ladies' Scottish Amateur Championships. It was the eighth occasion on which the Ladies' Championship had been played at Nairn, rather reflecting something of a change of attitude within the club which once notoriously had an entry in its suggestion book which read, 'women should be allowed in the clubhouse when the thermometer reaches freezing point'.

of three visits between 1910 and 1926.

Braid made his first visit to Nairn as early as 1901 as a player and the following year returned to set a new course record. It was clear that Braid was seen as the obvious choice to remodel Old Tom's layout but he was careful in his approach to the alterations, restricting himself mostly to making new tees and remodelling bunkers. One major change was the construction of a new green which is now the 16th.

In 1921 the Club was keen to revamp its reputation by then in decline, as it saw it, in comparison with other clubs in the region and it called Braid back north to make more radical changes. New

Safe to say that these days are long since gone on this stretch of the Moray coast and women have played a considerable part in the development of this forward-looking club for many years.

A new clubhouse costing £800,000 replaced the original wooden building so greatly loved by generations of visitors but which sadly could no longer stand the ravages of time. The ceilidh held to mark the old building's final fling before the bulldozers moved in was one which many, including the author, still remember with fond if rather hazy reflection to this day.

The Nairn layout is similar to St Andrews in that it is 9 holes out and 9 back, played in an anti clockwise direction with a little loop for minor variation. The prevailing wind is normally in the player's face on the outward journey, making the battle to the 8th green a daunting one, before there is a quick reversal of direction and then another battle against the wind up the 10th.

On the return journey the three holes between the 13th and the 15th are played around a little southerly horseshoe off the main loop and it is in this part of the course that the most magnificent views at Nairn are to be had. From the 14th tee at the top of the hill the view down this sharply descending and difficult par 3 and out across the Firth is quite awe-inspiring.

It was entirely fitting that Nairn should host the 1994 Amateur Championship as long-overdue recognition of this great links' standing as a genuine championship course.

Above: Gathering clouds behind the 12th at Nairn.

Below: Highest point of the course is the 13th green.

Royal Troon

ROYAL TROON

Established
1878 (Old Course)
Course details:
18 holes
7097 yards
SSS 74
Address:
Craigend Road
Troon KA10 6EP

Tel: 01292 311555
Fax: 01292 318204

The west coast of Scotland is less well endowed with great links courses than the North Sea coast but what it maybe lacks in quantity it more than makes up for in quality. Prestwick, birthplace of the Open Championship, Western and Glasgow Gailes, Turnberry and Royal Troon, together with a group of lesser known but also very fine courses, are contained within a relatively short stretch of coastline between Irvine to the north and Turnberry itself to the south.

Turnberry is slightly removed from the pack, enjoying some isolation, but of the main group the links of the Royal Troon Golf Club are perhaps now the most important, at least in championship terms, since Prestwick long since gave up any hopes of again being able to host the Open.

Royal Troon lies at the southern end of that beautiful stretch of Ayrshire coastline where golf was played long before the Troon Club was founded in 1878. There is evidence in Ian Mackintosh's excellent history of the club of a course of four or five holes as early as 1870 on which the holes were cut with a knife and 'were neither round nor square, but were large enough'.

Like so many other clubs formed around that period, the members met for the first time in a local hostelry. The Portland Arms Hotel was the chosen venue and the instigator of that first historic meeting was Dr John Highet.

Another of the founder members was James Dickie from Paisley on the outskirts of Glasgow who owned a summer house in Troon and was no

The 11th tee at Royal Troon provides one of the best views of the Firth of Clyde. Ailsa Craig is in the distance.

stranger to the town. He sought permission from the 6th Duke of Portland, the owner of the Fullerton Estate, to build a golf course on the land between Craigend and the Pow Burn. In the years since, the course has evolved into one of the toughest on the Open rota and boasts not only the longest hole in Open Championship golf but the shortest too, the famous 8th hole known as the 'Postage Stamp'.

Several famous golf course architects have been associated with the alterations and development of the course to its present layout. Willie Fernie, Open Champion in 1883, was instructed to make alterations when he was the club's professional, and James Braid, Dr Alister MacKenzie of Augusta fame and Frank Pennink are others who have left their mark on this famous links, although in Braid's case it appears that his contribution was restricted to some advice on bunkering.

Many illustrious names have been added to the Open Championship trophy after victory at Troon. Arthur Havers was the first in 1923 with Bobby Locke, Arnold Palmer, Tom Weiskopf, Tom Watson, Mark Calcavecchia and Justin Leonard completing the role of honour.

The most significant and perhaps the most spectacular of these victories was that of Arnold Palmer in 1962. Palmer had breathed new life into the championship by coming over in 1960 for the Centenary Open at St Andrews and narrowly losing to Australian, Kel Nagle. He had won the following year at Birkdale, bringing many more top American names with him to the championship. At Troon he spreadeagled the field with a scintillating performance on a dry, running course that was too difficult for most players to master.

Only six rounds under 70 were returned in the entire championship and three of them were by Palmer. Twenty years later, when Tom Watson won his fourth Open title, Arnold Palmer was honoured by the Royal Troon club with life membership, an honour richly deserved for his contribution to re-establishing the Open as the premier event in world golf.

It was fitting that the honour was made at Troon just across the fence from where the first Open Championship was played at Prestwick in 1860. The two courses sit end to end on this rolling stretch of Ayrshire linksland but are quite different in character. Prestwick is contained within a rather confined space whereas Troon is much more open and much bigger in scale.

There are few days on which the wind does not blow across this exposed links. The battle out is

Far left: The 7th green nestles between wild sand dunes as the players prepare to move on to the tee of the famous 'Postage Stamp'.

Royal Troon Clubhouse.
The Royal Troon Golf Club itself did not come into existence until March 1878 and was awarded its royal charter in 1978 – its centenary year.

ROYAL TROON COURSE RECORD
64 Greg Norman 1989; E Woods 1997

PAST OPEN CHAMPIONS

1923	Arthur Havers
1950	Bobby Locke
1962	Arnold Palmer
1973	Tom Weiskopf
1982	Tom Watson
1989	Mark Calcavecchia
1997	Justin Leonard

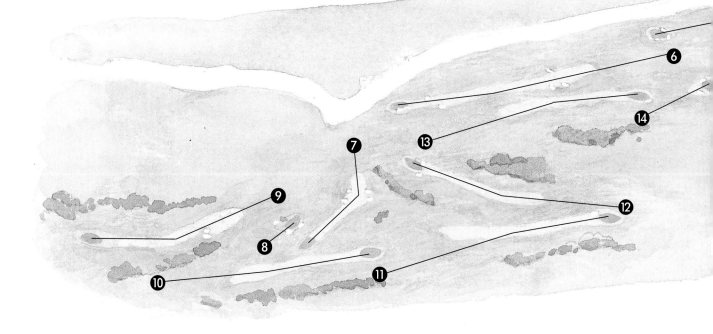

against the prevailing wind and challenging enough, but there then comes the long road home and the famous Troon finish, regarded as one of the toughest anywhere. When the wind is in the east it is an even more daunting prospect.

Two of the most renowned holes at Royal Troon, the 577-yard 6th, the longest hole currently in Open Championship golf, and the infamous 'Postage Stamp' have claimed many victims over the years.

The 6th famously ended the challenge of the young and virtually unknown American, Bobby Clampett, in the 1982 Open when he spreadeagled the field after two rounds, stumbled but still led after the third only to bury his chances in the bunker left and short of the green on the final day.

It was a graveyard for Clampett as it had been for many before him.

The Postage Stamp, the short 8th with its tiny green and fearsome surrounding bunkers, is known the world over. In the 1950 Open Herman Tissies, a German amateur player, had only one putt but required 15 strokes to hole out, including five from a bunker on the left, another five from a bunker on the right and three to escape from the original bunker for a second time!

There have also been memorable stories of triumph here, none more popular than the exploits of veteran Gene Sarazen, a winner in his time of all four major championships, when he made a sentimental trip back to Troon in 1973. Then in his 70s and playing in the company of two former Open

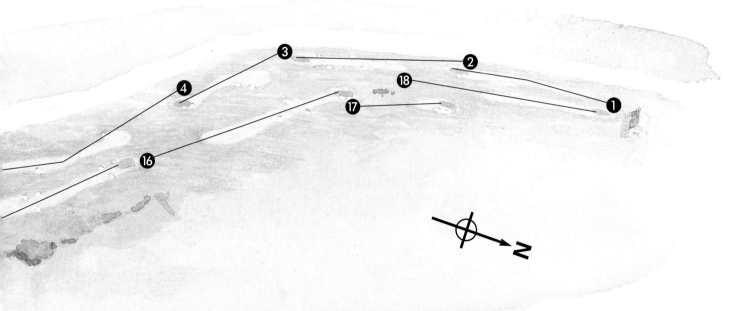

ROYAL TROON CHAMPIONSHIP COURSE

1st	Seal	Par 4	364 yds	10th	Sandhills	Par 4	438 yds
2nd	Black Rock	Par 4	391 yds	11th	The Railway	Par 5	481 yds
3rd	Gyaws	Par 4	379 yds	12th	The Fox	Par 4	431 yds
4th	Dunure	Par 5	557 yds	13th	Burmah	Par 4	465 yds
5th	Greenan	Par 3	210 yds	14th	Alton	Par 3	179 yds
6th	Turnberry	Par 5	577 yds	15th	Crosbie	Par 4	457 yds
7th	Tel-El-Kebir	Par 4	402 yds	16th	Well	Par 5	542 yds
8th	Postage Stamp	Par 3	126 yds	17th	Rabbit	Par 3	223 yds
9th	The Monk	Par 4	423 yds	18th	Craigend	Par 4	452 yds
Out:		Par 36	3429 yds	**In:**		Par 36	3668 yds
				Total:		Par 72	7097 yds

Above: The demanding par-3, 5th is surrounded by bunkers

Below: Evidence of early morning work by the Royal Troon greenkeepers.

Champions, Fred Daly and Max Faulkner, Sarazen holed his tee shot with a 5-iron in the first round and then holed a bunker shot in the second round for a birdie. His total for two rounds of the Postage Stamp was three strokes and he hadn't used his putter once!

Troon was the last of the royal golf clubs to be so honoured, gaining its title in its centenary year of 1978 and it remains the only 'Royal' club in the west of Scotland. The club had the support of the Scottish Golf Union when it wrote to the Secretary of State for Scotland in April 1978 requesting that a formal application for the royal title should be placed before the Queen. The following month confirmation was received by the club's then secretary, Major B.W.S. Boucher-Myers, that Her Majesty had been 'graciously pleased to accede' to the request.

Later the same year the Club petitioned the Lord Lyon King of Arms for the grant of arms to be used on the Club's crockery and cutlery and also on ties and blazer buttons. In a typically flamboyant reply from Herald's College the Lord Lyon granted the request and Royal Troon fell into line with all the other 'Royal' clubs of Scotland. The motto reads 'as much by skill as by strength'.

Troon's Royal title remains the only one to be granted by Her Majesty Queen Elizabeth II.

Southerness

SOUTHERNESS

Established
1947
Course details:
18 holes
6566 yards
SSS 73
Address:
Southerness
Dumfries DG2 8AZ

Tel: 01387 880677
Fax: 01387 880644

The best links golf of the west of Scotland is largely contained along the Ayrshire coast between Turnberry and the surrounds of Troon but there are other pockets where fine examples of the best in traditional golf can be found, albeit they are isolated and rather few and far between. One of the best examples is the links of the Southerness Golf Club tucked away in a corner of Dumfriesshire and certainly off the more heavily beaten tracks of Scottish golf.

Its location, deep in the south-west corner of the country, militates against the travelling golfer heading north towards Turnberry, Prestwick or Troon from stumbling across it by chance, for it is easily missed. Yet Southerness stands as one of the great links courses of Britain. It may be largely unsung but there are discerning players from far afield who make their way there almost religiously to pay homage to a classic links, and while they are there offer up a prayer for the remoteness that keeps it out of the wider gaze.

Southerness is truly one of Scotland's hidden golfing assets and would certainly command much greater respect than it does even now were it a little more easily accessible. Not that it is hidden away to the extent of, for instance, Machrihanish, but it does require a little effort to seek out.

Master architect Mackenzie Ross, who rebuilt Turnberry after it had been dug up to make way for an airfield during the Second World War, was the man responsible for this beautiful Southerness layout 15 miles south of Dumfries on the shores of the Solway Firth. He laid out a golfing treat on a flat stretch of land with sandy soil and heather lining many of the fairways.

The views across the coast of Galloway and inland to the mountain of Criffel are as spectacular as those across the Firth to the mountains of the Lake District and on a clear day even to the Isle of Man. It is a tranquil and a beautiful place and yet a

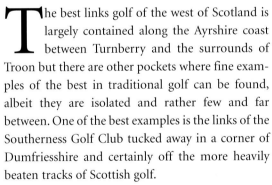

The beautiful surroundings and stern test of Southerness would command much greater respect than it already does if it were a little less remote. This is the 13th tee with the backdrop of the Solway Firth.

Above: The mountain of Criffel dominates this view across the 8th at Southerness.

Below: Golfers share the Southerness links with other animal life, canine as well as bovine.

challenging one. Southerness is arguably the only truly championship-standard seaside links to have been built on the British mainland since the Second World War.

There is little comfort here for lovers of the pristine and, some would argue, sterile style of golf course architecture so widely practised in the United States and whose influence continues to be seen in so many new golf course developments in Britain and Europe. Southerness is for the traditionalist, the golfing reactionary, the player who likes his golf open to the vagaries of the wind and weather and takes his lies on the fairway as Mother Nature left them.

There are humps and hollows and hanging lies, and no tally in the architect's report of how many million cubic yards of soil were moved to iron out the wrinkles. Southerness comes wrinkles and all, together with natural plateaux and shelves that Mackenzie Ross retained for green sites in the same way that that other member of the clan, Donald Ross, exploited to such great effect at Royal Dornoch.

Tight, crisp turf and naturally firm and fast greens are another of the Southerness hallmarks, as is the warm Borders welcome in the clubhouse from one of the friendliest clubs in the country.

There is solid challenging golf here too. Of the six par-4 holes on the front 9 only one is under 400 yards and at that only by a mere ten paces. On

the back 9 only two of the par-4 holes are under 400 yards and one of them, the 13th, is a monster only five yards short of par-5 status.

This gives the clue as to why Southerness has a nominal par of 69 and yet a standard scratch score of 73. There are only two par 5s, the 5th and the 18th and both are as close to 500 yards as does not matter. The two short holes in the last four add up to 400 yards between them with the 17th, although shorter than the 15th by some 40 yards, in many ways just as demanding.

Long irons, fairway woods and the sharpness of the short game are what come under scrutiny in no small measure on this testing layout.

In its original form Southerness was a classic out and back layout, but in 1974 the club built a new clubhouse in a new location. A revision of the layout around the new building made the original 6th hole the 1st hole, effectively splitting the course into two loops.

There is much in the way of Scottish historical interest to be found around Southerness, in addition to the excellent golf and the warmth of the welcome at the 19th, Mary Queen of Scots spent her last fateful night in Scotland at Dundrennan Castle not far away, and it was within a mile of Southerness that the infamous Admiral John Paul Jones was born.

Having thrown in his lot with the American revolutionaries in 1775 he terrorised the waters off his homeland coasts by harassing British shipping as far away as Lowestoft. Some time later he joined the forces of Catherine the Great of Russia as Kontradmiral Pavel Ivanovich Jones, before ending his days in impecunious circumstances in France.

There remains to this day evidence of his upbringing in Southerness and a well-known dance named after him is still popular in traditional circles.

Another aspect that makes this part of the Scottish coast so welcoming is the influence of the Gulf Stream, a significant factor in maintaining the Southerness links as an all-year-round golf course. It also made possible the creation of another of the great attractions of the area, the wonderful Arbigland Gardens at Kippford.

Crisp turf on the fairways and naturally firm and fast greens are Southerness hallmarks.

135

Turnberry

The world famous Turnberry Hotel stands on a headland looking out across the Firth of Clyde towards Ireland and down on one of the truly great championship golf courses of the world. It sits at the southern end of a strip of classic linksland along the Ayrshire coast 50 miles southwest of Glasgow amid scenery on the grand scale.

The hotel with its white façade and red russet roof is an imposing sight on this quiet stretch of the west coast countryside. Behind lies the rich agricultural heritage of the land of Scotland's national poet, Robert Burns, while across the Firth of Clyde the Isle of Arran rises stark and beautiful from the sea where once the great ships built on the Clyde were timed over the measured mile during their sea trials.

To the left of this panorama is the intriguing silhouette of the Ailsa Craig, known to the locals as 'Paddy's Milestone', a round island of granite that seems to float on the water like a huge marker buoy on the sea route between the Scottish mainland and Ireland.

Turnberry has had a chequered history. Twice this century the golf courses have been dug up to make way for aeroplanes. In the First World War it was the Royal Flying Corps who built a training airfield, then just before the start of the Second World War the Royal Air Force were the culprits, tearing up the links to build an airfield with three runways, parts of which can still be seen today.

The first reconstruction was undertaken by Major C.K. Hutchinson in collaboration with James Braid. The courses were essentially holiday layouts for the hotel until they were torn up to make way for a large aerodrome. After the Second World War there were serious doubts that the courses would

TURNBERRY

Established
1906 (Ailsa Course)
Course details:
18 holes
6976 yards
SSS 72
Address:
Turnberry KA26 9LT

Tel: 01665 331000
Fax: 01665 331706

Far left: The majestic hotel dominates the landscape at Turnberry, rightly judged one of the finest golf resorts in the world.

Left: Players silhouetted against the mountains of the Isle of Arran as they tackle the famous 9th hole from the forward tee.

The Ailsa course is by far the more famous of the two Turnberry courses but the Arran is a very fine test of golf in its own right and would be much more widely acclaimed did it not live in the shadow of its more eminent sister.

ever be rebuilt and it took a persistent campaign by Frank Hole, the managing director of British Transport Hotels, who were then the owners, to force the British Government into paying out compensation to enable reconstruction to be undertaken at all.

The world of golf owes a considerable debt to Frank Hole for his persistence. Hole brought in golf course architect Mackenzie Ross who, with the help of the hotel company's superintendent of grounds and golf courses, and a firm of English contractors, created in the Ailsa Course, one of the great championship links in the world.

The original course at Turnberry was very much different, however. It was of only 13 holes laid out by 1883 Open Champion, Willie Fernie, the professional at Troon further up the coast. The third Marquis of Ailsa, Captain at Prestwick in 1899 and after whom the championship course is named, leased land at Turnberry to the Glasgow and South Western Railway Company. The course was for the Marquis's private use.

A second 13 holes were laid out in 1905 and

TURNBERRY COURSE RECORD
63 M Hayes, Greg Norman 1986

PAST OPEN CHAMPIONS
1977	Tom Watson
1986	Greg Norman
1994	Nick Price

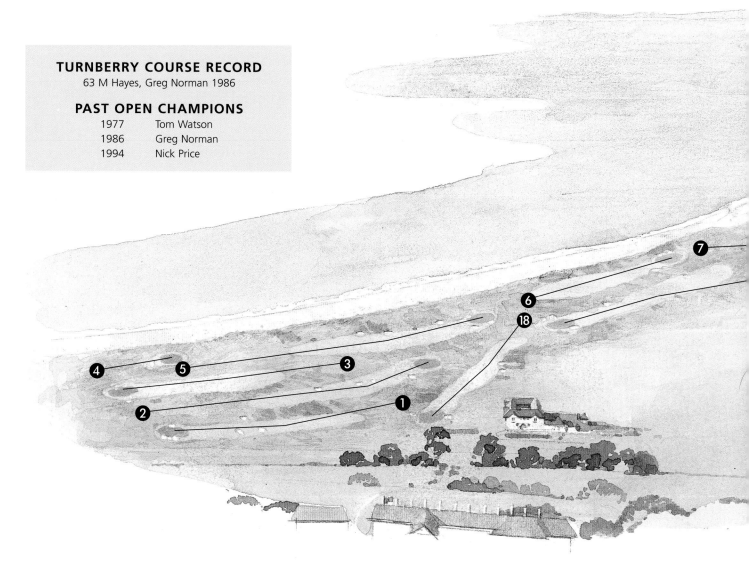

The evening sun highlights the lighthouse and Ailsa Craig as players putt out on the 9th green.

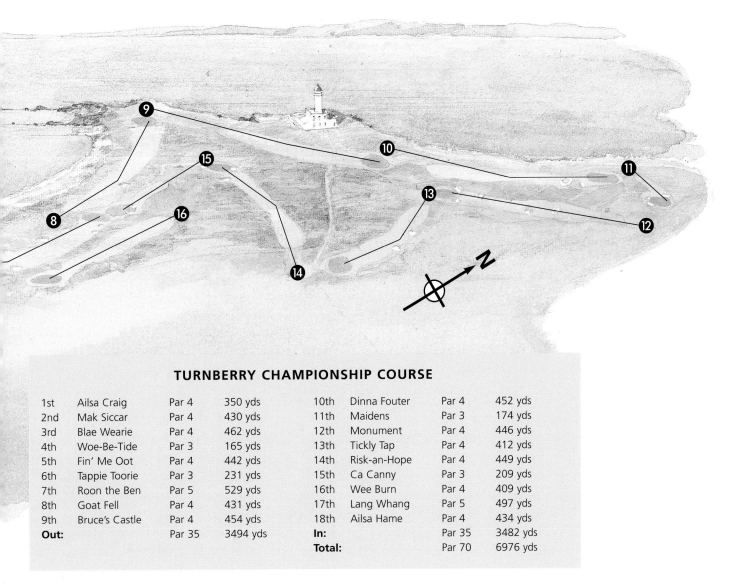

TURNBERRY CHAMPIONSHIP COURSE

1st	Ailsa Craig	Par 4	350 yds		10th	Dinna Fouter	Par 4	452 yds
2nd	Mak Siccar	Par 4	430 yds		11th	Maidens	Par 3	174 yds
3rd	Blae Wearie	Par 4	462 yds		12th	Monument	Par 4	446 yds
4th	Woe-Be-Tide	Par 3	165 yds		13th	Tickly Tap	Par 4	412 yds
5th	Fin' Me Oot	Par 4	442 yds		14th	Risk-an-Hope	Par 4	449 yds
6th	Tappie Toorie	Par 3	231 yds		15th	Ca Canny	Par 3	209 yds
7th	Roon the Ben	Par 5	529 yds		16th	Wee Burn	Par 4	409 yds
8th	Goat Fell	Par 4	431 yds		17th	Lang Whang	Par 5	497 yds
9th	Bruce's Castle	Par 4	454 yds		18th	Ailsa Hame	Par 4	434 yds
Out:		Par 35	3494 yds		**In:**		Par 35	3482 yds
					Total:		Par 70	6976 yds

The island bunker is a menacing hazard on the 10th fairway of the Ailsa Course.

when the Turnberry Hotel was completed, two years later, the railway company took over all the golf facilities.

Turnberry has hosted both the Amateur Championship and the Open Championship three times apiece. Sir Michael Bonallack won the first of his five Amateur titles in ten years at Turnberry in 1961 and the Walker Cup was played there two years later.

However, it was the famous 'Duel in the Sun' between Jack Nicklaus and Tom Watson in 1977 that confirmed Turnberry as a great Open Championship venue. It was the first time the Open had been played there and the huge galleries witnessed one of the greatest finishes in Open Championship history when Watson finished with two rounds of 65 to beat Nicklaus by one stroke. It was the beginning of a new era for Turnberry.

The Open was back again in 1986 when Greg Norman won the first of his two championships to date and Nick Price from Zimbabwe was the champion when the Open returned again in 1994, confirming

the Ayrshire links as a popular and long-term venue for the Championship.

There are many great holes on the Ailsa Course at Turnberry. The most famous is the 9th, a par-4 out by the lighthouse known as 'Bruce's Castle' after the nearby remains of a fortress where the Scottish king, Robert the Bruce, is said to have sheltered during one of his campaigns.

There are more difficult holes in championship golf, but none with a more spectacular or frightening tee shot. The walk to the tee is along a narrow finger of rock that juts out into the sea high above the Atlantic breakers. The player is separated from certain oblivion by a modest and fragile looking fence. With the wind blasting in from the sea as it so often does, it can be a frightening place.

It is the spot that prompted the eminent Scottish golf writer, Norman Mair, to coin the now immortal phrase 'for those in peril on the tee.'

The tee shot from this lonely eyrie must carry a considerable stretch of the Atlantic Ocean to reach the distant fairway but since it is normally down-

wind it is a carry that looks worse that it is in reality. It is the circumstances of the shot rather than the shot itself that can turn brave hearts to jelly.

The 220-yard 15th is another that has reduced many a strong man to a feeble wreck. 'Ca' Canny' it is called, and sage advice it is too. In the prevailing wind even a driver may not be enough to reach a green set in a great sand dune with perdition waiting to the right. It was here that Tom Watson delivered one of the vital blows that won him the 'Duel in the Sun' against Jack Nicklaus. He was off the green to the left and holed a 60-ft putt which rattled against the pin as it went in for a birdie.

Turnberry has it seems always been able to stir players to great deeds. Sir Michael Bonallack, Secretary of the Royal & Ancient Golf Club, launched his remarkable amateur career in 1961 at the start of a string of championship victories unsurpassed in modern times.

Eric Brown, Christy O'Connor and Dave Thomas have been worthy PGA match play champions there and Sandy Lyle found the inspiration for

a remarkable round of 65 on his way to victory in the 1975 European Open.

Ayrshire is one of Scotland's most beautiful and historic counties. Robert Burns was born not far from Turnberry and wrote much of the finest poetry in the Scots language.

Above: The menacing short 15th on the Ailsa Course has ruined many a promising score.

Below: The bag drop outside the lavish Turnberry clubhouse.

Western Gailes

WESTERN GAILES

Established
1897
Course details:
18 holes
6639 yards
SSS 73
Address:
Gailes
Irvine KA11 5AE

Tel: 01294 311649
Fax: 01294 312312

The narrow opening to the green emphasises the difficulty of the long 6th hole at Western Gailes.

Western Gailes is rather less well renowned than some of Scotland's great links courses but there should be no doubt that it is still one of the very finest. Were it not for the relatively close proximity of Royal Troon and Prestwick, Western Gailes would shine more brightly in that beautiful run of Ayrshire golfing country that stretches from Irvine to Prestwick and, with but a short interruption, to the mighty links of Turnberry itself.

There are two Gailes courses running cheek by jowl, and often there is confusion between them. Western's next-door neighbour is Glasgow Gailes, seaside outpost of the Glasgow Golf Club at Killermont and in similar vein. It was with a view to providing a links course for golfers who mostly played on inland courses in the Glasgow area that Western Gailes was also established.

The Glasgow Club had seen the value of this strategy some time earlier and established the Glasgow Gailes course in 1892. Five years later, four members from other clubs in Glasgow discovered the wonderful stretch of links next door to Glasgow Gailes between the Glasgow and South-Western railway and the sea, next to the Gailes railway station.

It was a perfect setting with easy access by rail from the city. An annual lease was secured from the Duke of Portland who owned the land, for the princely sum of £65, offset by £15 negotiated for the grazing rights.

Seven other golfers from Glasgow joined the enterprise and circulated a notice drawing attention to the proposal to build a new golf course on the 130-acre site at South Gailes. It was a bold and ambitious plan; however, unlike the Glasgow Club, which brought in Willie Park Jnr to design their layout, the new members at Western Gailes had no architect and had to leave the design work to the newly appointed greenkeeper.

The committee of the new club were in no doubt that success depended on attracting golfers who were already members of other clubs but who understood the value of having links golf not only as an alternative to inland golf, which most of them routinely played, but as a much more pleasant and drier underfoot alternative in the winter months. Subscriptions were set at a modest ten shillings and sixpence – a little over 50p in today's terms – with an equal amount levied as the entrance fee, to encourage a rapid take-up of memberships.

It was a sound strategy, and by 11 November 1897 the new greenkeeper began work on the club's daunting but promising land and by early in the following year 9 holes were in play. Work continued feverishly on construction and by June members were enjoying a full 18-hole layout.

Lavish it was not in those early days. There was no clubhouse and the members shared a small wooden shed with the greenkeeper as changing facilities. There was no bar and whatever food or beverage was consumed by the members was carried in on the journey there by train.

It was a situation that could last for only a short time and there became a clear need very quickly for a clubhouse to be built. By selling life memberships at £5 each, the club raised sufficient capital to build a substantial clubhouse at a cost of

£600. It was a wood and iron structure that served the members well until a much more ambitious design was authorised to be built in 1909. It is that building which is the basis of today's superb clubhouse with its wonderful panoramic view across the golf course and over the Firth of Clyde.

The hills of the Isle of Arran and the mysterious outline of the Ailsa Craig rise from the sea, prompting locals to explain to visitors that if the outline of Ailsa Craig can be clearly seen, it is going to rain, and if it cannot be seen then it is raining.

The wind, however, has always been the governing weather condition at Western Gailes rather than the rain. Certainly it can rain, and rain hard, although this is not an unduly damp part of the country. However, it certainly attracts its fair share of the wind.

The 600 members who had joined the club by 1901 were very well aware of that. So too were those responsible for keeping the golf course in good condition. The course in the early days was very vulnerable to winter storms and flooding when the sea breached the westerly dunes.

The Club needed a programme of reclamation to reverse the process and it was to be a long and expensive exercise. The well-tried method of driving rows of stakes into the ground at an angle to allow the prevailing wind to blow sand over them and create natural sand dunes, was employed. When further rows of stakes were added on the seaward side, the wall of sand became more consolidated and was anchored by the planting of the marram and bent grasses that flourish in this environment and form the basic structure of golf courses by the seaside.

It was a long-drawn-out process but a successful one and the Club was able not only to halt the advance of the sea but reclaim some land along the way.

All the effort of the previous years was almost destroyed in the terrible storm of 1926 and the Club had to raise more than £1000 for a concrete barrier to repair the damage in the aftermath.

In 1920 the Western Gailes club members had managed to buy the land on which their now well-established course stood for £3360, a fairly modest total even by the standards of the day. The following year there was a move to introduce seven-day golf at the Club where Sunday play had always been banned. It was a bold step but a little ahead of its time for it took another decade before a majority in favour of the move could be found. Even then the vote of 243 for to 219 against was a close one.

The quality of the Western Gailes course has been recognised by the staging of many important championships over its demanding 6700-yard layout. Harry Vardon won the first major event played here in 1903 with a remarkable score of 68, and since then the Club has played host to such events as the Curtis Cup, the PGA Championship, the Seniors', Scottish and Boys' Championships, and is regularly used as a final qualifying course for the Open Championship itself.

There is pure and unspoiled links golf to be found here, with lovely crisp turf on the fairways and firm, fast greens that have so far escaped the fate of so many of Scotland's fine links courses where over-watering and indiscriminate use of phosphate fertilisers has altered the natural and traditional character.

A calm sea is beautiful but a relatively rare sight from the 7th tee at Western Gailes where the wind is normally a constant factor on this exposed Ayrshire links.

CHAPTER FIVE

SCOTLAND'S HIDDEN GEMS

The great championship links are the icons of Scottish golf and rightly revered the world over, but the backbone of the game in the Home of Golf is formed of the dozens of lesser-known clubs largely hidden from the wider gaze.

From Dumfries to Durness there is a choice of courses as diverse in challenge and surroundings as can be found anywhere in the world. There are basic nine-hole layouts, there are great seaside links and sleepy inland courses, many of which have served their members faithfully for more than a century.

Among them are the hidden treasures of golf in Scotland; outstanding courses that do not enjoy the limelight of their iconic neighbours but which are a special joy to seek out.

The Shiskine course at Blackwaterfoot on the Island of Arran, is one classic example. To play there today is to play as Old Tom Morris did a century ago. It remains unspoiled and unchanging. There are courses like the James Braid classic at Brora in the Highlands and the delightful Pitlochry north of Perth, where the surroundings on a summer's day simply take the breath away.

This treasure trove has newer courses, too, like Whitekirk near North Berwick, built to a tight budget and a perfect example of what can be accomplished when the word 'championship' does not get in the way of planning. And there is the Duke of Roxburghe's creation on his estate in the Borders which comes with ambition to entertain championship golf and also fills a need for a more challenging course in the region.

The selection that follows is by no means the definitive collection of Scotland's hidden treasures, but it does represent a wide spectrum of courses that should be on every golf-course collector's wish list.

The great sweep of sand of Cruden Bay is a perfect feeding ground for hundreds of sea birds but the golfers have other matters in hand on the 15th tee of the historic golf course that bears its name.

Ayr

BELLEISLE

Established
1927
Course details:
18 holes
6477 yards
SSS 72
Address:
Belleisle Park
Doonfoot Road, Ayr

Tel: 01292 441258
Fax: 01292 442632

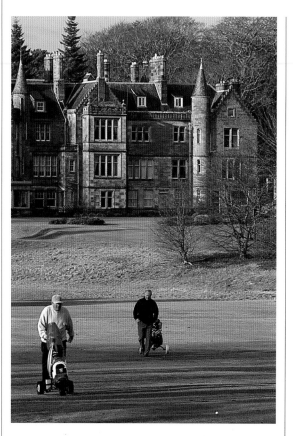

Belleisle sits in the splendid setting of the Belleisle Estate and is a product of the design genius of James Braid.

It is remarkable the number of occasions on which the name of James Braid crops up in discussion not only of the golf courses of Scotland but also of those throughout the British Isles. Braid had a prodigious output of new courses as well as refurbishment of long-established ones, nearly 200 in all.

At Ayr Belleisle, Braid was given a clean sheet to start with and produced what many believe to be one of the finest inland public links courses in Britain. It is laid out in the Belleisle Estate in Ayr where Braid came in 1927 to weave his magic by combining the natural features of the landscape into holes of genuine character and challenge.

There are many who travel to the Ayrshire coast and miss Belleisle in their headlong rush to sample the delights of Prestwick, Troon and Turn-berry. They are the poorer for the omission for there is excellent golf here in a beautiful, natural setting on a course that classically proves, as does the Old Course at St Andrews, that it does not have to be maintained in private hands to rank among the best.

Like St Andrews this is a public course that has staged important professional events including the qualifying rounds for the windswept European Open held at Turnberry in 1978.

Although it is not far from the sea, Belleisle is very much a parkland layout with mature trees lining many of the fairways that are normally much more lush and green than the links, for instance, at Troon just down the road.

A look at the score card tells the tale of just how demanding this Braid layout really is. At 6477 yards, with an SSS of 72, there are only two par 4s under 400 yards in length, the 8th and the 9th, and of the rest the majority are not only over the 400-yard mark but considerably over it at that.

Unusually, the course opens with two par 5s, albeit they are relatively short, and finishes with another that is anything but. Interspersed are four strong par-3 holes with the 3rd a particularly daunting test. Played uphill, its 176 yards play considerably longer than that and with bunkers right and left, and trees on either side, it is one of the most demanding tee shots on the golf course.

The burn across the fairway at the 16th hole, appropriately called 'Ca' Canny', has proved a watery grave for many a promising score in the testing trio of finishing holes that includes the tricky short 17th, also played across a burn, and that long 18th, 'Brown Carrick', a slight dogleg to the right of 532 yards.

A second 18-hole course in the Belleisle Estate, the Seafield, is a pleasant combination of links and parkland and a worthy complement to the Belleisle course, although quite a bit shorter.

Boat of Garten

There are many beautiful golf courses in the Highlands of Scotland but surely none fairer than the one to be found on the fringe of the Abernethy Forest at Boat of Garten. With a backdrop of the Cairngorms and a crumpled landscape of countless trees, this is a breathtaking place to pursue the royal and ancient game.

The air is clear and crisp, the mountains, purple and forbidding and capped with snow for most of the year, are constant companions and the golfer shares this glorious setting with a hundred species of wildlife that often wander the fairways, emerge shyly from the trees or fill the air with songs of approbation. The rare osprey can be seen here on occasions and deer have long since come to an amicable understanding with the golfing invaders of their natural habitat.

On a day when the sun shines in this northern setting the sheer beauty of the place is breathtaking and the challenge is no disappointment either. Not long by some standards, Boat of Garten is still a very fine test of golf, with demanding tee shots and hanging lies in the fairway in numbers more often associated with golf by the seaside.

Add to that the beautiful but wickedly clinging heather that fringes almost every fairway and it is not hard to see why the challenge is to keep the ball in the fairway from the tee and out of Braid's bunkers on the approach.

The original nine-hole course dates back to 1898 and served the locals and visitors well enough until the committee decided in 1930 that it needed to be extended to 18 holes. Inevitably it was James Braid who was called upon to make another of his long train journeys north to advise on the expansion, after additional ground had been acquired to make it possible.

He visited Boat of Garten in 1931 to draw up plans that were eventually implemented by John R. Stutt. The 6th hole is Braid's main achievement here and renowned as one of the finest holes in all of Scotland.

The course is only 5866 yards in length, with a par of 69 and only four of the holes more than 400 yards, but it is a tough nut to crack. Professional Gary Harvey has managed a 64 around the Boat but the amateur record remains at 67, testament to just how difficult it is to score well.

However, the score is not what matters here. The fresh mountain air, the tranquillity and beauty of the place and the feeling of being far away from it all are what really make the journey to Boat of Garten so worthwhile.

BOAT OF GARTEN

Established
1898
Course details:
18 holes
5866 yards
SSS 69
Address:
Boat of Garten
PH24 3BQ

Tel: 01479 831282
Fax: 01479 831523

Above: The beautiful Highland setting of Boat of Garten on the fringe of the Abernethy Forest.

Left: Winter snow still lingers on the mountains beyond the 17th tee.

Brora

The sight of a golfer suddenly stopping and stepping high in the air as he approaches a green with putter in hand is a very good clue that the golf course is the fine links of Brora, and that the player is climbing carefully over the electric fence that keeps cows and sheep off the putting surface. The fact that he steps so high is not so much a reflection of athletic prowess but more a concession to the fact that the fence is connected to the National Grid.

It has been said that there are two very good reasons to visit Brora in the very north of Scotland beyond even Dornoch itself. The first is the famous fishing tackle shop and the second a distillery that produces the Clynelish Malt Whisky. Golfers worth their salt know that, convincing as both reasons undoubtedly are, there is yet a third for which to venture this far north.

The links of the Brora Golf Club form one of the finest examples of Scotland's rich heritage of lesser-known golf courses to which those who would be true to their golfing souls have to make a pilgrimage at least once in their lifetime.

Apart from being a perfect base for a tour of the golf delights of the Highlands, Brora offers traditional links golf that has changed very little since James Braid was called in to upgrade the golf course in the 1920s. The five-times Open Champion took the train north to Brora from London, walked the course accompanied by Mr A.W. Sutherland, a member of the committee, and returned south on the next train.

The master architect's fee for his trouble was £25, plus of course his expenses, and the resulting upgrade of the layout was probably the best investment the Brora Golf Club made after it was founded in 1891 when Old Tom Morris travelled not quite so far from St Andrews to lay out the original first few holes.

The train still runs to Brora today and it is as good a way to get there as any, although the major improvements to the A9, and the opening of the Dornoch Firth bridge, have made this part of Scotland much more accessible than it used to be. Brora is now only an hour's drive from Inverness and sporting travellers are discovering this wonderful corner of Sutherland with its Royal Marine and Links hotels ideally situated beside the course to take care of their every need. There is wonderful and traditional links golf to be found at Brora with the cows and sheep for unobtrusive company just as it must have been when Old Tom staked out the first holes. Braid in turn left a heritage of fine golf holes through the hills and hollows of the dunes, together with a memorable finishing par 3 under the windows of the clubhouse.

BRORA

Established
1891
Course details:
18 holes
6110 yards
SSS 69
Address:
Golf Road
Brora KW9 6QS

Tel: 01408 621417
Fax: 01408 622157

Far left: Brora is one of the finest examples of Scotland's rich heritage of lesser-known golf courses which the connoisseur should take pains to seek out.

Above: Cattle have grazed the Brora course since long before James Braid upgraded the layout in the 1920s.

Left: Electric wire fences around the greens keep sheep and cattle off the putting surfaces. The electric fence around the 18th is clearly seen in the foreground as players climb the steep slope in front of the green.

Bruntsfield

BRUNTSFIELD LINKS GOLFING SOCIETY

Established
1761
Course details:
18 holes
6407 yards
SSS 71
Address:
The Clubhouse
32 Barnton Avenue
Edinburgh EH4 6JH

Tel: 0131 336 2006
Fax: 0131 336 5538

Despite its name the course of the Bruntsfield Links Golfing Society is not a links at all, at least in the Scottish meaning of the word. It is an out-and-out parkland layout and not at all a bad one at that in the suburbs of the city of Edinburgh.

It is an historic club of course, the 5th oldest in the world, dating back to 1761, and like several of its neighbours it has moved around a little in the intervening time. Originally the members played on the six-hole links at Bruntsfield but later moved to Musselburgh where they shared the public links with the Honourable Company of Edinburgh Golfers, the Edinburgh Burgesses and the Royal Musselburgh Club, not to mention a whole host of other minor clubs.

The Bruntsfield members moved to this parkland setting west of Edinburgh in 1898. The course shares a common boundary with the Royal Burgess Golfing Society.

There was something of a mass exodus by the major clubs from 1891 onwards when the Honourable Company started the trend by moving down the road to Muirfield, taking with them the Open Championship and not a little criticism in the process. The Royal Burgess Golfing Society moved to Barnton in 1894 and four years later the Bruntsfield members moved to their present course to the west of the city.

The course shares a common boundary with next-door neighbours, the Royal Burgess Golfing Society, but the courses are a little different in character. Bruntsfield is more undulating and is perhaps even more heavily tree-lined.

Willie Park is credited with the original layout,

but in 1971 Fred Hawtree was brought in to make alterations and modernise the course. He carried out some reconstruction work, made it longer and tougher than Willie Park had deemed fit in the days of the guttie ball, and introduced some new holes.

It can be fairly described as a modern parkland course which has not lost its historic setting and certainly there is good sport to be had here. The greens are large and undulating, if a little on the slow side, and even the fiercest boring shot with a driver will not be seen to scamper down the fairway to much extent. This is lush green, park golf and a formidable test when played from the 6407-yard mark with such little run.

The greens are large and undulating in character and require a more solid blow with the putter to get the ball up to the hole than might be the case elsewhere. However, shooting a score close to par is a major achievement as competitors in the Scottish Amateur Championship found to their cost in relatively recent times.

The surroundings make it a pleasant course to play, particularly on a fine summer's day, but the lasting memory for many is the Bruntsfield clubhouse.

There is no doubt upon entry to it that this is a club of great antiquity and of cherished history. However, it is also one of the great clubhouses in which to relax and dine after the exertions on the course.

It may not boast the mighty links of Prestwick or Muirfield but Bruntsfield stands alongside either of them when it comes time to take lunch.

Willie Park was the original designer but Fred Hawtree was brought in to modernise the Bruntsfield course in 1971.

Carnegie Club

CARNEGIE CLUB

Established
1995
Course details:
18 holes
6671 yards
SSS 71
Address:
Skibo Castle
Clashmore
Dornoch IV25 3RQ

Tel: 01862 894600
Fax: 01862 894601

Skibo Castle was once the home of Andrew Carnegie who, after making his millions in the United States, ended a long search to find his perfect Scottish retreat here on the banks of the Moray Firth.

Today Skibo Castle is the home of the exclusive Carnegie Club where a limited number of reservations are available for visitors who wish to sample membership. Without argument it is one of the great places in the world at which to stay.

The club has its own golf course which the present owner, Peter de Savary, ordained should be a resurrection of the course Carnegie built in 1898 to amuse himself when he returned from the United States to live in Scotland. In fact very little of the original course remained and architect Donald

Steel in effect created a new 18-hole layout.

There is spectacular and wild scenery here with views across the Dornoch Firth to Struie Hill and beyond in one of the finest settings in Scotland. The whole place has a great feeling of peace and

Above: The battered flag at the 8th is testimony to the winds that can whip across the Carnegie Club links.

Right: Donald Steel designed the new course for Peter de Savary at Skibo Castle to replace the original nine holes built by Andrew Carnegie to amuse himself after he returned from America to settle again in Scotland.

tranquillity about it and the aura of a great Edwardian sporting estate is carefully preserved.

Donald Steel's design lies close to the waters of the Dornoch Firth but it could not be described as a classic links layout in the manner of Royal Dornoch, for instance, only four miles along the road. There are links holes here of course but there are others with more of an inland feel to them making for an interesting contrast.

Thick rough and the prevailing wind are the course's main defences for it is not by modern standards a long course at 6671 yards from the very back tees. It is, however, a stern test for anyone, requiring a full repertoire of shots, particularly when the wind blows.

In keeping with its setting there is good sporting golf here for those fortunate enough to be able to take advantage of it. To it has been added a further nine-hole course known as the Parkland Course based on a unique concept with two options depending on which tees are used. It can be played either as a par-3 course or as a par-35 with an interesting mix of sporty par 3s, 4s and 5s.

The Golf House, the Clubhouse at the Carnegie Links course, is one of the most interesting in Scottish golf. It is modelled on the old farm steading which once stood on the site and nestles comfortably into the landscape. Open fires, an old bar, club dining area and the superb food and service for which Skibo Castle is renowned make it a memorable place to play.

It is, however, for the privileged few to enjoy. Visitors are allowed a one-night stay to sample the Carnegie Club, but have to join to make a return visit.

Crail

The Balcomie Links in the old burgh of Crail only eight miles or so from St Andrews is one of Scotland's finest golfing treasures. There is great antiquity here. The Crail Golfing Society was founded in 1786 at a time when there were only six other clubs in existence anywhere.

The links are set on an open and exposed corner on the most easterly point of the Kingdom of Fife, on a promontory known as Fife Ness. Old Tom Morris made the short journey from St Andrews to lay out the original nine holes at Balcomie in 1895 and returned four years later to add another nine. Prior to that the members played over a layout at Sauchope nearer the village and the Golf Inn was then used as a clubhouse.

Today the old course at Balcomie – it must be considered that now since an additional 18-hole layout has recently been added to the Crail portfolio – measures only 5922 yards soaking wet and hung out to dry. The par may be only 69 and the standard scratch 69, but this is a course that takes no prisoners, particularly when the wind whistles in from whichever quarter.

There is an abundance of short holes, six in all, but not one of them ever gives up par easily. There are three par 5s, two of them running consecutively on the homeward run with one of them always having to be played into the teeth of the wind.

Small greens that in the days before irrigation used to take on a summer shine players could almost see their faces in, and galloping fast fairways still to be found today, are the hallmarks of this classic piece of Scotland's golfing heritage.

Crail is known the world over and for many the pilgrimage here from distant airts is as much a part of the visit to the Home of Golf as to St Andrews itself. When the Open Championship is in the auld grey toon it is not unusual to see the famous faces of the game's greatest players pitting their wits against the unique challenge of Crail.

The sea is in view on every hole, often it is in play and there are wonderful views around two bays equalled only by the one from the clubhouse itself.

Crail is home to the famous Rankin Todd Bowl tournament played annually among the clubs of Fife. It is one of the great tests of golfing endurance, reducing the field to four qualifying clubs after the first round of stroke play in the morning, and then pits them against each other in foursomes match play during the rest of the day. The winner and the runner-up therefore play three rounds before taking the long climb back up the hill from the 18th green to the clubhouse which, if the truth be told, is tough enough after only one.

CRAIL GOLFING SOCIETY

Established
1786
Course details:
18 holes
5922 yards
SSS 69
Address:
Balcomie Clubhouse
Fife Ness
Crail KY10 3XN

Tel: 01333 450278
Fax: 01333 450416

Far left: The downhill, short 14th on Balcomie Links is exposed to the full force of the winds from the North Sea. The hills of Angus present the backdrop.

Above: Crail attracts players from all over the world to enjoy its wild and spectacular setting.

Left: A common sight at Balcomie; players retrieve golf balls from the beach, but only when the tide is out!

Cruden Bay

In a remote and beautiful area of rolling sand hills twenty miles to the north-east of Aberdeen is the unique links of the Cruden Bay Golf Club, a part of the very fabric of golfing folklore in Scotland, and a brooding seaside links like no other.

The original Cruden Bay Golf Club was founded in 1791 at Port Errol where it stayed for more than a century until moving to the present site in 1899. Up until the Second World War, Cruden Bay was a favoured holiday destination of the wealthy from the south, who journeyed up by train to a luxury hotel near the course long since demolished.

What remains from those golden days is a remarkable course offering glorious views out to sea as it winds its way alongside the sand of Cruden Bay, once described as being 'as smooth and firm as the floor of a cathedral'.

There is, however, nothing smooth about the Cruden Bay golf course. Massive sand dunes separate the winding holes, creating a sense of total seclusion for almost every hole is isolated. Tom Simpson laid out the original course in the days when the only way to move ground was with pick, shovel, toil and sweat. Simpson fitted the holes in where he could and an interesting job he made of it to say the least.

Here the player encounters just about every 'no no' in the modern golf course architect's text book. There is a host of blind tee shots and hidden greens – three in succession from the 13th – and the 15th is a blind par 3 where often the best advice is to lay up. But what wonderful, natural and compelling golf it is. It is golf the way it was played a hundred years ago and some would argue the way it should always be played. There is no chance of it changing either for the Cruden Bay Club members appreciate what they have, eccentricities and all, and jealously guard their heritage.

The scenery is breathtaking and it has been said by one eminent chronicler that 'you may never publicly have more fun in broad daylight' than at Cruden Bay. First-time visitors to the course have been known to become so enraptured with the place that they cannot take themselves away. It matters not that they may have emptied most of the contents of the ball pockets of their golf bags into the wild rough, or been frustrated by the uncertainty of it all, or been snarled up by bottle-necks of players; the sheer joy of the place brings them ever back for more.

Cruden Bay stands as one of the game's originals, the ultimate perhaps in natural golf save the Old Course at St Andrews itself, and a place where the memories last among the best in anyone's golfing life.

CRUDEN BAY

Established
1899

Course details:
18 holes
6395 yards
SSS 72

Address:
Cruden Bay
Peterhead AB42 0NN

Tel: 01779 812285
Fax: 01779 812945

Far left: Massive sand dunes and lengthening shadows make parts of Cruden Bay take on the look of the surface of the moon.

Above: The long strike for home. The 10th tee at Cruden Bay.

Left: The dunes that separate the holes create a sense of seclusion at almost every hole. This is the 14th.

Duff House Royal

DUFF HOUSE ROYAL

Established
1910
Course details:
18 holes
6161 yards
SSS 69
Address:
The Barnyards
Banff AB45 3SX

Tel: 01261 812062
Fax: 01261 812224

In 1637 the unfortunate soul of one Franceis Broun was returned to his maker courtesy of the hangman's noose after he received the death penalty for stealing golf balls. It is a matter of record that poor Broun 'pocketed golf ballis from the booth of Patrick Shand and reset them to one Thomas Urquhart, a servant'.

This harshest of penalties was handed down in the old town of Banff in Morayshire almost 250 years before golf became organised on this glorious stretch of golfing coastline. Indeed, there is some circumstantial evidence that some form of the game was being played more than a century even before the demise of poor Franceis Broun, but today there remains only the official record of his passing to confirm that the 'gouf' was being played

The tranquil surroundings of the Duff House estate are the setting for the parkland course of the Duff House Royal Club. The first Duke of Fife, Alexander Duff, gifted the land to the twin towns of Banff and Macduff in 1909.

at Banff and Macduff long before the Banff Golf Club came into existence.

The original club was founded in 1871, and just like St Andrews and many other courses along the east coast, the members did not have the links to themselves. Grazing sheep, fishermen drying and repairing nets and women drying their washing were hazards to the golfers as much as the whins and bunkers.

The original course was of eight holes, eventually extended to nine holes by the turn of the twentieth century.

In 1910 the Duff House Golf Club was founded after the first Duke of Fife, Alexander Duff, who married the Prince of Wales' daughter Princess

Louise, the Princess Royal, gave the Duff House estate to the twin towns of Banff and Macduff to provide land for a golf course and other recreational activity. Both were keen golfers, which goes some way to explain the Duke's remarkable display of generosity.

However, the 18-hole courses that was laid out in the estate was not very inspiring by all accounts. The square greens mown at the end of more or less straight fairways was not uncommon by the design standards of the time, but it was not the dullness of the layout which eventually sealed its fate, but the First World War. The course was turned over for agriculture and the golf club naturally went into decline.

It took a major fund-raising effort to re-establish the club's finances sufficiently to rebuild the course in 1923 but it was never a satisfactory layout. In that same year, the Duchess of Fife, who had been widowed in 1912, expressed the wish to become Patroness of the club and desired it to be known as the Duff House Royal Golf Club.

Two years later an amalgamation with the Banff Golf Club was agreed after that club had fallen into some decay. Dr Alister MacKenzie was brought in amid much controversy to lay out a new course and the Duff House Royal title was adopted for the new club.

Today it is a beautiful parkland course with little rough and large MacKenzie double-tiered greens. Not long at just over 6100 yards, it remains a severe but fair challenge to players of all abilities.

The 12th green at the Duff House Royal Golf Club, which is the 7th in line of Scotland's Royal clubs.

Durness

For those who seek out the relatively new course at Durness in Sutherland the experience might be likened to balancing on the edge of the world. Golfers simply can't get much further north in mainland Britain in pursuit of matters royal and ancient, Thurso and Reay perhaps being the exceptions, and even then by only a whisker.

If it is something of an expedition to get to Durness Golf Club the rewards for those who succeed greatly outweigh the effort to get there. There is pleasantly testing golf to be found here in dramatic scenery on a course that has been cleverly designed.

There are only nine greens, but two distinctly different sets of tees creating an interesting and exacting challenge of 5555 yards over the two circuits with an SSS of 69. It is not long by many standards, but it is difficult to score on. A measure of that difficulty is reflected in the fact that level fours was not officially broken in competition until 1996 when M. Mackay returned a 71, and that was eight years after the course was opened.

The area is more widely renowned for the mighty cliffs of Cape Wrath and the enchanting Smoo Cave than for its golf course, but the delights of Durness are attracting more and more attention as news of the hidden golfing treasure to be found there spreads. The course has now become very much the third attraction to this unspoiled corner of Sutherland.

The uphill opening hole affords a pleasantly uncomplicated start and holds in store a spectacular view over Balnakeil Bay when the green is reached. There are stronger holes to follow, however, with the 6th and 15th played to the same green but 420 yards and 505 yards respectively on the two circuits.

The majestic peak of Foinaven is the line for the 3rd and 12th holes and followers of the other sport of kings will recognise the name readily enough. The Duchess of Westminster took the name for her famous horse, which won the Grand National dramatically at Aintree in 1967.

The most memorable hole – indeed two holes – come at the end of each circuit. Played first time round the 9th is a modest short hole of only 108 yards, but second time of asking that gets stretched to 155 yards. In fact it matters little what distance it is played from, for the tee shot in both instances has to be played across the crashing waters of the North Atlantic where it has eaten its way into the cliff face over the centuries. The visitor who leaves Durness with two par figures on the card at these holes will have much to rejoice over.

DURNESS

Established
1988
Course details:
9 holes
5555 yards
SSS 69
Address:
Balnakeil
Durness IV27 4PN

Tel: 01971 511364

Left: The wild setting of the Durness Club on the very edge of Scotland.

Below: The green of the 8th and 17th holes.

Edzell

EDZELL

Established
1895
Course details:
18 holes
6348 yards
SSS 71
Address:
High Street
Edzell DD9 7TF

Tel: 01356 648235
Fax: 01356 648094

Edzell is regarded as one of Scotland's finest inland courses and lies at the very gateway to the Highlands.

E dzell is the most northerly of a coterie of great golf courses on Tayside that make the area such an appealing part of Scotland for the visiting golfer. There are the majestic links challenges of Carnoustie, Monifieth and Panmure Barry but there is great inland golf too, and Edzell is widely regarded as among the very finest examples.

The Edzell Golf Club dates back to 1895 when the course was laid out by Bob Simpson, a member of a famous Carnoustie family. It lies at the very gateway to the Highlands and enjoys a wonderful backdrop of mountains and one of the finest settings anywhere.

This is heathland golf on fine turf with heather and whin laid out on the outskirts of a delightful holiday village. It is an area also much beloved by hill walkers and those with a good eye and a shotgun.

It is one of Scotland's genuine hidden gems, not too widely known but greatly appreciated by those who have been fortunate enough to find their way to the town through the imposing arch that in less peaceful times kept the undesirable out.

Today there is no barrier to those who want to visit this lovely town and its equally lovely golf course. What they will find is a layout with large greens offering firm and fast putting surfaces and a warm welcome in the club itself.

The course covers quite a large area, almost 130 acres, a considerable area in the days when Bob Simpson was planning the layout.

It is, however, quite tight in parts and the players who succeed here are those who manage to keep the ball in play from the tee and heed club professional Alastair Webster's advice to take plenty of club for the approach shots to get the ball up on to the big greens.

A measure of how tight the course can be is the fact that on no fewer than eight of the holes out-of-bounds is an important factor, while on the 15th hole it is a double factor, for it appears down both sides of the hole. At the 9th the River West Water adds not only to the difficulty but to the scenic value as well.

Not that there is any lack of scenic interest at Edzell in the first place. Everywhere there are wonderful views in a rolling landscape and always the mountains to detract from concentration.

At a little over 6300 yards Edzell is not a long course but like so many of its vintage it is a challenge that has stood up admirably to the test of time, and the huge advancement in today's golf equipment.

It is a measure of the strength of the course that the professional record of 67, only two under the card and returned in 1992, has stood for so many years.

The course is mostly flat and easy to walk but there are a couple or three gentle climbs which only help to enhance the wonderful views.

Elie

Although James Braid was born within a mashie shot of the golf course and learned to play his golf at Elie, it is one layout that the master player and course architect had no hand in developing. Judging by the legal wrangles and rifts that surrounded the early days of golf in this beautiful corner of the Fife coast he was probably lucky to have avoided involvement.

The records of early golf on the links of Elie were lost when the charters of the Burgh of Earlsferry, to which Elie is joined, were destroyed by fire, but it seems likely that the game was played in its crudest form as far back as the infamous Act of Parliament of James II in 1457, which outlawed the playing of golf in favour of archery practice.

In 1770, after golfers had been roaming the links making up holes at their own whim, some semblance of order seems to have arrived in the proceedings with confirmation of the existence of a Long and Short course. However, there was to be no peace for the golfers to enjoy this move towards organisation for the owners of the Grange Estate bordering the links claimed that large parts of the territory were theirs, and ploughed up a large section of the middle of the golf course to reinforce their claim. Legal action was promptly taken by the Burgh of Earlsferry in August of 1812 but it was to

be another 20 years before the Court of Session in Edinburgh ruled against the Estate and ordered that a proper area for golf be marked out.

Interestingly it was decreed that the disputed golfing area should be 'as wide as the best player could hit the ball', but it seems that whoever was given the responsibility for that shot of defining width was not up to the mark on the day in question, for despite 20 years of expensive legal action, the golfers of Elie and Earlsferry ended up with a wholly inadequate neck of land to join up the two ends of their course.

The formation of the Earlsferry and Elie Golf Club in 1858 at last heralded the arrival of formal organisation of the game in the burgh and meetings of members were held in either the town hall or the Golf Tavern, a venerable watering hole that still exists to this day close to the 4th tee.

In 1873 four members of the club agreed to lease to the club a valuable additional piece of ground to provide three additional holes and a site for the first clubhouse. To raise funds for the building the Golf House Club was formed. The two clubs coexisted for four decades until the Earlsferry and Elie club was disbanded in 1912.

By 1878 all the legal wrangles had finally been resolved and by 1896 sufficient ground had been acquired to extend the course to 18 holes.

THE GOLF HOUSE CLUB

Established
1875
Course details:
18 holes
6261 yards
SSS 69
Address:
The Golf Clubhouse
Elie, Fife KY9 1AS

Tel: 01333 330327
Fax: 01333 330895

Above: Elie is unique in having a World War Two submarine periscope beside the 1st tee to enable the starter to see over the brow of the hill to sound the all-clear for waiting players.

Left: The beautiful short 3rd hole which is a daunting test into a strong west wind.

Fortrose & Rosemarkie

**FORTROSE &
ROSEMARKIE
GOLF CLUB**

Established
1888
Course details:
18 holes
5858 yards
SSS 69
Address:
Ness Road East
Fortrose IV10 8SE

Tel/Fax: 01381 620529

Fortrose and Rosemarkie
on the Black Isle is not only
a delightful golf course, it
also has the distinction of
being the place where the
famous march 'Colonel
Bogey' was composed.

Across the water from the delightful course at Fortrose and Rosemarkie on the Black Isle is Fort George, an army stronghold where in the early part of the twentieth century honorary membership was extended by the club to the soldiers. One of those who enjoyed this privilege was Bandmaster Rickets who regularly partnered his Colonel on the links.

During one round the bandmaster heard a fellow golfer whistle to attract the Colonel's attention. Later he remembered the whistle and used the notes in the opening bar of the famous march he wrote which he named 'Colonel Bogey'.

The Fortrose and Rosemarkie course lies out on the Chanonry Point, a sliver of land twelve miles or so north-east of Inverness jutting out into Rosemarkie Bay and guarding the entrance to the Moray Firth itself. The road to the lighthouse at the end of the peninsula splits the course in two, with just enough ground on either side to accommodate a layout that now measures 5858 yards with a Standard Scratch Score (SSS) of 69.

The club was founded in 1888 but it was not until the early 1930s that it was able to acquire enough ground to create a full 18-hole layout. James

Braid made the long train journey north from Walton Heath in 1932 to advise on the layout and was able to squeeze 18 holes onto a peninsula that is little more than 500 yards wide at its start and tapers to around 150 yards at the lighthouse end.

Two years after the opening the club was able to acquire still more land and Braid was asked again for his advice. He conducted a further survey and for the very modest fee of £12 10s (£12.50) produced a modified layout that extended the course essentially to that which exists to this day.

The course was officially opened by Sir Hector Monro in 1935, and after the opening the local newspaper reported that the new layout had 'great variety and necessitates much skill', adding that it was of such a sporting character that it was fully expected that the course would attract many visitors to the area. There is no doubt that over the years it has.

What the course lacks in length is more than compensated for by tightness and the ever-present dangers of the sea which threatens on seven of the holes, and some very dense whin and gorse. The wind is always a factor on this exposed peninsula and there are several holes that require a blind approach, notably out by the point close to the lighthouse.

The course has a rather macabre claim to fame as being the site of the last burning of a witch in Scotland. A stone on the 17th marks the spot, but since there is also a similar claim further up the coast at Royal Dornoch where there is a hole called 'The Witch' on the Struie Course, there is no certainty to which of the courses this rather dubious honour belongs.

There are several testing holes on Braid's layout. The 6th and the 11th share a large double green reminiscent of the Old Course at St Andrews, while the 12th has in more recent times been extended to nearly 400 yards bringing fairway bunkers, once bypassed by the modern game, back into play.

Grantown-on-Spey

Willie Park is credited with having laid out the little course at Grantown-on-Spey as far back as 1890, and a sterling job he made of it too, for this is one of the most delightful golf courses in the Highlands.

Never intended as a test of championship play, Grantown-on-Spey nonetheless offers enough of a challenge for most people and is in almost every regard the perfect holiday golf course. There are a few demanding par fours of more than 400 yards, two of them falling in succession at the 2nd and 3rd, but otherwise this is a test of accuracy and touch rather than power and length.

The course lies on the outskirts of the attractive little Highland town of the same name only 8 miles from that other example of superb Highland golf, Boat of Garten. They may be near neighbours but the courses are very different in character. Boat offers wonderful heathland golf among the heather while Grantown-on-Spey is more typically Scottish woodland and open parkland.

However, both courses share the common theme for this part of the world of spectacular mountain scenery. The Grantown course has been laid out through a delightful valley in the Cromdale Hills and enjoys wonderful views from several elevated tees looking down fairways to the dominant mountains behind.

In a course of this vintage there is the usual collection of blind shots to be played and out-of-bounds threatens on at least half of the holes. There are holes with wonderful names like 'Poor House', 'Wee Dunt' and 'Peezie's Nap', and there is 'Caper Cailzie', the 336-yard 10th that demands an arrow-straight drive leaving a blind approach to a green that slopes sharply from the left. Then there is the 'Bobby Cruikshank' hole, a real card-wrecker par 4 of 379 yards with trouble on either side of the fairway, and a bundle more round the green just for good measure.

The hole is named after the great Bobby Cruikshank, a native of Grantown, who emigrated in 1921 to become a top professional in the United States. Cruikshank fought a dramatic final round in the 1923 US Open forcing a tie with Bobby Jones with a birdie at the last hole.

In the play-off there was never more than one stroke between them, but Bobby Jones won his first major championship, beating the man from Grantown on the 18th with 76 to 78.

In 1932 Cruikshank came close to winning the US Open again, at Fresh Meadow Country Club in New York State. His final round of 68 would have been good enough for victory if Gene Sarazen had not returned a record 66 and played the last 28 holes of the championship in exactly 100 strokes.

The Grantown-on-Spey club has a recently renovated clubhouse and improvements continue to be made to the golf course to reinforce its standing as one of the Highlands' friendliest and most forward-looking clubs.

Like most Highland clubs there is little difficulty in acquiring a tee time at Grantown and handicap certificates are not required for play here. However, there are restrictions at weekends before 10am and during members' club competitions.

GRANTOWN-ON-SPEY GOLF CLUB

Established
1890
Course details:
18 holes
5710 yards
SSS 68
Address:
Golf Course Road
Grantown-on-Spey
Moray PH26 3HY

Tel: 01479 873154
Fax: 01479 873725

There is great heathland golf to be found at Grantown-on-Spey the home town of Bobby Cruikshank. He later emigrated to America and tied with the legendary Bobby Jones in the 1923 US Open, only to lose by two strokes in the play-off.

Lanark

**LANARK
GOLF CLUB**

Established
1851
Course details:
18 holes
6426 yards
SSS 71
Address:
The Moor
Lanark ML11 7RX

Tel/Fax: 01555 663219

Four portraits hang on the walls of the smoke room of the Lanark Golf Club to testify to the fact that golf was played in the ancient burgh long before the formation of the club itself in 1851. The subjects who sat for the portraits are the stalwarts who regularly played on the heath in the days before organisation came to the game. They are rightly honoured as the founding fathers of the Lanark Golf Club, one of the top 25 oldest golf clubs in the world.

Lanark is one of the genuinely hidden treasures of Scottish golf. The course is laid out on the sandy moorland turf of the Common Moor of the Royal Burgh and members are keenly aware of their fortune not only in having such a fine links so far inland away from the traditional heartlands of the

The historic course at Lanark is widely regarded as one of Scotland's finest courses away from the sea and the Lanark club is one of the 25 oldest golf clubs in the world.

game in Scotland, but also of their responsibility to maintain the great traditions of an historically important club.

The burgh of Lanark owned the ground on which the course is built from the twelfth century until 1995, when the club bought the course from the council. The benefits of considerable concessions in the cost of golf season tickets, which had been associated with the historic connection between the burgh and the club, remain the same under the new ownership.

The four founding fathers played over a short course of four holes. By the time two more holes had been added by 1851 there were 21 golfers who gathered together in the name of the game.

On 4 October that year the Lanark Golf Club officially came into being.

Just before the turn of the twentieth century the St Andrews example had virtually standardised golf courses to layouts of 18 holes.

Rather than be out of the fashion Lanark followed suit and drafted in Old Tom Morris from St Andrews in 1887 to lay out a small 18-hole course. Old Tom charged the club the princely sum of £3.10s (£3.50) for his services and laid out the course on the site of what is now the modern 9-hole 'wee' course.

In 1927, almost inevitably, James Braid was called in to suggest some alterations to the original Morris course.

It was a pattern that had been repeated many times around the country as the game expanded and equipment improved to the point where golf courses had to be improved too.

Braid, and his partner John Stutt created new holes at the 13th and 14th, and the course remains, with but a few minor alterations, much as it did after Braid and Stutt departed.

Lanark has been used on many occasions as a Regional pre-qualifying course for the Open Championship and one interesting aspect of the club's history is the Silver Claret Jug, one of its oldest trophies.

It was created in 1857, three years before the first Open Championship, but significantly bears a striking resemblance to the more famous claret jug which has been the Open Championship trophy since 1872.

The Lanark clubhouse overlooks ground that was owned by the Burgh of Lanark since the twelfth century. The club bought the course from the council in 1995.

Machrie

By the standards of the late nineteenth century, the course that architect Willie Campbell laid out at Machrie on the island of Islay, among the sand dunes and the long narrow valleys, was long indeed at more than 6000 yards. But it had been a conscious decision to make the Machrie course long and difficult rather than short and easy, because it was believed at the time that something special would be needed to attract visitors to this rather remote links.

The year was 1891 and Willie Campbell's challenge produced 18 holes without a single one of them under 200 yards long. But not content with having a course comparable in terms of difficulty with Machrihanish, Troon or Prestwick, two optional holes were provided to increase the length of the course by a further 650 yards!

An alternative 8th green was built north of the Glenegedale Burn, creating an unbelievable hole of 750 yards. The return hole back to the 9th green then became 620 yards.

History tells us not very surprisingly that there was little enthusiasm for such masochism and the holes just seemed to fade away. They were not even used during the match which officially opened the course.

There was never a bogey figure established for the longer of the two holes but some idea of what it would have been may be judged from a comparison with a long hole at the Lindrick Golf Club in Yorkshire, which also opened in 1891.

Based on the Lindrick example the 8th at Machrie would have been a bogey 8!

The first tee and the clubhouse were built at Kintra, the nearest point to Port Ellen where the majority of the visitors to Machrie would come, but the first hole, known as 'Mount Zion', was so difficult that the order of play of the holes was changed at the suggestion of the Rev. John Kerr.

The third hole became the first hole under the new layout making Mount Zion the 17th, an appropriate place for the most difficult hole on the course.

Harry Vardon later described it as 'the hardest hole I have ever seen'.

By 1894 further refinements to the course included the splitting of the 400-yard 10th hole to create two holes, one a short hole of 158 yards and another of 247 yards. The 15th was eliminated and the 16th realigned.

There were many more changes over the years, with the most recent of significance those recommended by Donald Steel in the 1970s. Improvements in the general condition of the course have been undertaken since new owners took over the course and the hotel in 1995.

Like Machrihanish, not far away as the crow flies, Machrie has suffered a little from its remoteness in terms of attracting prominent events.

That was not the case, however, in 1901 when Machrie hosted the richest open event of its time with a prize of £100.

The Great Triumvirate of James Braid, Harry Vardon and J.H. Taylor considered it of such importance that they all made the journey to Islay which lies some 15 miles off the west coast of Argyll, to play.

MACHRIE HOTEL & GOLF LINKS

Established
1891
Course details:
18 holes
6226 yards
SSS 70
Address:
Machrie Hotel
Port Ellen, Isle of Islay

Tel: 01496 302310
Fax: 01496 302404

Left: A conscious decision was made to make Machrie long and difficult when Willie Campbell laid it out in the late nineteenth century. It remains that way today.

Below: Fairways threaded between the great sand dunes and the spectacular scenery of Islay are what make Machrie so special.

Monifieth

Monifieth is an uncompromising links with tight fairways and well-protected greens.

No fewer than four golf clubs play over the Monifieth Golf Links a few miles to the east of the City of Discovery, Dundee. Their clubhouses stand proudly along the road beside the 18th green of the Medal Course, drawn up like a platoon of soldiers brought to attention.

There is proud golfing history here on the Angus coastline where Monifieth is the most westerly of that great triumvirate of majestic links courses of which Panmure Barry occupies the middle, while the mighty challenge of Carnoustie lurks only four miles further on.

There are two courses at Monifieth administered by a Trust with the Medal Course the principal, having been an Open Championship qualifying course in the year that Tom Watson won his first Open title at Carnoustie in 1975. It was also the venue, jointly with its illustrious neighbour, for the gale-ravaged Scottish Open Amateur Stroke Play Championship of the following year when the winning total was a record 299. The Medal Course also played host to the Scottish Amateur Championship in 1986.

The second course at Monifieth is the Ashludie, a par-68 layout of only just over 5100 yards which is popular with youngsters learning to play, ladies and those who seek a little respite from the demands of the Medal layout.

Like its near neighbours at Barry and Carnoustie, the Medal Course is a big, uncompromising links in the traditional vein. There are no airs and graces to be suffered here on its rough, natural links which like so many of the early seaside courses is bordered on the one side by the main railway line to the north.

There are simply no prisoners taken on this layout, particularly when the prevailing wind whistles in over the Firth of Tay from the direction of St Andrews, where it has already left its impression in the very Home of the Game itself.

Golf has been played on this rugged duneland between the great stands of whin and gorse since the early part of the seventeenth century, but the first signs of a real course date from 1850. The course has seen some changes, mostly in its overall length, but there has been no great sympathy with changing things in this part of Angus.

Par is a tight 71 over the 6650-yards and there are some wonderful holes scattered throughout the layout and some tight ones set alongside the railway line at the beginning of the round.

They demand length and accuracy at any time with rough that can become infuriatingly tough after a particularly wet spring, but are quite devilish when the wind swings round into the east and the battle to hold on to a score beyond the crucial 6th is hard won indeed.

Big greens that are normally fast, firm and true together with some clever bunkering are the hallmarks of this very much underrated links.

Monifieth is the home club of one of Scotland's true amateur players of the modern era. Unlike so many fine players who have used the amateur game simply as a stepping stone to the professional ranks, Ian Hutcheon always remained a genuine amateur player and was recognised as one of the finest exponents of real links golf.

Moray, Lossiemouth

In just the same way that the Old Course at St Andrews begins in the town, makes its way out around the links and returns to the place whence it began, so too does the fine Old Links of the Moray Golf Club at Lossiemouth on the Moray Firth.

This is classic links golf of symphonic proportions spread out from the old granite clubhouse, with its commanding views from above the 18th green. Seven holes march their way out along the coastline one after the other in perfect order towards Moray's version of the famous St Andrews loop. It is a slightly more complicated version, however, but it serves admirably to return the layout back along its outward path along the sea shore.

Old Tom Morris made the trip up the coast from St Andrews to lay out the original course in 1889 and essentially it has changed very little in the intervening time, although now a bit longer. The continued presence of some old-fashioned cross bunkering is testament to that although the fairways themselves are generous enough.

It is as well that they are so bounteous for the rough at Lossiemouth can be devastating when there is above-average spring rainfall. Fortunately that is not a regular situation for this is normally a very dry part of the country where the fairways are tanned, fast and running for most of the summer months, just as they are supposed to be. This is real golf here on the edge of the Moray Firth where there is a very good supply of it anyway.

There was a spell when overzealous use of irrigation and phosphates had turned the once spectacularly firm and fast greens into something considerably less than that. The pitch repairer, a tool that until then had only been found in the possession of visitors from less fortunate parts, suddenly began to make an appearance. However, a new regime has been in place at Lossiemouth in more recent times and the course is now well on the way back to being the great traditional links of old.

The Old Course at Moray shares many of the characteristics of the Old Course at St Andrews in addition to its start and finish in the town. There isn't a bad hole on the course and there is a succession of very great ones. Unlike St Andrews, however, all the trouble at Moray is in clear view and there is not a blind shot to be tackled anywhere.

Ten of the par 4s are more than 400 yards long, there are only two par 5s and just a solitary but very difficult par 3 on the course. The par of 71 over the 6643 yards is a demanding one, particularly when the breeze blows as it so often does, and concentration can be shattered in an instant by the sudden arrival of Jaguar or Tornado fighter bombers on their final approach into the nearby RAF Lossiemouth air base.

MORAY GOLF CLUB

Established
1889
Course details:
18 holes
6643 yards
SSS 73
Address:
Stotfield Road
Lossiemouth IV31 6QS

Tel: 01343 812018
Fax: 01343 815102

Crumpled fairways, classic links golf and the sound of jets is very much the mix at the Moray Golf Club. This is the 18th which comes back into the town in the same way as the Old Course at St Andrews.

Perth

**ROYAL PERTH
GOLFING
SOCIETY**

Established
1833
Course details:
18 holes
4746 yards
SSS 65
Address:
1/2 Atholl Crescent
Perth PH1 5NG

Tel: 01738 622265
Fax: 01738 441131

Above: King James VI
learned to play golf on the
North Inch at Perth and
the oldest of all the 'Royal'
clubs, the Royal Perth Golfing
Society, still plays there.

Right: Escape from the
trees on the North Inch.

The North Inch course at Perth has never been one of the most testing in Scotland's inventory of golf courses but it is one of the most historically important. There is on record reference to the game being played there as far back as 1599, but it seems certain that there were golfers on this stretch of the Tay River for a hundred years even before that.

King James VI, the son of Mary Queen of Scots who became King of Scotland in infancy after his mother was deposed, learned to play golf at Perth before acceding also to the English throne in 1603. There is a well documented tale of an early Perth foursome that incurred the wrath of the Kirk Session for playing golf on a Sunday. The date was 19 November 1599 and John Gardiner, James Bowman, Laurence Chalmers and Laurence Cuthbert confessed that they were playing at the golf on the North Inch 'at the time of the preaching afternoon on the Sabbath'. They were firmly rebuked and warned that they must attend the 'hearing of the Word diligently on the Sabbath in time coming' which they agreed to do and were then admonished.

The holes once played by King James VI have long since disappeared and over the centuries there have been many changes to the course. Originally it was only six, was then extended to nine and for a time ten holes constituted the round at the North Inch. Another three holes were then added before the course was finally extended to a full 18-hole layout.

The course runs alongside the River Tay and like the town of Perth itself has been prone to flooding over many years. In 1998 the local authority began work on a flood defence barrier which had the effect of closing half of the existing 18-hole course.

The North Inch will remain a 9-hole layout until work on the barrier is completed in the year 2001 and the new holes are opened for play.

The old 18-hole layout was of quite modest length at just under 5000 yards and there was nothing to indicate that this was one of the most historic sites in Scottish golf history. In fact the surroundings of the North Inch layout could not be more prosaic. It is flat, unexciting parkland shared by dog walkers and football and hockey pitches.

However, the changes forced by the flood defences should improve that situation and the new plans will incorporate the course into the flood barrier and make the river a more prominent feature.

All the great players of the second half of the last century have played at the North Inch from Young Tom Morris, and his father Old Tom, to Allan Robertson and Willie Park and Perth's most famous player, Bob Andrew, the man they called 'The Rook'.

The Royal Perth Golfing Society, the oldest of all the 'Royal' Clubs, older by a year even than the Royal and Ancient, still plays over the North Inch course.

Pitlochry

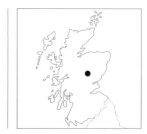

Scotland's reputation for beautiful and scenic golf courses is legendary, but nowhere in the country do they come much better qualified in either department than at the Pitlochry Golf Club, off the A9 between Perth and Inverness.

The members at Pitlochry may never be asked to host a Scottish Open, and there is as much chance of the good citizens of this hospitable Highland town entertaining the Ryder Cup as there is of finding a smile on the face of a bankrupt Aberdonian. However, that is exactly what makes this beautiful little course so special.

The royal and ancient game is in safe hands at Pitlochry. There are no frills and no pretensions to be anything other than a real and welcoming golf club, where visitors come to enjoy themselves and are never disappointed.

At first glance the opening holes bear an uncanny resemblance to the lower foothills of the Himalayas. However, as in everything worthwhile in life, the investment of effort pays its own dividends. The reward for scaling the first few holes at Pitlochry could not be more generous.

On the right day and once up on the plateau with the coronary arteries settling back to normal, the view and the surroundings are sublime. The air is as clean and clear as the Highland burns that wander down the hillside, the birds sing their approbation of the place and outward stretches a golf course ready and willing to gently flatter anyone's game.

At something less than 6000 yards even

stretched to its limits, Pitlochry is not the most testing golf course in the wide world of golf – and who is to say it is not the better for it – but it certainly is one of the most delightful to play. There are lovely holes here, challenging holes, tricky holes even, to accompany that ever-present feeling of well-being in what is quickly recognised as a rather special place.

A delightful little short hole brings the homeward golfer to a deceptive finishing hole below the old wooden clubhouse. The burn meanders in front of the green, the approach is played down the hill towards a welcoming and innocent-looking green, but many a promising score has come to grief in the minutes before the clubhouse is reached.

For those who fail to make par on the final green it doesn't really matter, for the hospitality, the welcome and the bill of fare in the club's venerable watering hole will quickly banish the memory.

The Pitlochry Club may not be home to a European Tour event but it does host the annual Highland Open Amateur Tournament for men and ladies, and excellent and highly recommended sport it is too.

PITLOCHRY GOLF CLUB

Established
1909
Course details:
18 holes
5811 yards
SSS 69
Address:
Golf Course Road
Pitlochry PH16 5QY

Tel: 01796 472792
Fax: 01796 473599

Above: The well-protected 6th green at Pitlochry with its stunning Highland backdrop.

Left: Wonderful scenery and a warm welcome in the clubhouse have made Pitlochry's reputation.

Portpatrick

PORTPATRICK GOLF CLUB

Established
1903
Course details:
18 holes
5882 yards
SSS 68
Address:
Golf Course Road
Portpatrick DG9 8TB

Tel: 01776 810273
Fax: 01776 810811

Clifftop golf at Dunskey has views to equal Pebble Beach and a cult following that comes back year after year to enjoy rolling moorland and seaside heath.

The Portpatrick Golf Club, or Dunskey as it is more commonly known, enjoys something of a cult following. There are groups of golfers who return time after time to this delightful corner of Wigtownshire to pit their wits against a layout that sits high on the cliff above the Firth of Clyde.

Like so many of Scotland's hidden golf treasures, the course simply evolved without much in the way of original help from the hand of man after the club was founded in 1903.

The present layout, however, is generally credited to C.W. Hunter, and an excellent one it is too, with some wonderful views to enjoy on the journey round. The coast of Ireland, the Isle of Man and the Mull of Kintyre are spread out on the panorama looking west from Dunskey and there is no doubt that this magnificent outlook contributes greatly to the popularity of a course that has been described in one golf magazine as 'the best holiday course in the south of Scotland'. There are few who have enjoyed its picture-book setting who would disagree.

The fishing village of Portpatrick sits on the coast below the course and benefits, like the course itself, from a micro-climate that encourages the growth of palm trees in the neighbourhood and makes it the dairy-farming centre of the United Kingdom. In fact so long is the growing season at Dunskey – some two months longer than most parts of the country – that the greenkeeper gets little respite from the mower and the course has more the feel and colour of the west of Ireland than the south-west of Scotland.

But Scotland it most certainly is, despite the fact that the Mountains of Mourne lie less than twenty miles across the Irish Sea, and Dunskey could easily be mistaken for an Irish club, so friendly and hospitable is the reception awaiting the visitor.

This is a course of rolling moorland and seaside heath. There is no linksland here. Meadow grass adorns the greens but they are always well kept and putt beautifully once the confusion of the nap is sorted out. The nap of the grass always runs towards the sea and many a short one has gone astray when that factor has been left out of the equation.

Recent changes to the course have included new bunkers and much bigger, multiple tees. Despite the changes the course remains relatively devoid of bunkers and relies for its defence on the wind that whistles in from the Irish Sea, and the thick rough and gorse that flourishes on the headland.

Modest of length at a little over 5800 yards, there is still enough of a challenge here for all but the gorilla and the foolhardy. Only two par 5s on the card make the SSS of 68 a tough mark and when that breeze gets up the hacker and the faint of heart are best advised to leave town.

The Roxburghe

The Borders form the natural barrier between Scotland and England. Most visiting golfers to the Home of Golf either fly over or drive through them in pursuit of their favourite game, for in truth it has never been an area particularly renowned for its golf courses. There are one or two of worthy note of course, but by and large the call of the mighty links of East Lothian and Fife, or the Ayrshire coast, is usually too strong to detain the traveller over long among the hills of a Border country much better known for great salmon and trout rivers, or the cashmere sweaters that keep Mr Faldo cosy from the snell draught.

His Grace the Duke of Roxburghe, however, has taken a giant step towards helping improve the image of the Borders as a golf destination by building The Roxburghe Course on his 56,000 acre estate, at Sunlaws on the outskirts of Kelso.

The Duke's family has lived at Floors Castle since 1721 and this glorious dwelling has been a long-time favourite haunt of the Royal Family. It is said that Prince Andrew chose the romantic setting of this historic Scottish castle to propose to Sarah Ferguson.

The 10th Duke, Sir Guy David Innes-Ker, is like Prince Andrew, a keen golfer, maintaining a single figure handicap at Muirfield and Sunningdale. His Grace called in former Ryder Cup player, Dave Thomas, to build the Roxburghe course through the rolling hills of the estate. There are wonderful views here, great woodlands and the River Teviot flows through the course.

There is a wide diversity of challenge on this Dave Thomas layout. There are doglegs galore in both directions, some straight holes, a few blind shots and a couple of very tough par 5s. In many ways it reflects Thomas's career as a player. Long game accuracy was the key to much of his success and there is much of the same requirement here in the undulating land where once the notorious Border Reivers war-mongered and cattle-thieved their way into Scotland's folk history.

The Duke was very clear in his remit to Thomas on the kind of course he wanted to build. It had to be of sufficient challenge to test the top players from the championship tees and yet be perfectly playable for visitors. At more than 7100 yards from the back tees he has clearly achieved the former but has made it very pleasantly playable for the mere mortal from the regular tees at not much more than 6500 yards. The ladies' length is 5733 yards making it a not insurmountable challenge for them either.

The Roxburghe is one of the new breed of Scottish golf courses built very much with an eye to the commercial, linked as it is to the very splendid Sunlaws Hotel.

THE ROXBURGHE GOLF COURSE

Established
1997
Course details:
18 holes
7111 yards
SSS 75
Address:
Kelso
Roxburghshire TD5 8JZ

Tel: 01573 450333
Fax: 01573 450611

Above: His Grace, the Duke of Roxburghe has built his course at Kelso with the ambition to hold major events. Certainly it is challenging enough and no more so than here at the long 14th.

Scotscraig

SCOTSCRAIG GOLF CLUB

Established
1817
Course details:
18 holes
6550 yards
SSS 72
Address:
Golf Road
Tayport DD6 9DZ

Tel: 01382 552515
Fax: 01382 553130

It may have been a case of unlucky 13 for the Scotscraig Golf Club in Tayport, 10 miles north of St Andrews, founded in 1817 when there were only 12 other clubs in existence. The club flourished quite successfully for about 17 years but the minute book recalls that in 1834 the gold medal was contested over the links of St Andrews because the Scotscraig course had been ploughed up.

The following year the members had to travel to Montrose to play their autumn meeting and thereafter the club went into abeyance for half a century.

In what might be described as its pre-plough period the club set very high standards, reflecting its rather exclusive bearing, and right from the outset there were gold and silver medals to play for.

The fascinating club minute books reveal that in those early days two uniforms were the order of the day. The playing version was 'a red coat with green velvet collar and a badge on the left breast with the same device as that on the gold medal'. For formal wear, such as the annual dinner, the members favoured 'a double-breasted green superfine cloth coat with black velvet collar and cuffs and gilt buttons bearing the same device as appears on the gold medal, five large buttons on each side of the breast and two small buttons on each cuff.'

Uniform was mandatory at all club meetings and for those who transgressed the fine was two bottles of port.

The fortunes of the club took a turn for the better when the land on which the original course was built was sold to Admiral Maitland McDougall, who called a meeting in the Templars' Hall in Tayport on 5 May 1887, when those foregathered resolved to reconstitute the club under its original name.

The Admiral was a legendary figure in Scottish golf at that time and eventually won no fewer than 16 Royal and Ancient Golf Club Spring and Autumn medals over the Old Course at St Andrews. In 1860 he won the Autumn Medal after rowing for five hours in an epic lifeboat rescue when the boat was one man short on the crew. The Admiral returned to shore, drilled a hole in his golf ball, inserted some buckshot to make it a little heavier and went out into the gale to win the Medal handsomely. To this day the first hole at Scotscraig is known as 'The Admiral' in his honour.

Following a merger with the Newport Golf Club in 1890, membership increased rapidly and a custom-built clubhouse was erected in 1896 to replace the old wooden building that had doubled as the Tayport Hospital up till that time. Eight years later the course was extended to 18 holes and by 1923 the members were able to buy the course. They made alterations and extensions under the expert supervision of James Braid, to create the course which is largely the one still played today.

Looking down the fairway of the 7th hole at Scotscraig.

Shiskine

On the island of Arran on the west coast of Scotland, only an hour by ferry from the mainland, is to be found one of the most unusual and great hidden gems in the wide world of golf. At the village of Blackwaterfoot on the west coast of the island is the Shiskine Golf Club, famous not for the championships that have been played there, for there have been none of any great importance, but for the fact that it is of 12 holes only and is one of the few truly unspoiled and genuine seaside links still surviving. The course can be found on Arran's south-west coast hard by the water's edge at Drumadoon Bay, on a sliver of land where golf has been played for more than a century.

While many of Scotland's finest links have had inflicted upon them the vagaries of the water sprinkler, or the pervasive ambitions of the green convener intent on leaving a mark, the Shiskine Golf and Tennis Club – for that is what it is properly called – has survived in essence, if not always in routing, as it was when it was first laid out by the 1883 Open Champion, Willie Fernie, thirteen years after he won the Championship.

Virtually every hole is blind, either from the tee or for the approach shot to the green, or in some cases, both. It has more signals to tell the player when to go and when to stop than a railway company and it has put up more markers than a dyslexic poker player.

It is a place where the modern school of golf-course architecture would cringe at the famous par 3, the 'Crow's Nest', played blind over a hill to a green set on a shelf in the side of a cliff 50 feet above

the tee. But who gives a jot for the modern school when there is to be found real golf; the golf that Old Tom Morris and Willie Park played, and Willie Fernie too, for that matter.

This is the true heritage of Scottish golf, of the challenge against wind and weather and nature and not against the sterile lumbering earth movers, computerised irrigation and nitrates, never mind $1 million designer fees.

What joy it is to be greeted by Fiona Brown in the golf shop she has run for almost two decades and have her outline the 'route' around Shiskine on the back of an old yellow scorecard. What wonder unfolds in her explanation that the white flag at the 'Craw's Nest' hole is not the flag for the hole at all but the signal flag that the player must remove from its own hole at the top of the hill and replace only when he leaves the green. The marker for the real pin stands on a ledge high above, much in the manner of the famous 5th at Prestwick.

She will explain how to play the 'Twa' Burns', the 'Shelf', 'Hades', 'Paradise' and all the others, and reveal that the cost of this great rubbing of shoulders with the game of golf as it used to be played is the best golfing value to be found in any day's march.

SHISKINE GOLF CLUB

Established
1896
Course details:
12 holes
2990 yards
SSS 42
Address:
Shiskine
Blackwaterfoot
Isle of Arran KA27 8HA

Tel: 01770 860226
Fax: 01770 860205

Above: Shiskine is golfing ground of such purity, owing only the barest influence to the hand of man, that to play here is to enjoy a unique experience.

Left: Fiona Brown has run the golf shop at Shiskine for almost two decades.

179

Whitekirk

WHITEKIRK

Established
1995
Course details:
18 holes
6520 yards
SSS 72
Address:
Whitekirk
North Berwick EH39 5PR

Tel: 01620 870300
Fax: 01620 870330

Above: The relatively
new course at Whitekirk
is a tribute to what can
be achieved on a modest
budget with prudent
planning and expenditure.
This is the tricky 2nd hole.

Right: Whitekirk sits high
on the hill above North
Berwick and enjoys spectacular views across the Firth
of Forth. The Bass Rock
dominates this view of the
5th green.

There are so many fine golf courses in the Lothians of Scotland it was hard to identify a need for any more when Yorkshire farmer George Tuer announced that he was going to build a golf course to stand four square against the likes of Gullane, North Berwick, Dunbar and, let it be whispered, the mighty Muirfield itself.

This is historic golfing country and Mr Tuer's decision that he was going to add another because there is demonstrable need was bold to say the least. Indeed only Daniel's decision to slip into the lions' den can have come anywhere close to matching it.

He knew that if his course was to succeed it would have to be built at the right price and provide first-class facilities at affordable prices, for his project was not to be a private club but a course open to all on a pay-and-play basis.

The result is the Whitekirk Golf Course, situated a couple of miles east of North Berwick, and it can quite rightly claim to be one of the finest new golf courses built in Scotland for many a long day. It genuinely is a welcome and worthy addition to the already excellent golf facilities in the area.

It is also a tribute to what can be achieved on a modest budget. The construction of the golf course

and the superb modern clubhouse for an outlay of little more than £1 million, at a time when some big-name golf course architects are charging similar sums just to put their names on the design board before the ground is even broken, is a tribute to prudent planning and expenditure.

The course sits high on the hill above North Berwick and enjoys commanding views around East Lothian, across rich farmland rimming the course and past the famous landmarks of the Bass Rock, Berwick Law and Tantallon Castle and to the hills of Fife across the Firth of Forth.

Architect Cameron Sinclair made an excellent job of the layout on what was part of George Tuer's extensive farm. The layout is a little over 6500 yards with a demanding par of 71 and is just about as tough as anyone would want to play.

Sinclair cleverly used the natural water hazards and the many changes in elevation to produce a good challenge that becomes greater still with even the slightest breeze. Many of the tees are elevated to make the most of the glorious views.

The greens have been built to USGA specifications, there are four teeing grounds on each hole, the course has returning nines and buggies are available for rental for those who prefer to ride rather than walk in the good fresh air.

Whitekirk has been a major success story. The clubhouse is so popular the visitor needs to be sharp to find a table in the dining room, and a good majority of the customers are not even golfers!

Indeed so popular is the clubhouse as a meeting point that on days when the weather is inclement there are very often more people in the dining room and the bar than on the course itself. That's hardly surprising either since there is good honest golfer's fare to be enjoyed here and cheerful, friendly staff to serve it. Visiting parties have their own private function room with its own bar for prize-giving ceremonies and private dinners. Another illustration of Whitekirk's modern and sensible approach to pay-and-play golf.

CHAPTER SIX

SCOTLAND'S MOST FEARSOME HOLES

Scotland's golf courses are littered with intimidating holes. It is the nature of the game in the country that invented it to make life on the links for those who pursue it an eternal frustration. There will be almost as many 'collections' of holes in Scottish golf to strike fear into the soul as there are players who continually take on the challenge.

From Wick to Wigtown there are golf holes that remain largely hidden from the wider view, constantly frustrating those who have to deal with them on a regular basis and which could just as easily qualify for inclusion in the rogue's gallery of Scotland's most fearsome holes. However, there exists a small collection which by general consensus and wider exposure represent not only some of the most famous as well as intimidating holes in Scotland, but anywhere in the world where the game of golf is played.

Among that exclusive group the selection of nine that follows is a totally subjective one. It is in no way an attempt to list the nine most difficult holes in Scotland, but more simply to take a voyage of discovery through Scottish golf's rich heritage of great golf holes recognised internationally for their difficulty or reputation, or, just as likely, where famous incidents have carved out for them a special place in the lore of the game.

There are long holes and there are short holes. There are holes that appear to pose little threat but claim countless victims and there are holes that appear terrifying at first sight, only to become even more terrifying when they are played.

It may not be the definitive list of Scotland's most frightening or inspiring holes, but there is enough intimidation here to get most people's attention for a very long time.

The famous Postage Stamp at Royal Troon where German amateur Herman Tissies once took 15 strokes, including a single putt, and the legendary Gene Sarazen played the hole twice in the 1973 Open in only three strokes and didn't need his putter at all.

The Road Hole: St Andrews

ROAD HOLE

17th, Old Course, St Andrews

461 yards

Par 4

With the exception of recent resurfacing of the road behind the green little has changed on the Road Hole over the decades, as this photograph from the 1940s confirms.

The 17th on the Old Course at St Andrews – the Road hole – is the most famous hole in the world of golf. Countless dramas have been played out over the 461 yards of its tortuous length. It is a hole that many golf course architects have tried to copy and incorporate into courses around the world but none has ever succeeded.

The Road hole has tested the greatest players in the history of the game and found most of them wanting at one time or another, for like so many other holes on the Old Course, there is more than one way to get into serious trouble playing it.

What is it about the 17th on the Old Course at St Andrews that carries such menace? Why is it that this menace hangs over every golfer's head like the Sword of Damocles from the very moment he steps on to the first tee until he reaches this famous stretch of golfing turf and yet all the while he can hardly contain his excitement at the prospect of reaching it?

Is it excitement tinged with fear, or is it the other way round? Only those who have played it and been victim to all the misfortunes and vicissitudes that can befall those who take on the challenge can even begin to know.

It is not just the drive, intimidating as it is, that makes this hole so special. True, it must be struck long and true, and pass over much real estate

belonging to the hotel and not the course, and therefore out-of-bounds.

If the wind is in the prevailing south-west, the benefit of having the ball pushed away from the hotel is nullified by the prospect of it finishing in the rough to the left of the fairway, from where the chance of reaching the green is so remote as to be not worth considering.

With the wind in the east, residents in the hotel who venture on to their balconies to observe the efforts of others tackling the Road hole come under grave risk of injury in the fusillade of balls that are launched and, wind assisted, inevitably rattle against the Old Course Hotel masonry.

Even for those who find the middle of the fairway, the challenge is really only just beginning. The shot to the angled plateau green, with its steep little bank in front, and the infamous Road bunker that, in the words of Bernard Darwin, 'eats its way into its very vitals', is a stroke of fearsome prospect.

For those who steer a wide course from the dreaded bunker, the road, from which the hole takes its name, lies menacingly in wait.

Sadly in 1998, the powers-that-be saw fit to entirely cover the old road with tar macadam and by so doing remove the rough and stony ground at the bottom of the bank behind the green which was so much part of the character of the hole. It was an act of vandalism which those with any understanding of the place could scarcely believe. However, it remains as ever a threat to be avoided at all costs.

Conventional wisdom calls for a second shot played to the front of the green, leaving a chip and run to the hole which is always cut behind the bunker when the course is in competition livery.

Even the carefully placed approach to the front fringe does not guarantee that all danger has passed. The inexperienced – and many who should know better from experience – often under-hit this most testing of running shots. A deep swale to the right of the Road bunker gathers anything marginally under-hit with the unerring tenacity of the income tax collector and dumps it in the bunker. The result, as the unfortunate Tommy Nakajima discovered in the 1978 Open Championship, can be utter disaster.

The Road bunker is a pit so deep that once in there, it is hard to see daylight above. Escape is often

Constantine Rocca tries to escape the vertical face of the Road bunker in the play off for the 1995 Open against John Daly. Unfortunately for the Italian, the ball remained in the bunker.

only effected in a backwards direction, and the road waits like a vulture to snap up the tattered remains of the player's score if the escape is forwards and even marginally over-hit.

The Sands of Nakajima

The Road hole bunker has claimed many victims in its time but none perhaps so infamously in modern times as Japanese professional, Tsuneyuki 'Tommy' Nakajima. In the 1978 Open Championship this oriental philosopher of some experience, who is also a very fine player, opened with rounds of 70 and 71 and came to the 17th needing two par 4s for another 71 and a good chance in the championship the following day.

He played the Road hole sensibly, with a good drive followed by a carefully crafted approach shot to the front edge of the green. From there he had a long approach putt to the hole, but he was playing well and confident of making his par.

He carefully studied the line of the putt and set the ball on its fateful journey towards the hole. As it climbed the bank and slowed its pace it began to swing to the left and, as so many have done before and since, it curled inexorably into the waiting jaws of the Road bunker.

The unfortunate Nakajima required four strokes to extricate himself from the pit before bravely holing out for a nine.

His Open dream lay in tatters, graphically illuminated in his own footprints at the bottom of the notorious Road bunker.

The Cardinal Hole: Prestwick

THE CARDINAL HOLE

3rd, Prestwick

482 yards

Par 5

Prestwick, birthplace of the Open Championship, has been variously described as a 'museum piece' and 'old fashioned'. No less a person than the learned golf writer, Leonard Crawley, wrote in *Golf Monthly* in June 1952 that it was 'out of date'.

Whether Crawley was feeling a little liverish when he penned this attack on the course, or whether his criticism was more directed at the decision to play the Amateur Championship there that year, we can only speculate at this distance.

On the face of it, it was a strange comment from one so deeply steeped in the game, for it seemed to deny the enviable antiquity that only a handful of truly great golf courses possess, and which none in the modern game could ever hope to emulate.

Prestwick is of another time, perhaps, but it stands up there beside the Old Course at St Andrews in importance and influence in Scotland's golfing heritage, and although it has changed much since the original 12 holes were laid out, and has not been able to cope with an Open Championship since 1925, it has classic holes still among its wild humps and hollows.

The Cardinal hole, the 3rd at Prestwick, remains one of the great holes in world golf. *The Golfer's Handbook* once rated the Cardinal and the Road hole at St Andrews as the 'two most famous holes in world golf'. That was a few years ago, and might not be their pairing today, but the Cardinal is still as fearsome a test now as it was a century and more ago.

In 1882 the Cardinal hole was 436 yards long, a formidable journey with a hickory shaft and a gutty ball. By 1987 it was stretched to 505 yards for the

The sheer intimidation of the Cardinal bunker is clearly apparent in this view of the 3rd hole at Prestwick. It was off the vertical face of the bunker in the foreground that James Braid almost lost the 1908 Open Championship when seemed to be 'playing racquets against those ominous boards' according to his followers.

Even when the Cardinal is passed there is still work to be done at the 3rd. The short approach to the green is a delicate one from the humps and hollows in the only safe ground beyond the Cardinal bunker.

return of the Amateur Championship that Crawley argued should never darken Prestwick's door again, while today it is played to 482 yards for medal play.

Perhaps the terrors of the Cardinal are not quite as severe as once they were but the drive remains a fearsome prospect, with the dark and wide wall of the Cardinal Bunker shored up by sleepers dominating the forward view. In a stiff east wind it is possible to drive into the first part of the Cardinal from where the par figure of 5 will seldom be accomplished.

In normal conditions a drive well placed leaves the terrifying prospect of the shot over the vast, frowning expanse of the Cardinal bunker with its black, vertical face of railway sleepers broken only by a many-stepped ladder for access.

The great Harry Vardon wrote of the Cardinal in 1905: 'The third hole at Prestwick is one that stirs the soul of the daredevil golfer, for, after he has dispatched the ball well and safely from the tee, he finds a big, gaping bunker, the famous Cardinal, ahead of him for his second – an ugly brute that gives a sickening feeling to the man who is off his game. Defy this bunker, be on the green with your brassie, put a 4 on your card and you have done something which should make you happy for the morning.'

No doubt it was within the compass of Vardon to find the green with his second shot over the pit of the Cardinal, but for mere mortals the task of avoiding this graveyard is far from easy, and perhaps best achieved today with an iron club rather than the present-day equivalent of Vardon's brassie.

The simple fact is that just clearing the Cardinal is not enough, although everyone heaves a huge sigh of relief when it is accomplished. There is little fairway to land in for sanctuary and even if the fairway is found there remains to be played the most delicate of chip shots to a narrow green that confirms as readily as any other on the course that Prestwick greens have a character all of their own.

The 3rd at Prestwick, unlike most of the other great par 5s in Scottish golf, has never been holed in two shots, according to the club's record, and rarely indeed in three. The great American amateur, Lawson Little, is one player who had that distinction, on his way to winning the Amateur Championship at Prestwick in 1934. Following a long and well-placed drive he let loose a majestic second shot that whistled across the Cardinal and just reached the small green surrounded by a series of hummocks. The putt went in for one of the few eagles ever recorded on this infamous hole.

The legendary James Braid was less fortunate during the 1908 Open Championship which he eventually won but almost threw away at the Cardinal hole. Braid's supporters watched in anguish as their hero tried to give the championship away by 'playing racquets against those ominous black boards'.

Braid finally escaped and went on to victory but he could so easily have been just another victim of one of Scottish golf's most intimidating holes.

Barry Burn: Carnoustie

BARRY BURN

16th, Carnoustie

250 yards

Par 3

Golf in America owes much to the men of Carnoustie. Its early development was influenced by a stream of emigrants from the north shore of the River Tay, who at various times held every American State title there was to win. Since the last years of the nineteenth century around 300 young men from the Angus town have become professional golfers with a large number of them crossing the Atlantic to seek fame and fortune.

Players like the Smith brothers, Willie who won the US Open once, brother Alex who won it twice, and perhaps the best of the three, Macdonald, who sadly would never win it at all, although he came desperately close often enough, all learned to play on the mighty links of Carnoustie, one of the great championship golf courses in the world and the one with perhaps the toughest finish of them all. The last three holes at Carnoustie taught them the truth of the old adage that no round of golf, and no championship, is over until it's over.

The dramas of Carnoustie in its Open Championship history, and at much lower levels than that, and for much longer too, have nearly all been played out over this famous stretch of Angus links.

Deep bunkers protect the narrow green at the 16th. One notable Canadian amateur was once heard to say that the green was so narrow that his group had had to march on to it in single file.

The first of the deadly trio of finishing holes is the famous 16th, a short hole that is not short at all and one of the most demanding par-3 holes in the game. By any standards it is a ferocious hole. The tee is slightly elevated and the view is across rough and uncompromising ground with the Barry Burn, after which the hole is named, just close enough to be threatening on the left for the pulled tee shot.

The green is long and narrow with undulations that try at every turn to throw the ball back off the green even if it reaches there in the first place. The entrance to it is so narrow that one notable Canadian amateur was once heard to say that his group had had to march onto it in single file.

There is sand everywhere and not just any old sand. It is sand contained in a series of six pits spread around the green. James Braid, during his reconstruction of the course in the 1920s, may have filled in around 80 bunkers but he left this grouping intact to strike fear into the hearts of many who would follow.

Bernard Darwin once voted the 16th at Carnoustie the best hole on the golf course, although

it was not then quite in the form that it exists today. He didn't play it as a par 3 either, it was valued at a shot more than that in his day and his tactical plan called for a drive out to the right on to a narrow neck of fairway, followed by a tricky little pitch up to the hole from there. It was what he once described in relation to St Andrews as 'being inclined to approach on the instalment system'.

When James Braid was called in to remodel the course in 1926, and create the hole as it now exists, it was a par 4 even then. It was the same length then as it is now from the back tee but the improvement in golf equipment in the three-quarters of a century since has turned it into a one-shot hole, albeit one of such immense challenge.

The ability to find the green by threading a shot between the barriers of sand with a very long club, for that is what is invariably required (and there are times when there is not a long enough club in the bag) is given to but a few souls. For the rest the theory that even a blind pig must occasionally stumble upon a truffle is usually the only hope.

Even the great Tom Watson, who won the first of his five Open Championship titles here in 1975 in a play-off against Jack Newton, failed to make a par on any of the four rounds of the Championship proper.

In the famous finish in the 1968 Open, when Gary Player and Jack Nicklaus fought out a remarkable final 5-hole drama, the 16th was all but out of range for the entire field. Into the breeze only Nicklaus was able to smash a driver on to the green and get the ball past the pin at the back. Player finished short and in the bunker to the right but with his wonderful dexterity from sand extricated himself well enough to hold on and eventually win by one stroke.

James Braid was responsible for creating the 6th as it now exists. He was called in to make changes to the entire course in 1926.

The Postage Stamp: Royal Troon

THE POSTAGE STAMP

8th, Royal Troon

126 yards

Par 3

Perched among the sand dunes on the formidable links of the Royal Troon Golf Club on the Ayrshire coast there is a slender plateau of land surrounded by cavernous bunkers that holds a very special place in the annals of Scottish golf. It is the green of the shortest hole in Open Championship use and is known throughout the world simply as the 'Postage Stamp'.

It is a disconsonant name for a hole that can generate feelings so much more strident than those usually reserved for the local sub post office. History is not at all clear who actually gave the 8th at Royal Troon this sobriquet, but while it lends impression to the physical size of the difficulty it certainly does far less than justice to the overall gravity of the problem.

'Ignorance, is bliss' says the proverb and nowhere has that assertion more pertinence than here in this cunning corner of the Ayrshire countryside where the views out across the Firth of Clyde to Ailsa Craig and the mysterious Isle of Arran can be staggeringly beautiful.

Standing on the tee for the first time the player is confronted with a green of very small proportions certainly, a shot of a mere 126 yards from as far back as the tee box will go. It is a flick, a mere waft with some sort of short iron, at least at first sight, requisite only of more careful consideration should the wind

It is clear from this view why the 8th at Royal Troon is known as the 'Postage Stamp'. It is a short hole by most standards but the landing area is tiny while the penalty for missing the green is huge.

be blowing strongly enough to encourage some account to be taken of it. Certainly the target area is small, but, for goodness sake, can a 120-yard pitch be all that difficult?

Could that have been the feeling that enveloped the unfortunate German amateur player, Herman Tissies, when he stood on the tee at the Postage Stamp in the 1950 Open Championship and scanned the modest yardage in front of him? If it was, then Herman was a wiser man when he finally reached the end of the 126 yards, for he had required no fewer than 15 strokes before his ball mercifully disappeared beneath the ground in the one place that mattered, underneath the pin, for in truth he had been in just about every other hole around up till then.

The obvious question was asked of the unfortunate Herman as to how it could have taken him 15 strokes for the shortest hole in Open Championship golf. With true Teutonic stoicism he informed all those who wanted to hear that he had holed not only a good putt but his only putt on the hole!

Herman was not the first, there have been many more since and will be just as many in the future, who have spent considerable time ping-ponging across the green from bunker to bunker in their efforts to find the putting surface. Herman, no doubt, fully understood why Henry Leach once wrote that the Postage Stamp is 'as full of wickedness as it is of beauty'. It has been the graveyard for many a promising score in Open Championships and for many, many more.

However, for one eminent golfer the Postage Stamp will forever have much happier memories. The legendary Gene Sarazen, a winner in his time of all four of golf's major championships, had arrived at Troon as the reigning US Open Champion in 1923 at the age of 22, with every intention of adding the Open on this side of the Atlantic to his portfolio. Caught in a gale of wind, however, he scored 75,

85 in the qualifying rounds – these were the days when everyone had to pre-qualify – and failed to win a place in the Championship.

Half a century later Sarazen returned to Troon at the age of 72 for the 1973 Open Championship. Sir Ian Stewart, Captain of the Royal & Ancient Golf Club, made a presentation on the eve of the Championship of inscribed silver cigarette boxes to Sarazen and to Arthur Havers, the winner of the 1923 Open.

The following day Sarazen reached the 8th in the company of former Open Champions Max Faulkner and Fred Daly, to once again confront the Postage Stamp. Into the wind Sarazen punched a 5-iron which took one hop onto the green short of the flag and went straight into the hole. The following day Sarazen reached the Postage Stamp again but this time his tee shot with the same club took the more well-trodden route by finishing in a deep bunker to the right of the green.

Undaunted, the 72-year-old inventor of the sand iron so many years before, took his current version of the implement into the bunker and proceeded to hole his bunker shot for a two! Over the two days he had required only three strokes for the hole and hadn't used his putter at all.

It was a remarkable train of events on a hole that has witnessed so much drama in its history. Sarazen celebrated by presenting the 5-iron to the Royal & Ancient Golf Club and it remains on display in the Trophy Room of the Club to this day.

A classic problem on the 'Postage Stamp'. The prospect of making par, or even holding the green from this position, is very remote.

The Long Hole: St Andrews

THE LONG HOLE

14th, Old Course,
St Andrews

567 yards

Par 5

The shape of Hell bunker
may have changed a little
over the last century, as this
photograph c.1890 clearly
shows, but its menace to
many promising scores
is just as real today as it
was then.

The Road hole may be the one which comes up most often when the dangers of the Old Course at St Andrews are up for discussion, but the evidence of the Open Championship over the years points to the 14th as the Old Lady's most formidable line of defence. The 'Long Hole Home' is what it is called and throughout its very long history it has assembled an impressive list of victims.

It is of course the other half of the fairway shared with the 5th, known now as the 'Hole o' Cross' or the 'Long Hole Out', from the days when there was only one fairway and the holes simply retraced the path of those on the way out. Today there is more of a division, but the 14th is as often played from the fairway of the 5th as it is from its own Elysian Fields, the landing area of the 14th fairway on a shallow plateau bordered by the old stone dyke that separates the Old Course from the Eden Course.

There are almost as many opinions on how to play this dangerous hole as there are players who have ever tried to find a way to do it without courting disaster. And disaster is certainly what can befall the unwary – and the wary too for that matter – over its 567 perilous yards.

Who can forget the mighty Jack Nicklaus, no less, pinned down in Hell bunker in the 1995 Open Championship, slashing away at his ball to a point of frustration that saw his club exit from the bunker more quickly than normal decorum should allow. The Bear climbed from the pit in a black cloud. Yet who could blame him, for this awesome crater had detained him to the point where double figures were inevitable and the 14th had yet another victim to add to its list.

Hell bunker is the most notorious of the craters that pock-mark the journey along the 14th, although there are at least 15 others that have to be taken into account when plotting the route. The group of four known as the 'Beardies' is the first consideration. They are most devastatingly in play from the very back tees, although less of a hazard from the medal tee, unless the wind is strong and against. They must be avoided at all costs.

The author can vouch with some authority as to their magnetic powers, having at one time felt obliged to name his house 'The Beardies' to reflect the fact that he was as often in one as the other.

The various schools

of thought on how to play this hole are divided, more or less, into three groups. There are those who favour the left all the way, including a drive over or to the left of the Beardies, those who favour the right all the way and those who favour a combination of the two. Irrespective of which is ultimately employed the dangers and difficulties are manifest.

Central to the strategy has to be a way of avoiding the dreaded Hell bunker. Those who favour the all-the-way-left approach take it out of play by progressing down the 5th fairway, provided they have avoided the Beardies at the outset. Those who favour the right must carry Hell, or the rough and other nameless pits of sand to its right. The right-left-right brigade, which we might describe as the military option, drive on to the Elysian Fields and then turn half left to miss Hell on its port side and approach from over the Grave and Ginger Beer bunkers.

In short it is almost impossible to play the 14th safely. Somewhere along the route sand has to be carried. There may be less of it down the starboard side but the approach to the green must then carry over a high mound on the front right of the green to a putting surface that slopes sharply towards the back from that point.

Among the great players who have found to their cost how difficult it is to pass this fearsome hole safely was four-times Open Champion Bobby Locke who, in 1939, was five under par when he reached the Long Hole Home. His hooking drive was carried by the gusting wind into one of the Beardies. His first attempt at escape with a 7-iron failed. He escaped with the next but then hit a wooden club shot into Hell and ran up an eight.

Six years earlier Gene Sarazen was at the height of his powers and looking for a birdie at the 14th after a long and arrow-straight drive on to the Elysian Fields. His second shot with a brassie was struck out of the heel and the ball finished inevitably in Hell bunker. Only a hundred yards from the green Sarazen caught his shot from the sand a trifle thin and buried the ball in the face of the bunker. He required three putts for an eight and left St Andrews a wiser man.

Central to any strategy when playing the 14th on the Old Course is to find a way to avoid Hell bunker.

The 9th: Muirfield

THE 9TH

9th, Muirfield

504 yards

Par 5

A procession of bunkers
down the right hand side on
the approach to the green
forces many a second shot
too close to the out-of-
bounds wall on the left.

For the modern tournament player the traditional par 5 has all but ceased to exist. There are very few that they cannot reach in two strokes, very often with an iron club for the second. In the relatively rare cases where they cannot reach in two, the second is usually a lay up shot purely to make progress along the hole before the final pitch to the green.

The great par-5 holes demand much more than that. They may still be reachable in two given the right conditions but they always retain that element of danger that separates them from the run of the mill.

The 9th at Muirfield is a classic example. There are many demanding holes on this famous links, home to the Honourable Company of Edinburgh Golfers, and regular Open Championship venue, but few have caused as much havoc to score cards at all levels over the decades than this one.

Of the many factors that together make this hole

the devil it is, length is not one of them, for this is not by any means the longest hole in Scottish championship golf. At 505 yards it is well within the range of many players, amateur or professional, but with even the hint of a breeze the 9th at Muirfield can cause immense problems.

The hole follows the line of an old grey stone wall down the left-hand side, but a huge swathe of thick rough and hummocks sweeps into the fairway half way along, effectively turning the hole into a dog-leg to the left. Where the rough cascades in to meet the fairway two separate bunkers stand guard to force the tee shot to the right where more of the notorious Muirfield rough lurks in wait.

Between the bunkers and the rough on the right is a narrow neck of fairway that has to be safely reached before there is any prospect of reaching the green in two. If the wind is against, the first bunker cuts off the short line to the hole: if it is from

194

behind the second bunker comes into play to do the same job.

The tee shot is therefore vital, as the great Arnold Palmer found to his cost in 1966 when he was well placed in the Open and elected to go for length from the tee. He came to grief when he failed to reach the narrow neck of the fairway and his resulting six critically damaged his chances.

At other times when the wind is helping and a dry spring has produced plenty of run on the course, the tee shot is considerably easier. This was the case in 1972 when Lee Trevino and Tony Jacklin fought out their memorable finish in the Open Championship.

In the last round Trevino and Jacklin were locked in an epic battle with Jack Nicklaus when they arrived at the 9th tee. Both drove into the rough but it had been a dry spring and it was not as thick as it might have been. Both were comfortably long enough to reach the green in two and both did with iron clubs. The shots were struck to perfection, pitching twenty or so yards short of the green before running up on to the putting surface. Each holed out for an eagle.

When the wind is against, however, and that is the prevailing direction, the 9th takes on an altogether more sinister cloak. The second shot has to be laid up safely, and herein lies the key to the difficulty of the hole.

A diagonal line of bunkers to the right forces a shot towards the old stone wall with out-of-bounds beyond it. The rolling approach to the green may seem easy enough to hit but into the wind any shot pulled slightly is a candidate to finish over that 5-feet high ribbon of stone.

Five-times winner of the Open Championship, Peter Thomson, is one who knows that better than most. In the 1959 Open he was the defending champion, having won four times in the previous five years, but his chance of making it five from six virtually ended at the 9th. His second shot with a wooden club was slightly pulled and the curving shot, exaggerated by the wind, flew over the wall and out-of-bounds. There are many more similar and equally sorry tales to be told of the 9th at Muirfield.

Even with an inch-perfect drive and a carefully placed second shot, the player is even then not entirely out of the wood.

In a stiff breeze the third shot to the green can be shrouded in as much danger as either of the ones before. It takes a steady nerve and firm control to play an approach into this green when the wind can so easily grab the ball in flight and dispatch it across the wall.

The test is one of patience and sound technique, knowing when to gamble with the drive or the second shot and when to play for safety.

The temptation to try for the rewards attached to reaching the green in two must always be weighed very carefully, for nowhere can a potential four be turned into a six or seven, or much worse, than here almost in front of the windows of the famous Greywalls Hotel.

Nick Price came perilously close to the wall during the 1992 Open Championship but played a remarkable recovery shot left-handed.

Redan: North Berwick

REDAN

15th, North Berwick

192 yards

Par 3

The Redan has earned its reputation not for its looks but for the searching test it presents, and the remarkable configuration of the hole itself.

It is not given to many holes in the world of golf to have had such an influence on the design of so many others that they become the generic name for the style. One such, and the most famous of them all, is the 15th at North Berwick, known as the Redan. No hole in golf has been copied more often than this famous par 3 on the ancient Lothian links.

While many short holes are remembered for their spectacular location – the 7th at Pebble Beach, the 5th at Loch Lomond or of course the 16th at Cypress Point, regarded by many as the most beautiful golf hole in the world, are obvious examples – the Redan is unlikely ever to appear in such a list. The 15th at North Berwick has earned its reputation not for its looks but for the searching test it presents and the remarkable topographical configuration of the hole itself.

It is a configuration that owes nothing to the hand of man. It evolved, as the rest of the golf course did, from the earliest days of the game when golfers played where they could and set what challenges they desired on the ground available. They had little choice, for in those evolutionary days two or more centuries ago they had no means of altering the countryside even if they had felt the need.

The mounds and ridges and depressions left on the links by the recession of the sea and the erosive effect of the wind were what the earliest golfers at North Berwick were given to play with, and as such the golf course was formed rather than built as it would be in the present day. The Redan is quite simply an accident of nature.

The players who decided that the Redan should be a hole were those who followed their featherie golf balls to a point where they chose to hole out. Such sites were chosen to offer a challenge to the skill levels of the players, without making it too difficult for them to complete. An obvious site for such a holing-out area was any ridge that ran across the path of play.

The green of the Redan hole sits on just such a ridge where, over the years, it has evolved into the famous hole that has prompted so many golf course architects to copy it.

The Redan at North Berwick is 192 yards long and the plateau green sits on a diagonal across the line of play and on a slope. It is

guarded by a deep bunker set into the shoulder under the left-hand side of the plateau, with more bunkers defending the other side.

The challenge is in the decision to attempt to carry the ball to the green or to manoeuvre a way there by instalment which may not elicit a par but which will not be otherwise too damaging. The former option requires the most precise tee shot, for there is very little hope of recovery if the green is missed. The second requires a carefully placed shot to the front right of the green, but the putt from there is savagely difficult if the pin is cut on the left.

The wind, as ever at North Berwick, is another critical factor in the decision on how to play the hole and it is the diversity of all these tactical considerations that has made the Redan almost a benchmark in par 3 design.

The first golf course architect to take what nature had created and apply it to his own design philosophy was Charles Blair Macdonald, the father of American golf course architecture. Born in Niagara Falls, New York, but brought up in Chicago, he entered the University of St Andrews at the age of 16 where he fell in love with golf. When he returned home he built two golf courses for the members of the Chicago Club, one at Belmont in 1893 and another at Wheaton in 1895. They were the first two 18-hole golf courses in America, and the course at Wheaton, now the Chicago Golf Club, ranks today as one of the finest in the United States after having been renovated by Macdonald's protégé, Seth Raynor, in 1923.

After the turn of the century Macdonald began to put together his plan to build a golf course patterned on some of the best golf holes in Britain. Eventually he found a suitable piece of land on Long Island, next door to Shinnecock Hills, and

began construction of the course he called The National Golf Links of America. It was a grand name for a grand vision, and one of the major elements in his design was his interpretation of the Redan hole at North Berwick.

The 4th at the National is not a replica of the 15th at North Berwick, more a copy of the elements that make the Redan such an outstanding hole. Almost the same length, the 4th at the National has a long green falling off diagonally to the left with the same deep bunker tucked in under the escarpment upon which the green is set. It is a superb hole and many consider Macdonald's Redan to be better than the original.

The Redan design has been copied many times since, most notably by A.W. Tillinghast on the 2nd at Somerset Hills in New Jersey. The 7th and 17th at Shinnecock Hills show a marked resemblance, as too does the 17th at Pebble Beach, although the slope is in the opposite direction. No matter how many times architects try to copy the Redan there remains only the one original. Contours can to some extent at least be copied, but environment and climate cannot. The truth is that the Redan is such a fearsome hole not just because of its topographical layout but because of all the elements that come together to make up the whole.

The slightly elevated green and ring of protective bunkers at the Redan have been copied many times around the world.

197

Bruce's Castle: Turnberry

BRUCE'S CASTLE

9th, Turnberry

454 yards

Par 4

Ailsa Craig stands guard as Greg Norman plays his drive from the forbidding eyrie that prompted the immortal comment 'for those in peril on the tee'.

In terms of the great holes in world golf the 9th at Turnberry rates highly indeed, although it lacks perhaps the mystique of, for example, the Road hole at St Andrews, the 12th at Augusta National or the finishing hole at Pebble Beach. Some American visitors, familiar with the Monterey Peninsula, tend to draw comparisons with Pebble Beach when they first encounter the 9th at Turnberry because this part of the course certainly has shades of the cliff-top golf found in northern California.

Turnberry, however, is not the western seaboard of the United States. This is classic Scottish links golf on the Ayrshire coast and the 9th is only one of many great holes on a course that is a tribute to architect Mackenzie Ross and to Frank Hole, a former managing director of the British Transport Hotels, who between them recreated the layout from the debris of the Second World War when the Turnberry courses were dug up for the second time in their history to create an airfield.

The 9th is not just a memorable hole. It is one that strikes fear into the stoutest heart not simply because of its difficulty – and that certainly is not in question – but for the famous tee shot played from a tiny outcrop of rock falling off the very edge of Scotland.

There are few if any more spectacular or beautifully sited tees in the world than here at the apex of the triangle that makes up the Turnberry layout.

The walk up from the 8th green gives no hint of what lies in wait. A narrow strip of turf leads the player out on to the tee where a fragile-looking fence is the only protection from the oblivion waiting on the rocks and the crash-ing breakers blow.

For some people the journey on to this fear-some tee is akin to that of the high diver mak-ing his way to the edge of the board, with the only consolation that they do not have to bal-ance on their toes on the edge. They may have problems with balance anyway if the wind is howling across the links as it can at Turnberry and that fragile-looking fence takes on an even more brittle appearance.

If the view down towards the water is scary then the one in the direction of the hole itself is just as bad. The tee shot has to carry a sizeable chunk of the Atlantic Ocean as it pounds in to the little cove around which the hole is built. In terms of actual length it is not perhaps all that far but given the cir-cumstances of its execution it presents one of the most fearsome shots in world golf. It is the very spot which prompted the eminent Scottish golf writer, Norman Mair, to coin the now immortal line dur-ing a television commentary: 'Oh hear us when we cry to Thee; For those in peril on the tee.'

Since the carry is not enormous and the tee shot is often played with at least a favouring wind, often enough a howling wind, it is the circumstances of the shot, rather than the shot itself, which can turn strong men into quivering wrecks.

It is as much a test of nerve as of shot making with the crash of the waves resounding in the ear, the sight of the cliffs and the abyss below and the certain knowledge that any mis-hit will not only be disastrous to the score but massively so to self-respect as well. The 9th tee at Turnberry is no place to be with a faint heart and dodgy swing.

Even if and when the chasm has been safely car-ried, and the player has climbed unscathed from the eyrie, what remains of the hole is no sinecure either. The wind of course is the critical factor but if it is not too strong the drive is aimed at a marker stone on the crest of the upslope far ahead from where the hog's back fairway runs slightly downhill to the green.

On the left the imposing Turnberry lighthouse casts its all-seeing eye across the tangle of rough between it and the fairway, proclaiming a warning just as relevant to the land-lubber golfer as to the seafarer it was built to protect. The lighthouse dominates the hole, bringing to mind the story of one of the Turnberry caddies – and there are many notable characters among them – who was once asked by his American employer if the lighthouse still worked.

'Aye, sur', said the caddie, 'but only at night'.

To the right the rough makes it very difficult to reach the green in regulation for those who eschew the challenge from the tee. Hit it long and straight from the tee is the only advice on the hole known as Bruce's Castle, after King Robert the Bruce, the revered Scottish monarch who is said to have used the old castle, the remains of which are still visible, as a resting place on one of his campaigns.

The all-seeing Turnberry lighthouse proclaims a warning not only to mariners but also, it seems, to golfers playing the hole they call Bruce's Castle.

Long: Carnoustie

LONG

6th, Carnoustie

570 yards

Par 5

In the lexicon of world golf no word has been more devalued or abused than 'championship'. Every new golf course developer adds it as a matter of course to his project publicity, even if his creation rates no more than a pitch and putt in a cow pasture.

There is one place, however, where 'championship' means exactly that; where the course rates among the truly great and where only true champions have ever been crowned in the oldest and greatest golf championship in the world.

Carnoustie is that place. The very name sets the pulse racing in the hearts of even the strongest because they know what lies in wait on the flat, uncompromising Angus links. There is no place at Carnoustie to hide. Every hole is a battle to be fought in a war in which the player may survive better than his opponent but never, ever taste lasting victory.

Of all the great holes at Carnoustie – and there

are many – the 6th is a classic and among the finest of all the par-5 holes in world golf. It ranks up there with the Road hole at St Andrews, the 9th at Muirfield or the 18th at Pebble Beach. It knocks the 13th at Augusta into a cocked hat.

There are times, of course, when weather conditions can take some of the sting out of its 570 yards but there is seldom a day on the north shore of the Firth of Tay when the wind does not blow, and it needs very little wind to make the 6th at Carnoustie a fearsome prospect.

There are three elements that make the hole such a prodigious challenge. The first is the pair of bunkers that dominate the field of view from the tee. They are deep caverns where to escape with the loss of only a single stroke is considered a victory. The left-hand of the pair – and the nearest to the tee – rears up from the centre of the fairway like a black hole intent on sucking everything into its gaping mass. Slightly to the right, and a little further on, its compatriot is not quite so stark of appearance but just as dangerous. To the left of both, the boundary fence marks an out-of-bounds that runs the full length of the hole, and indeed the one that follows.

The second element is a drainage ditch. A modest enough stream of water as Scottish burns go, but one which eats insidiously and diagonally into the fairway from the right, and which is marked at the end of its course by a single little yellow marker. From

The wide but relatively shallow green runs diagonally across the line of play and is well protected by deep bunkers.

there the stream dives underground and goes we know not where.

Into the prevailing wind the ditch can easily consume any second shot struck a little too far to the right, forcing the player to seek safety in a narrow gap of fairway between the end of the ditch and the boundary fence, a task calling for a steady nerve and precise stroke.

The third element is the wide but shallow green with its subtle shelf, a dangerous bunker on the front right and a long and

nasty sand pit behind the green that swallows any shot just marginally strong. Into a stiff breeze the third shot to the 6th with a longish club is one of daunting prospect, while downwind those who attack it with a long second find the narrow green just as difficult to seek out.

On a windless day it is true that much of the threat can be compromised but, like the Road hole at St Andrews, the 6th at Carnoustie has that strange habit of jumping up and inflicting the severest of bites just when least expected.

It was, however, a calm day in 1953 when William Benjamin Hogan from Dublin, Texas, set out on the final two rounds of the only Open Championship he was ever to play in Britain. Still recovering from the car accident which almost ended his life, and that of his wife Valerie, Ben Hogan was persuaded to make the long journey to Carnoustie to win the championship the world said he needed to win to confirm his standing as the greatest golfer of his era.

He came early to Carnoustie to practise. He moved out of his hotel and found another where he could soak in a hot bath for hours to ease the pain in his shattered legs. He disliked the food and ate lunch in his car and he practised on a hard and running course that American journalists described

as like playing golf on the moon.

In 1953 the final two rounds of the Open were still played on the one day and those who watched his masterful performance always remember the way Hogan reduced that fearsome 6th to just another hole on his dogged road to victory.

Morning and afternoon Hogan screamed drives through the heavy, grey air into what the great American golf writer, Al Barkow, once so beautifully described as 'Hogan's personal channel in the sky'. Both times the ball flew down the right and past the two threatening bunkers in the fairway into what would become known as 'Hogan's Alley'; twice he followed up with brassie shots just short of the putting surface; and twice he got up and down for birdie fours.

It was golf of frightening precision that left the field struggling in his wake. His final two rounds had been 70 and 68; each round in the championship had been lower than the one before and he beat Frank Stranahan, Dai Rees, Peter Thomson and Antonio Cerda by no fewer than seven strokes.

His clinical destruction of the 6th over the final two rounds of the 1953 Open was simply a reflection of his mastery in that memorable championship.

Ben Hogan reduced the 6th to just another hole on his way to an historic victory in the Open Championship at Carnoustie in 1953.

CHAPTER SEVEN

GREAT EVENTS AND MEMORABLE OPENS

The history of Scottish golf is littered with great events and memorable moments. From the days of the great money matches between Allan Robertson and Old Tom Morris and the Dunns of Musselburgh, through memorable Amateur Championships and lesser events, to the great dramas played out in the Open Championship, the Home of Golf has seen it all.

Today the Open Championship remains one of the great sporting occasions in the world and the only one that does not impose restrictions on the numbers who come along to watch. It is the people's championship, where anyone can turn up at the gate, pay their admission money and watch the greatest players in the world battle it out for the oldest and greatest golf title in the world.

In the early days of golf there was no crowd control whatsoever. The galleries walked the fairways with the protagonists and in the first years of the Open Championship the members even continued to play on the course while the Championship was underway!

It was not until huge crowds engulfed the Open at Prestwick in the fateful Championship of 1925, in their keenness to support expatriate Scot Macdonald Smith against Jim Barnes of the United States, that the need to control galleries became a major issue. Today many thousands attend the Open Championship and many other events and dutifully stay outside the roped-off fairways. There have been historic moments, too, that had nothing to do with daring feats on the golf course. The most famous of them all was in 1958 when the Freedom of the City of St Andrews was conferred on Bobby Jones.

Spanish passion. Seve Ballesteros holes his birdie putt on the last green to win the Open Championship at St Andrews in 1984.

203

The Amateur Championship 1899

Freddie Tait of St Andrews and Hoylake's Alan Ball, two of the great amateur heroes around the turn of the twentieth century, fought out what probably remains to this day the epic battle in the history of the Amateur Championship.

Tait was the defending champion at Prestwick in 1899, and after the first round of the final he was three up and a strong favourite to win again.

Like so many before him, however, he was an immediate victim in the second round of the wall down the right-hand side of the first. His lead was immediately cut and reduced again at the Cardinal hole, when he couldn't match Ball's five.

From there the battle raged on until the players came to the famous Alps hole, the 17th, with the man from Hoylake one hole in front. It was here that one of the most remarkable dramas was acted out.

A deep bunker sits just short of the green with a vertical bank shored up by railway sleepers in front. It is a formidable pit, and on this occasion was filled with water after previous heavy rain.

Freddie Tait's approach fell short of the carry over the bunker and finished floating in the water (some golf balls floated in these days). John Ball also went for the carry over the bunker, but he too failed to make it and his ball rolled back off the face of the bunker into the wet, clinging sand, an inch or two above the water line.

Freddie Tait had no option. One behind with two to play he had to play the ball as it 'floated' to have a chance to save the hole. The man from St Andrews did not hesitate. He waded into the water 'well over his boots' to attempt the escape.

Tait played a miracle shot. Taking the floating ball cleanly from the surface of the water he not only escaped from the bunker but managed to find the green into the bargain.

Hardly had the cheers subsided than John Ball played a shot almost as miraculous from the heavy sand while also standing in the water up to his ankles. The ball climbed almost vertically over the face in front of the bunker and on to the green alongside the ball of Freddie Tait.

The hole was halved and Tait made a marvellous three at the last to take the match to the 19th. The players moved to the first tee again and the excitement was so intense that some of the Hoylake stalwarts supporting Ball stayed in the clubhouse where, in the words of Bernard Darwin: 'they waited for news, presumably groaning dismally like Mr Winkle with their heads under the sofa cushions.'

They had no need to fear. Freddie Tait's impeccable four, thanks to a deft chip from the back of the green, was not good enough. Ball's approach shot landed safely on the green and Bernard Darwin described the winning putt.

'John Ball holed a putt, not an enormous putt but a very, very good one, perhaps 8 feet, perhaps 10, for a three at the 37th. From between somebody's legs I believe I saw him strike the ball, but I only heard it go in.'

Young Tom Morris

Young Tom Morris became a romantic idol in St Andrews from the day in 1867 when he went with his father, Tom Morris Snr, the Open Champion that year, to Carnoustie to play in a professional match. 'Whit hae ye brocht the laddie for, Tom?' Willie Park is said to have asked.

'Ye'll ken whit for soon enough,' replied Old Tom.

And so it turned out. Young Tom beat the best players in the world that day at Carnoustie and Scotland was agog at such precocious talent.

The plot of Young Tom Morris's short life is the stuff of high melodrama. That he was a golfing genius there is no question, but more than that he had what might have been called in a later era, film-star quality.

Tall and handsome and incredibly strong, he was often known to break a golf club shaft just below the handle by the simple act of waggling it. He was modest and idolised by a St Andrews following who had a hero with a genius never before seen in golf.

If it was Allan Robertson who first introduced an iron club to the armoury for pitching, it was Young Tom Morris who perfected its use. He was the master of the niblick, his favourite club, and the first golfer to learn to make the best use of it to stop the ball quickly on a hard green.

His record of four consecutive Open Championship victories has never been equalled, and is never likely to be, but his greatest triumph was probably the third victory when he made the Championship Belt his own property at Prestwick in 1870.

A measure of his domination of the field in all three Championships was the fact that he finished an average of nine strokes ahead of his nearest rival in each of them. There were fewer competitors then of course, but his scores were remarkable in their own right given the equipment and the rough courses of the day.

His winning total in 1870 for the 36 holes – three rounds of the Prestwick course – was 149, which meant that he had achieved the seemingly impossible feat of twice breaking 80 for 18 holes. His winning margin was an amazing 11 strokes.

He returned to St Andrews with the Belt, which under the rules of the tournament became his property after winning it in three successive years, to a hero's welcome. The celebrations were hardly less contained when he returned to Prestwick in 1872 – there was no Open in 1871 – to have his name inscribed as the first on the famous claret jug which has been the trophy since Young Tom made the Belt his own property.

Seven short years after he won his first Open Championship the hero of St Andrews was dead,

diagnosed the victim of pneumonia, but everyone believed a broken heart was the real cause following the deaths of his wife and first child in childbirth a few months before.

OLD COURSE MARATHON

Allan Robertson and Willie Dunn had many memorable encounters but surely none of longer duration than one match in July 1843 over the Old Course at St Andrews. The battle was joined over ten consecutive days, except Sundays when the course was closed, and each day over two rounds. Day after day they battled on until on the tenth day, Allan Robertson was ahead by one round. On winning the 19th round on the morning of that final day he was two rounds ahead with one to play and declared the winner.

Matches then were played either over a number of rounds, a number of holes or a number of courses. It would be many years before stroke play entered into the equation of competitive golf.

Many today still believe that match play is the only real game of golf and that in foursomes is to be found the true manifestation of it.

Allan Robertson, the first heroic figure in golf. Old Tom Morris once said of him: 'The cunningest bit body o' a player, I dae think, that iver haunled cleek an' putter'.

The Famous Foursome

There has never been any contradiction of the boast made for Allan Robertson and Old Tom Morris that they were never beaten in a foursome. They were the most formidable partnership in the great days of the money matches before the first Open Championship in 1860, but they came to the very brink of defeat in the most famous foursomes match in Scotland's golfing history.

Their opponents were old adversaries, the identical twin brothers, Willie and Jamie Dunn, pride of Musselburgh. The stake for the match, to be played over 36 holes on each of three greens (courses), was the astonishing sum for 1849 of £400, and there were very heavy side bets. The whole of Scotland, which in effect was the whole world of golf at that time, wanted to see it.

The first leg was played at Musselburgh and the Dunns trounced the St Andrews pair by 13 and 12. The second was at St Andrews where the local pairing won, although narrowly. The third and showdown match was over the neutral links of North Berwick. Crowds flocked from near and far. The popular route from Fife was by boat from Leven on the north shore of the Firth of Forth and it must have been a terrible journey for those who made it for it began as a terrible day of rain.

The match was of 36 holes, five rounds of the course plus one hole more. The rain had stopped but a strong wind blew from the south-west. Both teams had their supporters with the Musselburgh contingent outnumbering those who had had to

The Dunn twins, Willie and Jamie, are among this group of professionals gathered for a grand tournament at Leith Links on 17 May 1867. Willie Dunn holds a club over his shoulder while brother Jamie is seated on the right of the photograph.

make the journey by boat across the Firth.

So intense was the atmosphere that as soon as a shot was played the crowd was on the move after it to see the outcome and establish which ball lay in better position. It was a Titanic encounter with the Dunns having much the better of the early exchanges to the point where they were four holes up with only eight to play. However, by the time the match reached the 16th it was all square.

Allan Robertson's drive at the 17th lay very badly while the Dunns were in perfect position further ahead. Three strokes later Robertson and Morris were still in a bunker short of the green while the Dunns were off the green to the right on a cart track and close to a kerb stone, having played two shots fewer.

The Dunns wanted the stone moved and sent for a spade! Sir David Baird, the referee, would have none of it and ordered the ball played as it lay, on the grounds that it was off the course and the stone was a fixture.

Twice the Dunns in turn attacked the ball with an iron without moving it. They had played the

same number of strokes as their opponents. Reports of the match say that the Musselburgh men completely lost their composure, but worse than that, they lost the hole and the St Andrews men were one up with one to play.

The last was a formality. Old Tom and Allan won that one too for victory by two holes, completing one of the greatest comebacks in golf and maintaining their unbeaten record.

Freedom of the City for Jones

There have been many great occasions in the history of golf in Scotland. Most have been associated with great deeds on the golf course, victory over adversity or great feats of scoring. Perhaps the greatest, however, did not take place on the Old Course at St Andrews, or on any other course, although it did take place at the Home of Golf itself.

The year was 1958 and the Younger Graduation Hall of the University of St Andrews was packed to overflowing to see Robert Tyre Jones of Atlanta, Georgia, declared a freeman of the city of St Andrews.

It was an occasion unique in the annals of golf. Bobby Jones had become a hero in St Andrews after

The grand old man of golf, Old Tom Morris. With Allan Robertson he was never beaten in foursomes play and continued to play golf until he was in his 80s.

Bobby Jones, pictured with Provost Leonard of St Andrews, after he was given the freedom of the city in an emotional ceremony in the Younger Hall in 1958.

207

winning the Amateur Championship over the Old Course on his way to his famous Grand Slam of golf, winning the Amateur and Open Championships of Britain and the United States in the same epoch-making year of 1930. He was not only the toast of St Andrews, but then the most popular sportsman in American history.

In 1936, six years later, after he had retired from tournament golf, Jones made a sentimental return to St Andrews as an ordinary holiday-maker, to have another round on the Old Course with some friends. Word spread around the old town like wildfire, and when Bobby Jones arrived on the first tee at 10 o'clock in the morning a huge crowd of spectators – variously estimated between two and five thousand – had gathered to watch their hero play. Hundreds more joined the throng as he progressed.

At the Younger Hall, confined to a wheelchair and in sadly declining health, he recalled that day 22 years earlier when the crowds came to greet him.

'That spontaneous welcome was bound to be touching and it did something to me,' he said. 'I played golf as I had not done for more than four years or ever since.'

The packed hall cheered as Jones rose slowly from his wheelchair to tell them: 'I could take out of my life everything except my experiences at St Andrews and I would still have had a rich, full life.'

The honour done to Bobby Jones by the people of St Andrews was unique in sport. Few men had been honoured with the freedom of the city, a measure of the esteem in which this great sportsman was held not just as a player but for his much greater contribution to the game as a whole. Only one before him had been an American: Benjamin Franklin, honoured by the city of St Andrews as a freeman nearly a hundred years before, in October, 1759.

Jones concluded his emotional address in the Younger Hall with these words: 'I like to think of it this way, that now officially I have the right to feel at home in St Andrews as in fact, I always have done.'

There was a long and spontaneous standing ovation for the lawyer from Atlanta, the greatest golfer of his age and some say of all time. When next the citizens gathered together in the name of their hero it was in the old Town Church less than 14 years later for a memorial service to their friend and freeman who had died and been released from a terrible wasting illness a few months before.

The 1938 Walker Cup at St Andrews

The Walker Cup began in 1922 between the amateur players of the United States and Great Britain and Ireland. The tenth playing of the biannual matches was at St Andrews in 1938. Until that year the Britain and Ireland team had been outclassed by the Americans who were able to field very strong teams, none more so than when they were headed by the legendary Bobby Jones. Jones was in the first five Walker Cup teams. He played ten matches, won nine and lost the other in a quite remarkable record.

There was no Bobby Jones at St Andrews in 1938, but it was nonetheless a formidable team that arrived at the Home of Golf. In the American side was Charlie Yates, like Jones, from Atlanta, Georgia. He arrived in St Andrews fresh from winning the Amateur Championship at Troon two weeks earlier.

Good crowds followed the matches, cheering and hoping for the first victory by a GB & I team. The home side made a very good fist of the first day's play, winning the 36-holes foursomes by two points to one, half points not counting in those days.

It was a great opening day for GB & I but it might easily have been marred had it not been for the swift action of veteran English player, Harry Bentley. After lunch in the match between Bentley and his long-hitting Irish partner Jimmy Bruen, and the American pairing of Johnny Fischer and Charlie Kocsis, the Americans were three up and had a chance to go four in front if Fischer could hole a 12-ft birdie putt at the 3rd. Fischer left the ball a foot short of the hole and in disgust walked up to the ball and tapped it in.

He had played out of turn and Jimmy Bruen quickly called the referee's attention to this breach of the rules and claimed the hole. Bentley intervened immediately and told the referee that the hole had been halved because he had conceded the Americans the short putt.

It was an act of great sportsmanship, preventing this international match from being soured by what

John Black (left) captain
of the GB & I team with the
American captain, Francis
Ouimet after the historic
Walker Cup match at
St Andrews in 1938.

the great American golf writer, Herb Warren Wind, later described as 'some inappropriate technicality'. Eventually the match ended, perhaps appropriately, in a tie.

The GB & I team carried their first day lead into the second with renewed confidence and won five of the eight 36-hole singles matches to record an historic victory.

Huge crowds cheered the players on both sides, the home side for a memorable victory and the Americans for their friendliness and dignity in defeat. The formal presentations were made on the steps in front of the R & A clubhouse, but after the events were concluded no one would leave. The crowd kept calling for players from both teams, and particularly Charlie Yates from the American team who had become so popular with the Scottish galleries.

Yates had a quick discussion with Gordon Peters, a Scottish member of the winning team, and together they stood on the steps in front of the clubhouse and sang the old Scottish favourite 'Just a wee doch-an-doris'. Thousands joined in a moving and fitting end to a rare and memorable occasion in a town that has been blessed with so many of them.

1998 CALCUTTA CUP

In a remarkable career W. C. (Bill) Campbell from Huntington, West Virginia, has been one of the United States's greatest amateur players. He played on seven US Walker Cup teams and was non-playing Captain of another. He won the US Amateur in 1964 and was a beaten semi-finalist twice. In 1954 he lost in the final of the British Amateur and has won a host of other titles. He has been a member of the USGA Executive Committee, and won the Bob Jones Award for Sportsmanship.

However, it is a remarkable fact that in 47 years as a member of the Royal & Ancient Golf Club, Bill Campbell was never able to win a single Club competition. He graced the R & A as Captain in 1987, but not one single trophy carried his name – that was until 1998 when Bill Campbell broke his R & A duck.

At the age of 75, and having had his handicap just reduced from three to two, he battled through desperate weather in the early part of the week and won the R & A's Calcutta Cup, partnered by former R & A Rules Secretary and Irish internationalist, John Glover. For John Glover, who played in six Home Internationals between 1951 and 1970, it was also his first R & A competition victory. Bill Campbell celebrated by comfortably beating 'his age in the R & A Medal two weeks after his Calcutta Cup win.

Memorable Opens

Sir Henry's Greatest Triumph

Of the three Open Championships won by Henry Cotton, his first in 1934 at Sandwich most readily comes to mind because of his wonderful scoring in the first three rounds and in the qualifying. His 65 remains one of the great rounds in the history of the event and prompted Dunlop to name a golf ball in its honour.

However, it was Cotton's second victory in the Championship, at Carnoustie in 1937, that was really a triumphal march. His Sandwich win had been slightly anticlimactic because of the hard work he made of the last round when he almost threw away a seemingly impregnable lead. It was an incomplete victory in some ways and few Americans were present in the field.

At Carnoustie it was a different matter entirely. The whole American Ryder Cup team, fresh from their victory at Southport, was there as Henry Longhurst put it, 'in full array', and the weather was simply appalling.

Cotton's 146 on the opening day – it was then still two rounds on each of two days – left him trailing Reg Whitcombe by four strokes. In the morning round of the second day Cotton reduced the leeway by one with a 73, and as the players set out on the final round the rain lashed across the Angus links driven by a ferocious wind.

Water began to gather in great pools on the greens and there was a grave danger that the whole day's play would be wiped out. Whitcombe finished with a superb round in the circumstances of 76 when many could not put together anything like a decent score because they could not keep hold of their clubs. He looked for all the world like the winner, and the press were already writing their stories.

Cotton was some way behind and knew what was required to win. What he produced on that dreadful day at Carnoustie prompted Henry Longhurst to describe it as 'the greatest single round of golf I ever saw'.

Henry Cotton finds the green with his approach from a poor lie at the 2nd hole at Carnoustie in 1937. Fifty years later Sir Henry made his only return visit and explained to the author how he had used a 'hit and stop' shot with a No 2 iron to reach the green, and that it had been a key shot in the round.

The Maestro manufactured fours with wonderful pitching and putting at holes he could not possibly reach in two in the conditions. His incredible round of 71 contained only 26 putts and he won in the end by two strokes.

In 1987 he was knighted for his services to golf but died before the honour could be conferred.

The Duel in the Sun

Tom Watson's greatest single triumph produced one of the most sensational finishes in the long history of the Open Championship. It was the 106th, the 1977 at Turnberry, and the first time the Open had been played on this great Ayrshire links.

In a week of high sunshine there was even higher drama as Watson and Jack Nicklaus fought out an epic struggle that left them so far ahead of the rest of the field that it became a simple head-to-head battle, forever to be remembered as 'The Duel in the Sun'.

For four days the galleries witnessed the most incredible head-to-head shot making and low scoring the game of golf has ever seen.

For 70 holes Watson had never had his nose in front against the dour, ice-cold determination of Nicklaus, but The Bear could not shake him off. They had identical rounds of 68-70-65 heading out on the last round together, jointly in the lead by three strokes over the rest of the field who might as well have been playing on the Ailsa Craig for all the chance they had of catching up.

It took a 60-ft birdie putt from off the green at the devilishly difficult par-3 15th for Watson to get back on level terms with Nicklaus after he had gone behind. The ball positively rattled against the pin as it went in and the two looked at each other. Dan Jenkins, the wonderful American golf writer, recounted the exchange as Tom smiled at Jack and said: 'This is what it's all about, isn't it?'

Jack smiled back and said 'You bet it is.'

They halved the 16th, then with a raking 3-iron to the par-5 17th, Watson set up a birdie that Nicklaus could not match. For the first time Watson was in front and they were going to the last hole.

Watson fired a 1-iron to the perfect spot in the fairway. Nicklaus, who under other circumstances would surely have followed suit, had to gamble and he went with a driver. The tee shot was blocked

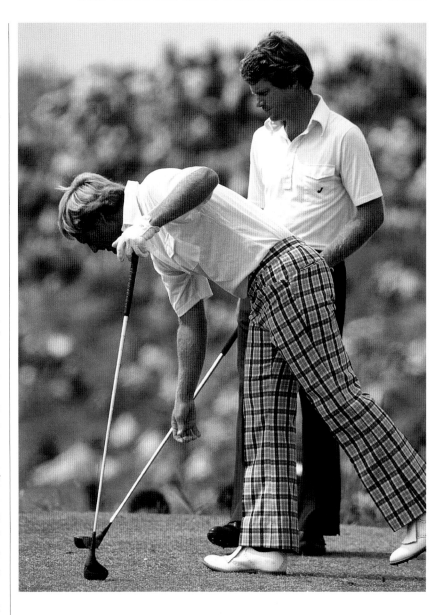

Jack Nicklaus and Tom
Watson took the game of golf on to a new plane when they fought out the famous 'Duel in the Sun' at Turnberry in 1977.

slightly and finished under some whin bushes on the right.

Watson then delivered the *coup de grâce*, an arrow-straight 7-iron which nailed into the green and finished two feet from the hole. It did not matter that Nicklaus produced a miracle shot to scramble the ball on the green and then, as only Nicklaus could, hole a snaking 40-footer for a birdie.

Watson's two-footer was a formality and the greatest finale in the history of the Open was over, a victory for the new generation over the old. It was a new era and the record books had to be comprehensively rewritten. Watson's 65-65 finish for 268 was a new record by an electrifying eight strokes.

Above: Australian Kel Nagle, winner of the Centenary Open at St Andrews in 1960.

Right: Jim Barnes was a surprise winner of the 1925 Open at Prestwick when Macdonald Smith was engulfed by the crowd and lost a five stroke lead in the final round.

The Centenary Open

The Centenary Open at St Andrews in 1960 marked the first steps in the revival of the Championship after it gradually went into decline after the Second World War. It was the presence for the first time of Arnold Palmer that did more than anything else to encourage it and his victories at Birkdale and Troon in the following two years cemented the process. Palmer would not win at St Andrews in 1960 but he would come very close.

One hundred years after Willie Park won the inaugural Open at Prestwick in 1860 there was a great sense of occasion at St Andrews and famous names from the past arrived with Arnold Palmer for a memorable Championship. Gene Sarazen, the 1932 Champion, now 58, and 76-year-old Jock Hutchison, the 1921 Champion, were two of them and they acquitted themselves well.

Sarazen had a splendid 69 round the Old Course and a 72 on the New Course before scratching from the Championship proper with his honour well satisfied. Hutchison had planned to play only a token nine holes but he played so well he was not for coming in at the turn and finished the round in 82.

In the end it was an Australian to whom all the honours belonged in the Centenary Open at St Andrews. Kel Nagle from Sydney in New South Wales was the hot man that week with the putter. He opened with a 69 and added a 67 to be two strokes behind Roberto de Vicenzo at the halfway stage. A 71 put him into the lead after the third round on the Friday morning of what should have been the final day.

Nagle had posted his third-round score just

before a tremendous cloudburst flooded the course. The Valley of Sin in front of the 18th green was flooded to a depth of 3 ft and it took the Fire Brigade an hour to pump it out. The final round had to be delayed until Saturday morning.

Palmer made the charge everyone knew he would from four strokes behind and reduced the leeway to two at the 17th where he had a four for the first time that week. Then, as Nagle was preparing to try to hole a 10-footer for a par at the 17th, a huge roar went up as Palmer finished with a birdie at the last.

The Australian had to make the 10-footer and a par at the last for victory. He calmly rolled in the putt at the Road Hole and followed it with a majestic pitch to only three feet at the last for a memorable victory.

Prestwick's Swan Song

The 1925 Open at Prestwick was one of the saddest Championships in history. It was here that this great Championship had been inaugurated in 1860, but on one fateful day in 1925 the long association between the Open and the historic

Ayrshire links came to an end forever. If there was sadness over that there was nothing short of despair for an exiled Scot by the name of Macdonald Smith who should have won that last Open at Prestwick, but didn't.

Smith had long since departed his native Carnoustie to seek fame and fortune in the United States and so too had Jim Barnes, originally from Cornwall, the winner by a mile of the 1921 US Open. For both men it would be a memorable Championship but for totally different reasons.

In the opening round Macdonald Smith was almost left stranded by a 76 against Barnes' opening round of 70, but on the second day the tables were completely reversed; Barnes had 77 and Smith a marvellous 69. Smith led by two going into the first round of the final day and when Barnes slumped to a 79 against his 76, Smith was five shots clear and seemingly home and dry going into the afternoon final round.

Barnes was out early and returned a creditable 74 but it was clear to everyone that it would not be good enough. Smith needed only a 78 to win, or a 79 to tie.

Then fate and the enthusiasm of the Scottish crowds took a hand. It was the classic confrontation, the exiled Scot and the expatriate Englishman back home to fight out the final round of the Open Championship. The crowds were massive and in the words of Henry Longhurst, 'In their combined determination to see the play at all costs (or, in the case of those who did not pay to come in, at no cost) and to cheer their hero home, they lost him the ambition of a lifetime.'

Hordes trampled over poor Macdonald Smith, desperate to see every shot. He was never given enough room to play and never saw the outcome of any long shot he played during the round.

He left the course a sad and embittered man with a score of 82 in a Championship that he had all but won before he was trampled into defeat by a well-meaning, but over-enthusiastic crowd.

The lack of adequate stewarding compounded by the tightness of the Prestwick course to accommodate such huge crowds, was a major embarrassment to the Prestwick Club. And never again would the Club be asked to host the Championship.

Ice Man at Carnoustie

Ben Hogan called it the greatest year of his life. It was 1953, a vintage year anyway, the year of the Coronation of Queen Elizabeth II, the year Sir Edmund Hillary and a sherpa by the name of Tensing conquered Mount Everest and the year that the man they called the 'Ice Man' or the 'Hawk' came to Carnoustie to play in his one and only Open Championship.

It is widely held that Hogan did not really rate the Open Championship; that his reason for coming to challenge the famous Angus links had more to do with appeasing those who said he could not claim to be the greatest player in the world

Ben Hogan, the man they called the 'Hawk' shot every round lower than the one before when he won the Open at Carnoustie in 1953.

unless he won an Open Championship in Britain.

By all the odds William Benjamin Hogan should have been dead before then. His recovery from a desperate car crash on 2 February 1949 was little short of a miracle. Sheer determination made him walk again after chilling hospital reports that he was unlikely to survive after his car's head-on collision with a Greyhound bus.

But recover he did and Hogan arrived at Carnoustie having already that year won the Masters and the US Open. No one before or since has won three of the modern day 'major' championships. Hogan was about to.

Carnoustie was a culture shock for Hogan and in as much contrast to his native Texas as it was possible to get. The food was different so he ate lunch in his car. The wind swept across the exposed Carnoustie links and Hogan had to play the smaller British ball for the Championship.

The Ice Man coldly charted his way round. In practice he sent his caddie to the front of the green at the long 6th, then hit three raking 2-iron shots, one to the right, one to the left and one exactly in the middle, and demanded his caddie to check which way each bounced on to the green. As one eminent Scottish golf writer who witnessed the performance asked at the time: 'Who else is going to win?'

Hogan won all right with every round lower than the one before – 73 down to a last round of 68. He returned home to a ticker-tape parade and a chat with President Dwight D. Eisenhower.

Palmer Charges at Troon

The revival of the Open Championship in Britain can be laid at the feet of one player, Arnold Palmer. It was Palmer who led a long trail of top American players back into the world's oldest championship, bringing with them a new breath of life to an ailing patient.

Palmer only just failed to win on his first visit to St Andrews in 1960, putted into second place by the unflappable Australian, Kel Nagle. At Birkdale the following year he triumphed but Arnold Palmer's greatest victory in the Open Championship came in 1962 at a hard and fast Royal Troon on the Ayrshire coast.

The dry conditions which produced the occasional bizarre bounce on the fairways were hardly conducive to Palmer's all-out aggressive approach to the game of golf. Careful planning and subtle execution were not in the Palmer lexicon. Hit it hard, find it and hit it hard again was more the Palmer way. If there was a challenge to be taken on, no matter how apparently futile or foolhardy, the great man would take it on. Most times he succeeded and that made him the most exciting player in the game.

He opened at Troon with a fairly conservative round of 71, one behind Peter Thomson, but got into gear the following day with a 69 that was only equalled by Peter Alliss. He then spread-eagled the field with a 67.

Arnie simply gave everyone a lesson in how to play a fast running course that none of the other leading contenders could cope with. Gary Player couldn't handle it at all and missed the cut. Jack Nicklaus finished 29 strokes behind at the finish and the only danger to Arnie on the final day was himself. He needed something to shoot for and was encouraged by his wife to make sure he made it two Open victories in a row, 'because not many had done that before'.

The incentive worked well enough and Palmer outclassed the field with a 69 in the last round for an aggregate of 276. His winning margin over Kel Nagle of six strokes was a fitting revenge for his defeat by the Australian two years previously, and it is a mark of how much he outclassed the field that Phil Rogers and Brian Huggett, tied for third place, were 13 strokes behind the winner.

Arnie's total mastery of the long and difficult 11th hole alongside the railway line will always be remembered from that Open. Nicklaus once got into double figures there, but in six rounds, including two qualifying rounds, Arnold Palmer was six under par.

Mexican Hat Dance

It was many years before Tony Jacklin would actually admit that Lee Trevino's outrageous victory over him in the 1972 Open at Muirfield was a key factor in cutting short his major championship career. Jacklin had won the Open Championship in 1969, the US Open the following year and might easily have won the 1970 Open at

St Andrews had rain not caused an abandonment of play after he had gone to the turn in 29 and lost his momentum when he returned to finish the round the following day.

Two years later at Muirfield he had a great chance to win a second Open Championship, a victory that might well have taken him on to greater things. He was the great hope of European golf at a time when the Americans were again dominant. Trevino changed all that.

They were level on 141 after two rounds with Jack Nicklaus an ominous figure one stroke behind them. In the third round Jacklin and Trevino were paired together.

'I've never really been a fatalist,' said Jacklin sometime afterwards, 'but I have always believed that if you work hard enough and keep trying even when there seems to be no hope, you will get your just reward.'

Jacklin's faith in just reward for effort came under severe strain that third round. Trevino birdied the last five holes with two huge putts, a thinned bunker shot at the 16th which hit the pin and went straight in the hole and a chip into the hole at the last from 30 yards for another birdie. Jacklin dug in against the slings and arrows of outrageous fortune, birdied three of the last five holes himself and was proud of the way he had held on.

In the final round Nicklaus made a charge but in the end it came down to Trevino and Jacklin. They were level with two to play and Jacklin felt he was gaining the upper hand. He had battled away, taken everything that Trevino threw at him, and when Trevino uncharacteristically hooked his drive into a bunker and then had to play out sideways, Jacklin felt that at last he had worn the Mexican down.

Fate took a hand again. Trevino's third was hooked into the rough. His fourth ran through the green into the fringe rough and he admitted later he had mentally conceded. Jacklin's third to the par 5 was a little short but on the green, and he sat on the grass while Trevino walked ahead and took no time to play his chip back down the green. The ball ran down the slope and straight into the hole to save par. It was the third chip shot he had holed in two rounds.

Jacklin was devastated. He three-putted the 17th and finished weakly at the 18th to leave

Trevino the unlikeliest winner.

Jacklin was like a heavyweight boxer who had taken one punch too many.

'Essentially that was the point at which my challenge for the major championships finished,' he reluctantly admitted many years later.

Locke Survives Rules Drama

It was two years after Peter Thomson won at St Andrews that the Open Championship was back at the Home of Golf, unexpectedly, in 1957. The late switch from Muirfield was a direct result of the 1956 Suez crisis and Britain's attack on Egypt in early November that year. By the end of the month petrol rationing had been imposed,

South African Bobby Locke replaced his ball on the last green in the wrong place but was still adjudged the champion at St Andrews in 1957.

private motoring was restricted to 200 miles per month and there were reductions in public transport.

Muirfield was far too inaccessible for the Open, for the Championship Committee, the contractors and the public, so the venue was switched to the Old Course.

The 1957 Open was the first to be given full television coverage and it was the first time the leaders were sent out last in pairs for Friday's final two rounds.

It was the portly figure of South Africa's Bobby Locke who took advantage of the warm weather conditions to stamp his authority on the Championship with a wonderful third round of 68 to add to his halfway total of 141 and take a three-stroke lead into Friday afternoon's final round. Only Peter Thomson, trying to equal Young Tom Morris's record four in a row, and Scottish favourite Eric Brown, had any realistic chance of catching the South African.

Locke meandered round at his usual lethargic pace and his only testing moment came at the long 14th when his third was bunkered in front of the green. However, he recovered brilliantly to save par and no one really had a hope of catching him after that.

There was drama still to come at the 18th, however, although no one realised it at the time. With a comfortable lead Locke swept his trademark, hooking approach shot on to the last green to a yard or so from the hole. His ball was in the line of his playing partner, Australia's Bruce Crampton, who asked the South African to mark the ball a putter's length off his line.

In the excitement of the moment Locke replaced his ball that putter's length away from where it originally lay. No one spotted his error at the time; it was only the evidence of the television cameras that later confirmed the mistake.

The Championship committee did not take much time to decide that Locke had gained nothing from the mistake, and with a three-stroke advantage should not be penalised. It was a decision made 'in equity and the spirit of the game' and one with which there could be no quibble.

Locke, seeking to remind himself for the rest of his career of the Committee's compassion for a genuine error, never wore his trademark plus-fours again.

The luckless Doug Sanders gets a hand on the old claret jug held by R & A Captain, Lord Whitelaw, but it was Jack Nicklaus (right) who emerged the winner after a play-off in the 1970 Open at St Andrews.

Thirty Inches From Glory

Between 1955 and 1972 Doug Sanders from the United States won a total of 20 US Tour events and was regularly among the top 60 money winners. However, in his flamboyant career it would be safe to conclude that Doug Sanders did not achieve the success in the game that his talents deserved.

He came close to winning major championships. He was runner-up in the US PGA Championship in 1959, finished second in the US Open in 1961, fourth in the Masters in 1966 and runner-up behind Jack Nicklaus in the Open Championship at Muirfield the same year.

In 1970 at St Andrews, Sanders was battling it out again with Nicklaus for the Open Championship, only this time he looked to have The Bear at his mercy. They had started level going into the final round but at the 16th Nicklaus dropped a shot and Sanders was at last in the lead.

He shied back from disaster at the famous Road Hole when he played the shot of the Championship from the Road bunker to make a miraculous four and take his one-stroke lead up the last. A four would surely give him the Championship.

His drive at the 18th downwind was perfect. It came up 50 yards short of the green but his pitch was a little long leaving him a good 12 yards past the flag.

It is a difficult putt from that back part of the 18th green; often slower than the player anticipates and Sanders left his approach putt that now famous three feet short of the hole.

What happened next was a nightmare for one of golf's endearing characters. He was hesitant about the left to right putt and stopped after he had settled to make his stroke.

He recalled it afterwards: 'I was over the ball and when I looked down I thought I saw a spot of sand on my line. Without changing the position of my feet I bent down to pick it up. It was a piece of brown grass. I didn't take the time to move away and get reorganised. I mis-hit the ball – I hit it in the neck of the putter – and pushed it right of the hole.'

For the first time since the Open had become a 72-hole event in 1892, the play-off was over 18 holes instead of 36. Sanders fought long and hard and ironically, as it happened, made a text-book three at the 18th, holing a putt of the same length he had missed the previous day.

But it was a putt too late. Nicklaus had famously removed his sweater on the tee and driven the ball through the green to the rough at the back. He chipped down to within eight feet and holed the putt for victory.

End of the Road for Watson

In the long history of the Open the Road hole at St Andrews has played many a decisive role, but none in more public gaze than in the final round of the 1984 Championship. Millions of viewers around the world watched the dramas of the 17th hole all week and Tom Watson, looking down on the most famous hole in golf from his Old Course Hotel balcony, knew that it would be a key factor in this Championship as in every other. The road, the wall and the bunker were on everyone's mind.

By the halfway stage six strokes covered the top dozen players, with Seve Ballesteros, Nick Faldo, Bernhard Langer, Lanny Wadkins and Tom Kite among them. Jack Nicklaus had struggled to make the cut, but out in front was Australian, Ian Baker-Finch, ten under par and three strokes clear.

After the shake-out of the third round Baker-Finch was still there after a 71 and was joined in the lead on 205 by Watson who had returned a glorious 66 to come from five strokes behind, helped by a superb 2-iron to the 17th to make par. Langer and Ballesteros were two behind and paired together for the final round.

The final day of high drama began as early as the first hole when Baker-Finch hit what looked like the perfect approach shot to the green, only to watch in horror as the ball pitched close to the pin and spun back off the green into the Swilcan Burn. His challenge was finished from that point.

Seve Ballesteros salutes the the crowd after his popular win over the Old Course in the 1984 Open Championship.

Nick Faldo watched his drive intently on his way to a memorable victory at Muirfield in 1992.

It became a battle between the young Spaniard, who had won at Royal Lytham in 1979 and would win there again in 1988, and Watson trying to become the first person to equal Harry Vardon's record six Open Championship victories.

A superbly flighted 6-iron from the rough on the left found the green at the 17th and ensured the par he promised he would make in the final round. Watson following hit his drive much further right, flirted with the hotel grounds but found the perfect spot in the fairway. His 2-iron approach, unlike the day before, slid on the wind and finished against the wall behind the green. His recovery, good as it was, was 30 ft from the hole. Just as he played it there was a thunderous roar from the crowd. Ballesteros had holed his putt for birdie.

Watson needed to hole his 30-footer, and birdie the last for a tie, but it was too much to ask.

Ballesteros was the new Champion and the 17th had taken its toll once again.

Faldo's Best Round Ever

In the second round of the 1992 Open at Muirfield, Nick Faldo went out in 33 and home in 31 for 64, for what he described later as 'the best round of my life'. Added to a 66 from the first round, it took him three clear of Gordon Brand Jnr and American John Cook. It also broke the record set by Henry Cotton at Royal St George's back in 1934, and equalled by Faldo and Greg Norman at St Andrews in 1990.

While Faldo was rewriting the record books, Jack Nicklaus was walking up the final fairway, where he had won his first Open 26 years earlier, to a tumultuous reception from the crowds and to only his second missed cut since his first appearance in 1962.

Faldo's third round of 69 was almost shabby by comparison with his first two rounds but 199 was a daunting target for those bravely trying to keep up.

John Cook was the closest, four strokes back, but his chance seemed to have gone when he drove out of bounds at the 9th where he had chipped in for an eagle on the Saturday. He was still four behind Faldo at the turn as flurries of rain and a cold wind swept across the exposed Muirfield links. Then the whole complexion of the Championship changed.

Faldo, three ahead with eight to play, suddenly plunged to two behind Cook with four to play. A negative wedge shot into a bunker at the 11th, three putts on the 13th and a drive into a bunker at the 14th, hadn't helped his cause.

It was then that the world was to see what makes Faldo the great player that he is. He knew he had to grind out the best four holes of his life to retrieve the situation. And no one is a better grinder than Faldo as Paul Azinger had found in the 1987 Open at Muirfield when Faldo manufactured 18 consecutive pars in miserable conditions on the last day to win his first Open title.

Nick set to the task. A glorious approach to the 15th left only a three-foot putt for a birdie. He chipped to save par at the next and set up a chance of an eagle at the 17th with two glorious shots between the banks that guard the green. Two putts gave him another birdie while Cook, playing ahead of him, was dropping a shot at the last, and that after catastrophically missing from two feet for a birdie at the 17th.

Faldo needed par at the last for the title and although his second was a little strong he made no mistake with two solid putts for victory.

The Arrival of Wild Thing

In 1991 Big John Daly came from out of nowhere as a first alternate to win the US PGA Championship in a way that no Hollywood scriptwriter would have dared to write. He became that year's

leading the Open Championship and would have won it easily enough in regulation play if Constantino Rocca had not made a total nonsense of his short pitch to the last green and then redeemed himself by holing an outrageous putt from the depths of the Valley of Sin for a birdie to force a play-off.

The play-off was a tribute to Daly's wonderful appreciation, until then unseen, of how to play winning links golf.

He holed a 30-foot putt with a three feet borrow at the 2nd extra hole but it was his exquisite pitch and run with a 9-iron, low with right to left spin to the heart of the 17th green that was the stamp of a master who knows what links golf is about.

It was a sweet moment when he raised the old claret jug aloft.

For once Wild Thing had tamed the one thing that stood between him and victory – himself, and he had surprised everyone with the dexterity of its doing.

John Daly was an 80-1 outsider for the 1995 Open at St Andrews but won with a virtuoso display of links golf.

St Andrews 1995 and the end of an era. Arnold Palmer salutes his 'army' from the old Swilcan Bridge as he bids farewell to the Open Championship he graced for 35 years.

US PGA Rookie of the Year.

When he won at Crooked Stick, Indiana Daly had a reputation as a hell-raiser and a guy who had once played Russian roulette in his car by running through 17 red lights in a row. They called him 'Wild Thing'.

Big John arrived at St Andrews for the 1995 Open with his big reputation as a big hitter and a big drinker but no big hope of victory. The Tour's 'Bad Boy' was an 80-1 outsider.

Daly wasn't a newcomer to links golf. He had been humiliated at Muirfield in his first Open Championship, after shooting 80 in the third round and eventually finishing last. He finished tied for 14th the following year at St George's and was in the winning United States Dunhill Cup team at St Andrews. Then at Turnberry in 1994 he finished last again during a year in which he claimed drug abuse was common on the US PGA Tour and he got involved in a punch-up in a car park at the World Series in Akron, Ohio.

It was a different John Daly at St Andrews, however. In the last round the driver stayed in the bag and he used an iron three times off the tee to preserve the lead he had painstakingly built up. The incredible was about to happen. Wild Thing was

'I GUESS IT'S OVER...'

Arnold Palmer, who had graced the Open Championship with 22 appearances in 35 years, took his final bow standing on the Swilcan Bridge at the end of his second round in the 1995 Open at St Andrews. The R & A changed the wording of the Rules to allow the most popular player in the history of the modern game to play a final farewell. The famous Arnie's Army, which had followed him faithfully for more than three decades, cheered him wherever he went and it was an emotional moment when he stood on the old stone bridge to wave a final goodbye. They knew they would not see the likes of him again.

CHRONOLOGY

1457 King James II proscribes golf by Act of Parliament and demands archery practice in its place.

1471 King James III repeats the ban on golf.

1491 James IV's parliament passes a statute ordaining that 'in a place of the Realme there be used Fute-ball, Golfe, or uther sik unproffitable sportis'.

1502 James IV signs Treaty of Perpetual Peace with England, gives in to the inevitable and buys 'Gowf clubbes' from a bow maker in Perth.

1513 Scots archers no match for their English counterparts in the Scots ignominious defeat in the Battle of Flodden.

1553 Archbishop John Hamilton confirms St Andrews townspeople's rights to play golf over the Old Course at St Andrews.

1567 Mary Queen of Scots incurs the wrath of the church for playing golf in the field beside Seton with the Earl of Bothwell after the murder of her husband, Lord Darnley.

1582 Patrick Learmont, son of a Provost of St Andrews, takes a pot shot at Archbishop Adamson who was disporting himself 'at the goff' when he should have been preaching.

1598 St Andrews town church complaint of congregation playing golf during hours of church service.

1599 Miscreants fined small sums for playing golf on the Sabbath.

1606 Unsubstantiated claim as the date a group of Scots founded the Royal Blackheath club.

1618 First improvement in golf equipment – the arrival of the feather ball, or 'featherie' as it is known. King James I & IV grants monopoly for 21 years to James Melville for the manufacture of golf balls, provided that he does not charge more than four shillings a ball. The King also decrees that golf should be allowed on Sundays after the golfers had 'first done their duties to God'.

1629 Marquis of Montrose recorded as playing golf at St Andrews.

1642 King Charles I heard the news of the Irish Rebellion while playing golf at Leith.

1691 St Andrews described as the 'Metropolis of golfing'.

1735 Claimed as the inaugural date of the Royal Burgess Golfing Society of Edinburgh, but the club has no written records before 1773. There is some evidence in the *Edinburgh Almanac*, however, to support the 1735 date.

1744 Founding date of the Gentlemen Golfers of Leith, now the Honourable Company of Edinburgh Golfers, when the City of Edinburgh presented a silver club for competition.
First 'Articles & Laws in Playing Golf' drawn up.
John Rattray appointed first captain of the Gentlemen Golfers after winning the Silver Club on 2 April, probably the first championship in golf's history.

1745 John Rattray wins Silver Club for second time but is captured at the Battle of Culloden and saved from the gallows by fellow Leith member, Duncan Forbes.

1754 Society of St Andrews Golfers, now the Royal & Ancient Golf Club of St Andrews, formed.

1759 First reference to stroke play in the Rules.

1760 According to *The Gazateer of Scotland* published in 1832 there was a golf club in Crail near St Andrews on this date but no records exist.

1761 Bruntsfield Links Golfing Society founded.

1764 First introduction of the 18-hole round.

1774 Royal Musselburgh Golf Club founded.

1777 First rules for teeing the ball.

1780 Royal Aberdeen Golf Club formed.

1786 Crail Golfing Society officially comes into being on or prior to 23 February.

1787 Glasgow Golf Club inaugurated.

1794 Inauguration of Dunbar Golf Club.

1797 St Andrews Town Council, deeply in debt, sells the ancient birthright of the citizens, the Links of St Andrews, to Mr Thomas Erskine for £805.
Start of a hundred years' war to regain possession of the links.
Burntisland Golf Club founded.

1806 Society of St Andrews Golfers change the convention that the winner of the Silver Club becomes captain for the year and make captaincy elective.

1812 First revision of the Rules of Golf of 1744.

1815 Birth of Allan Robertson, golf's first professional, in St Andrews on 11 September.

1817 St Andrews Thistle Club, first tradesman's club, founded.

1821 First survey of the Old Course at St Andrews completed.
Birth of Tom Morris Snr on 16 June.

1832 Old Course St Andrews greens doubled in size to speed up play.

1833 Perth Golfing Society becomes the first 'Royal' golf club when King William IV becomes patron of the club which is then to be called the Royal Perth Golfing Society and County and City Club.

1834 King William IV, who was also Duke of St Andrews, grants the title 'Royal and Ancient' to the Society of St Andrews Golfers but at first declines to become patron of the club. The King relents when it is pointed out to him that he is already patron of the Perth club and that the St Andrews Club is 'entirely composed of a great portion of the nobility and gentry of Scotland'.

1836 Longest drive with a featherie recorded at 361 yards at St Andrews.

1838 First rule for lost ball penalty is introduced.

1843 St Andrews Golf Club instituted under the name of Mechanics Club.
July – Allan Robertson and Willie Dunn battle each day for ten successive days, except Sundays, over 36 holes in an historic match. Robertson is declared the winner after he takes the 19th round on the morning of the final day.

1845 R & A fights plan for proposed railway line to cut through the

St Andrews Links at the Burn Hole and succeeds in having it re-routed.

1848 Watershed date in the advance of golf equipment. Gutta percha ball introduced after 200 years of the featherie. Cheap price means golf for all.

1849 Famous foursomes match between Allan Robertson and Tom Morris against Willie and Jamie Dunn played over three courses, Musselburgh, St Andrews and North Berwick, for a £400 stake.

1851 Railway arrives in St Andrews with line built alongside the links.
Birth of Young Tom Morris, on 20 April.

1854 Sir Hugh Lyon Playfair masterminds the building of the Royal and Ancient clubhouse.

1855 Two greens instituted at the High Hole at St Andrews. A new rule includes provision for lifting a ball if bed linen being washed or dried.

1857 Foursomes event played at St Andrews is regarded as the first ever championship.

1858 Allan Robertson scores 79 over the Old Course, the first player to break 80.

1859 First steward at a golf match.
Death of Allan Robertson.

1860 First Open Championship at Prestwick.

1861 Amateur players allowed to play in the second Open Championship at Prestwick making it a truly 'open' event.

1865 Old Tom Morris appointed first professional at the Royal & Ancient Club.

1867 Young Tom Morris, at the age of 16, defeats all the leading professionals including Willie Park and Robert Andrew at Perth.
First ever ladies' golf club formed at St Andrews.

1868 Young Tom Morris wins his first Open at Prestwick and scores the first ever hole-in-one in the Championship.

1869 Patent hole cutter invented and presented to Old Tom Morris.

1870 Young Tom Morris wins the Open Championship belt outright after his third successive victory.

1871 No Open Championship because there is no trophy to play for.

1872 Prestwick Golf Club, the R & A and the Honourable Company of Edinburgh Golfers subscribe for a new open Championship challenge trophy, the famous claret jug.
Young Tom Morris wins his fourth successive Open Championship.
Musselburgh fish ladies form golf club.

1873 First Open played over the Old Course at St Andrews.
Tom Kidd uses first ever deliberately grooved club in the Open.

1875 Tragic death of Young Tom Morris at the age of 24.

1876 Bob Martin wins mismanaged Open at St Andrews when the Championship contestants had to share the course with weekend players. Martin wins in a walk over when David Strath refuses to contest the play-off after a dispute.
R & A and Union Clubs amalgamate.

1885 R & A approached by other clubs to form an Association under one set of rules.

1886 Left hand circuit of the Old Course at St Andrews used for the first and only time because of administrative blunder.

1888 R & A issue Rules of Golf to all clubs.

1890 First canvas golf bag in use.
John Ball from Hoylake becomes the first amateur and the first player not of Scottish birth to win the Open Championship in the 30 years of its existence.

1894 St Andrews Town Council regains possession of the links. New Parliamentary Order sets out arrangements with the R & A.

1895 The New Course at St Andrews opens.

1897 R & A given sole control of Rules of Golf Committee.

1900 Freddie Tait shot by sniper in South Africa. His 1898 diary had recorded 99 days of golf, nearly all of 36 holes.

1902 Sandy Herd uses new Haskell rubber-core ball to win the Open Championship.

1903 Willie Park, winner of the first Open, dies at the age of 69.

1904 Jack White from North Berwick becomes the first player to break 300 for four rounds of the Open.

1905 Tom Morris acts as starter for the Open Championship for the last time.

1908 Old Tom Morris dies at the age of 86.

1910 James Braid wins his fifth Open Championship title.

1913 First charge for golf levied on visitors to St Andrews.

1914 The Open Championship at Prestwick follows the American pattern of two qualifying rounds rather than one and Harry Vardon earns his sixth championship at the age of 44.
The Eden Course opens at St Andrews.

1915 Prestwick Golf Club insures itself against aircraft bombardment.

1918 Votes for women over 30 in Great Britain.
On 11th November, Germany signs armistice.

1919 R&A takes over management of British championships.
15 June – Alcock and Brown's first flight across the Atlantic.

1920 R&A takes over responsibility for Amateur Championship.
Scottish Golf Union formed.

1921 Jock Hutchison wins the Open and takes trophy across the Atlantic for the first time.
Standardisation of the small, heavy 1.62 in-diameter ball.

1922 Prince of Wales plays in, not too well, as Captain of the R.&A.
J Wilson wins the first Scottish Amateur Championship at St Andrews.
Prestwick Golf Club donates £20 for cost of team of British golfers visiting USA.
21 May – Prestwick Golf Club decides not to put sheep back on the course.

1924 Prestwick Golf Club approves installation of electric light in the clubhouse.

1925 Professionals given access to the clubhouse at Prestwick for the Open.
Jim Barnes wins Open marred by poor crowd control.
Prestwick taken off Open Championship rota.

1927 'The Jazz Singer', the first talking picture is released.
Scottish ex-patriot, Tommy Armour, wins play-off in US Open.

1929 R&A legalise steel shafts in Britain.

1930 The Duke of York plays in as Captain of the R&A.
Bobby Jones wins Amateur Championship over the Old Course as part of his Grand Slam.

1933 Spectators are charged gate money for the first time at the Open.

1936 20 January – Accession of King Edward VIII to the throne; abdicates 10 December.

Bobby Jones makes a nostalgic return to St Andrews.

1937 Henry Cotton's 71 over a rain-drenched Carnoustie on his way to his second Open Championship is described by Henry Longhurst as 'the greatest single round of golf I ever saw'.

1938 29 September – Chamberlain and Hitler sign Munich Agreement.

Great Britain and Ireland win first victory in the Walker Cup at St Andrews.

1939 Ministry of Aircraft Production requisitions part of the Prestwick Clubhouse.

1941 Japanese attack Pearl Harbour.

Prestwick members concerned about course condition – no fertilisers and shortage of staff.

1945 USA explodes first Atom Bomb in New Mexico.

Prestwick rough ordered to be cut because of a shortage of golf balls.

1946 General Dwight D. Eisenhower elected Honorary Life Member at Prestwick.

End of free golf at St Andrews.

Introduction of crowd control for tournaments.

1949 Lord Brabazon of Tara pulls the first caddie cart on the Old Course at St Andrews.

1950 Death of five-times Open Champion, James Braid.

1951 R & A and USGA abolish the stymie rule.

R & A and USGA agree a code of rules for the game worldwide.

Mr Francis Ouimet is elected first Captain of the R&A.

1952 The Golf Foundation comes into being to provide coaching for British youngsters. Henry Cotton is a prime mover in the initiative.

Mr Francis Ouimet is elected honorary life member at Prestwick.

1953 Ben Hogan wins the Open at Carnoustie on his one and only visit.

1954 Death of William Lowell, the dentist who invented the wooden tee peg. He died poor, having spent much time and money in contesting patent suits.

1955 First televised Open Championship broadcast from St Andrews.

1957 Bobby Locke wins Open at St Andrews despite wrongly replacing his ball on the last green.

1958 Bobby Jones granted the Freedom of St Andrews.

First Eisenhower Trophy played over the Old Course at St Andrews.

1960 Kel Nagle wins the Centenary Open Championship at St Andrews.

1961 Central heating installed at Prestwick Golf Club.

Yuri Gagarin makes first manned space flight.

1966 First colour television coverage of golf in Britain from Gleneagles, Carnoustie and St Andrews.

1967 First Sunday play allowed on the Old Course at St Andrews for the Alcan Tournament and future Open Championship replays.

1969 Neil Armstrong and Buzz Aldrin land on the moon.

11 June – Suggestion made in Prestwick Golf Club suggestion book – 'That Societies of Riveters and Pipefitters, whose Articles of Association would appear to forbid them from dressing properly, or observing the etiquette governing behaviour on a golf course, be restricted to using the course on midweek evenings after 5pm, during the months of November, December and January.'

1970 21 July – Doug Sanders misses short putt on the last green to lose the Open at St Andrews to Jack Nicklaus.

1971 Admiral Alan Shepard plays golf on the moon during the Apollo 14 expedition.

1972 The 10th hole on the Old Course, St Andrews is named 'Bobby Jones'.

Memorial Service for Bobby Jones is held in St Andrews town church.

1976 Death of Fred McLeod (94) from North Berwick who beat Willie Smith in the play-off in the US Open in 1908.

1977 Tom Watson and Jack Nicklaus fight out their famous 'Duel in the Sun' in the Open Championship at Turnberry.

Cairn to mark the first Open Championship at Prestwick is unveiled by Henry Cotton.

1978 The world's favourite golf commentator, Henry Longhurst, dies after a long battle against cancer.

1982 In the Open at Troon, little-known American Bobby Clampett posts the best 36-hole score, 67, 66, since Henry Cotton's 132 in 1934, but Tom Watson is the eventual winner.

1983 Sir Michael Bonallack takes over as Secretary of the Royal and Ancient Golf Club.

1985 Replica of the original Open Championship Belt is presented to Sandy Lyle after his victory in the Open at Royal St George's.

1987 Nick Faldo pars every hole in the final round at Muirfield to beat Paul Azinger and claim his first Open Championship victory.

1988 Sandy Lyle becomes the first British player to win the Masters.

1990 The gardener at the Old Course Hotel in St Andrews starts wearing a tin helmet for protection from ambitious players taking too tight a line down the right side of the fairway on the Road hole.

1992 Nick Faldo wins his third Open Championship at Muirfield and in his victory speech thanks the press 'from the heart of my bottom'.

1993 Bernard Gallacher agrees to third term as Europe's Ryder Cup Captain.

Scotland lose 2–1 to Paraguay in the Alfred Dunhill Cup at St Andrews – the shock result of the year.

1994 The Honourable Company of Edinburgh Golfers marks its 250th anniversary by playing a match in period costume.

The first known golf trophy, a Spode Bowl, won in 1814 by John Pitcairn at the Bow of Fife Golfing Club, was sold for £16,100 at auction in Chester.

1995 'Wild Thing' John Daly from the United States is the 80–1 winner of the Open Championship at St Andrews after a play-off with Constantino Rocca.

1997 The world of golf mourns the passing of Ben Hogan.

1998 Colin Montgomerie wins record sixth consecutive European Order of Merit.

INDEX

AUTHOR'S ACKNOWLEDGEMENTS

I am greatly indebted to Mike Rensner and the staff of Colin Baxter Photography for their
unfailing support and encouragement during the development and production of this volume.
Glyn Satterley has worked with great diligence to produce new and superb golf course images to accompany the text, and
I am particularly grateful to him for his tenacity when weather conditions placed such a huge strain on photographic schedules.
My thanks also go to all golf club Secretaries who gave of their valuable time to help with editorial queries
and made their golf courses so readily available for photographic purposes.
I am particularly grateful to Sir Michael Bonallack for his generous foreword, and finally I owe, as ever, a special debt of gratitude
to Jane McCandlish without whose unfailing support and encouragement this project would still be on the drawing board.